First World War
and Army of Occupation
War Diary
France, Belgium and Germany

47 DIVISION
142 Infantry Brigade
London Regiment
23rd (County of London) Battalion
1 March 1915 - 9 May 1919

WO95/2744/2

The Naval & Military Press Ltd
www.nmarchive.com
Published in association with The National Archives

Published by

The Naval & Military Press Ltd

Unit 10 Ridgewood Industrial Park,

Uckfield, East Sussex,

TN22 5QE England

Tel: +44 (0) 1825 749494

www.naval-military-press.com

www.nmarchive.com

This diary has been reprinted in facsimile from the original. Any imperfections are inevitably reproduced and the quality may fall short of modern type and cartographic standards.

© Crown Copyright
Images reproduced by permission of The National Archives, London, England, 2015.

Contents

Document type	Place/Title	Date From	Date To
Heading	WO95/2744 Mar 15-May 19 1/24 London Regt		
Heading	47th Division 142nd Infy Bde 1-24th London Regt Mar 1915-May 1919		
Heading	142nd Inf. Bde. 47th Division War Diary 1/24th London Regt March 1915		
War Diary	Hatfield	01/03/1915	22/03/1915
War Diary	St Hilaire	23/03/1915	27/03/1915
War Diary	Lapugnoy	28/03/1915	31/03/1915
Heading	142nd Inf Bde 47th Division War Diary 1/24th London Regt April 1915		
War Diary	Lapugnoy	01/04/1915	19/04/1915
War Diary	Richebourg St Vaast	20/04/1915	26/04/1915
War Diary	Letouret-Rue De Lepinette	27/04/1915	30/04/1915
Heading	142nd Inf Bde 47th Division War Diary 1/24th London Regt May 1915		
Heading	War Diary		
War Diary	Trenches Section D I (c). d	01/05/1915	03/05/1915
War Diary	Essars	04/05/1915	30/05/1915
Miscellaneous	Narrative For 25th-26th May		
Miscellaneous	Narrative Of Events 25th-26th May 24th Ban London Regt		
Miscellaneous	To 142nd Inf Bde 26		
Heading	Operation Orders		
Miscellaneous	Preparatory Orders	08/05/1915	08/05/1915
Miscellaneous	The 6th Lon Inf Bde (Less 22nd 23rd Bns) Will Support The Infantry Advance		
Heading	142nd Inf. Bde. 47th Division War Diary 1/24th London Regt June 1915		
Miscellaneous	War Diary	01/06/1915	01/06/1915
Heading	142nd Inf. Bde. 47th Division War Diary 1/24th London Regt July 1915		
War Diary		01/07/1915	31/07/1915
Heading	Operation Order No. 9		
Operation(al) Order(s)	Operation Order No. 9	05/07/1915	05/07/1915
Heading	142nd Inf. Bde. 47th Division War Diary 1/24th London Regt August 1915		
War Diary		01/08/1915	26/08/1915
Heading	142nd Bde. 47th Division War Diary 1/24th London Regiment September 1915		
War Diary		01/09/1915	30/09/1915
Heading	142nd Inf. Bde. 47th Division War Diary 1/24th London Regt October 1915		
Miscellaneous	D.A.G 3rd Echelon Reference Your No.140/LXVI	26/12/1915	26/12/1915
Miscellaneous	D.A.G 3rd Echelon	10/01/1916	10/01/1916
War Diary		01/10/1915	30/10/1915
Heading	142nd Inf. Bde. 47th Division War Diary 1/24th London Regt November 1915		
War Diary		01/11/1915	30/11/1915
Heading	142nd Inf. Bde. 47th Division War Diary 1/24th London Regt December 1915		

Type	Description	Start	End
Heading	War Diary Of 24 London Rgt The Queens for December 1915		
War Diary		01/12/1915	31/12/1915
Heading	24 London Regt Jan 1916 Vol X		
War Diary		01/01/1916	31/01/1916
Heading	24 London Regt Feb 1916 Vol XI		
War Diary		01/02/1916	29/02/1916
Miscellaneous	Herewith War Diary For Month Ending March 31st 1916	05/04/1916	05/04/1916
War Diary		01/03/1916	31/03/1916
Heading	1/24 London Regt Vol XIII April 1916		
War Diary		01/04/1916	30/06/1916
Heading	142nd Brigade 47th Division 1/24th Battalion London Regiment July 1916		
Miscellaneous	Herewith Please Receive War Diary For July 1916	01/08/1916	01/08/1916
War Diary		01/07/1916	31/07/1916
Heading	142nd Brigade 47th Division 1/24th Battalion London Regiment August 1916		
Miscellaneous	Herewith Please Receive War Diary For August 1916	02/09/1916	02/09/1916
War Diary		01/08/1916	31/08/1916
Miscellaneous	Headquarters 142nd Inf Bde	20/09/1916	20/09/1916
War Diary	High Wood	01/09/1916	30/09/1916
Map	Map		
War Diary		01/10/1916	31/03/1917
Miscellaneous	H.Q. 142 Inf Bde	05/05/1917	05/05/1917
War Diary		01/04/1917	30/04/1917
Operation(al) Order(s)	1/24th London Regiment O.O. 149	11/04/1917	11/04/1917
War Diary		01/05/1917	31/05/1917
Miscellaneous	1/24 Batt London Regt (The Queens) Minor Enterprise On O4 A87.85 And O4.a 87.80		
Miscellaneous	Report On Work Done In Company's Sections During Tour Of Company		
Miscellaneous	Ref. O.O.155		
Miscellaneous	Headquarters 142nd Infantry Brigade		
Map	Map		
War Diary		01/06/1917	30/06/1917
Miscellaneous	Narrative Of Attack London Regiment "The Queens"	07/06/1917	07/06/1917
Map	Map		
War Diary		01/07/1916	31/10/1916
Miscellaneous	Headquarters 142nd Inf. Bde.	02/12/1917	02/12/1917
War Diary		01/11/1917	30/11/1917
Miscellaneous	Report On Raid Carried Out on November 4th 1917	04/11/1917	04/11/1917
Miscellaneous	1/24th London Regiment Report On The Raid	07/11/1917	07/11/1917
Operation(al) Order(s)	24th Battalion London Regiment O.O No.196		
Miscellaneous	Appendix 1 Time Table		
Miscellaneous	Appendix II Administrative Instructions in connection with 34th Battalion Instructions No. 1.		
Miscellaneous	Appendix III		
Map	Map		
Operation(al) Order(s)	O.O No.197	02/11/1917	02/11/1917
Miscellaneous	Headquarters 142nd Inf. Bde.	03/01/1918	03/01/1918
War Diary		01/12/1917	28/02/1918
Heading	47th Division 142nd Infantry Brigade War Diary 1/24th Battalion London Regiment March 1918		
War Diary		01/03/1918	31/03/1918

Heading	142nd Brigade 47th Division War Diary 1/24th Battalion The London Regiment April 1918		
War Diary		01/04/1918	02/05/1918
Miscellaneous	H.Q. 142 Inf Bde	17/04/1918	17/04/1918
Heading	1/24th Battalion London Regiment "The Queens" Narrative Of Operations At Aveluy Wood March 29th 1918 To April 7th 1918		
Miscellaneous			
War Diary		01/05/1918	31/07/1918
Heading	142nd Bde. 47th Div 1/24th Battalion London Regiment August 1918		
War Diary		01/08/1918	09/05/1919

WO 95/2744
Mar '15 - May '19
1/24 London Regt

47TH DIVISION
142ND INFY BDE

1-24TH LONDON REGT
MAR 1915-MAY 1919

47TH DIVISION
142ND INFY BDE

142nd Inf. Bde.

47th Division.

Battⁿ. disembarked
Havre from
England 16.3.15.

WAR DIARY

1/24th LONDON REGT.

M A R C H

1 9 1 5

24th Bn. C. Hants Regt.

Army Form C. 2118.

WAR DIARY
INTELLIGENCE SUMMARY.
(Erase heading not required.)

Instructions regarding War Diaries and Intelligence Summaries are contained in F. S. Regs., Part II and the Staff Manual respectively. Title pages will be prepared in manuscript.

Hour, Date, Place	Summary of Events and Information	Remarks and references to Appendices
HATFIELD		
March 1st 1915.	Battalion Training. Formed in of Bivouac. + assembly formation. 3rd class drill of A Company on Hatfield Range.	C9u.
March 2nd "	Battalion Training. Recruits from Hatfield marks to Downs for Ridge. Occupation of a defensive position. 3rd class drill of B Company on range. Company Training + medical examination of whole Battalion. 3rd class drill of D Company fired.	C9u. C9u.
March 3rd "	Battalion Training. Digging in Hatfield Park. C. Company. 3rd class drill fire.	C9u.
March 4th "		
March 5th "	Battalion Training. (digging) Night operations. Occupation + reinforcing a trench + to rest.	C9u.

24th Bn. C. [?] Regt.

Army Form C. 2118.

WAR DIARY
or
INTELLIGENCE SUMMARY.
(Erase heading not required.)

Hour, Date, Place	Summary of Events and Information	Remarks and references to Appendices
HATFIELD		
March 6th 1915.	Inspection by K.O. of whole battalion on marching order. Inspection of kits etc. Order received that 24th London Division to be held in readiness to proceed for abroad immediately.	CGW
March 7th 1915.	Sunday. Church parade. Men drawn from A.O.D. at Pimlico.	
March 8th "	Battalion Route march. Received General Service boots & drums of further issue etc. Battalion at HATFIELD.	CGW
March 9th "	Battalion drafts & route march. Arms & Stores continued to be drawn	CGW

2nd Bn. Bedfordshire Regt.

Army Form C. 2118.

WAR DIARY
INTELLIGENCE SUMMARY
(Erase heading not required.)

Instructions regarding War Diaries and Intelligence Summaries are contained in F.S. Regs., Part II. and the Staff Manual respectively. Title pages will be prepared in manuscript.

Hour, Date, Place	Summary of Events and Information	Remarks and references to Appendices
March 10th 1915.	Inspection of whole battalion by C.O. Drums & arms of Officers, harness etc.	—
March 11th 1915.	Inspection of battalion by G.O.C. 6th Lan. Inf. Bde.	—
March 12th "	Completing of battalion to full establishment of horses etc. Stores received. G.O.C. 2nd Lan. Div. inspected all transport final.	—
March 13th "	Company training & issue of war stores etc. Orders received for battalion entraining in 2 trains at HARPENDEN on evening of 14th.	—
March 14th "	A. Coy & B Coy. Company paraded 11 pm, marched to HARPENDEN and entrained for SOUTHAMPTON. Remainder of Coys under Major Law paraded at 12.30 am. Battalion at full strength, less 45 men for first reinforcement.	—

24th Bn. C. Platoon 15 V.

Army Form C. 2118.

WAR DIARY
INTELLIGENCE SUMMARY
(Erase heading not required.)

Instructions regarding War Diaries and Intelligence Summaries are contained in F.S. Regs., Part II and the Staff Manual respectively. Title pages will be prepared in manuscript.

Hour, Date, Place	Summary of Events and Information	Remarks and references to Appendices
March 15th 1915	Battalion arrived at SOUTHAMPTON. Stayed on ship (Berth 39) at Docks all day. Embarked at 6 p.m. on "Empress Queen" for HAVRE.	—
March 16th	Arrived HAVRE 4 a.m., but did not disembark till 9 a.m., marched to Rest Camp No 6 where stayed all day.	—
March 17th	Paraded 6 a.m. & marched to GARE DES MARCHANDISES HAVRE where entrained for unknown destination. (Capt 2 platoons 13.11.14) which followed by next train)	—
March 18th	Train arrived at ST OMER 5:30 a.m. & we learnt that destination was ARGUES. Detrained there and marched to BLENDECQUES where went to billets at 6 p.m. received orders to send billeting party to KILLERS & St HILAIRE	—

24th Br. C. of Entry
Reg.

Army Form C. 2118.

WAR DIARY
or
INTELLIGENCE SUMMARY.
(Erase heading not required.)

Instructions regarding War Diaries and Intelligence Summaries are contained in F.S. Regs., Part II. and the Staff Manual respectively. Title pages will be prepared in manuscript.

Hour, Date, Place	Summary of Events and Information	Remarks and references to Appendices
March 19th 1915.	Battalion paraded at 8.15 am & marched as rear Batt of 6th Inf Bde to ST HILAIRE. Very cold work enroute & place then found fires hard. March on & were rather tired on arrival. 10 men fell out. ST HILAIRE proved to be a gaoled village, much inferior to Begnis villers & BIENVILLERS. Went into billets on arrival (about 2.30 pm)	
March 20th	Rearrangement of billet areas. The Battalion share St HILAIRE with the 23rd Batt taking Northern half. Several rest & clean up	
March 21st	Sunday. Church parade at 11 am. Address by the C.O. Hostile aeroplane dropped bombs on LILLERS about 3 miles off	
March 22nd	Inspection of battalion & transport by Lieut. Genl. In afternoon practice clipping & machine	

(73989) W.4141—463. 400,000. 9/14. H.&J.Ltd. Forms/C. 2118/10.

24th B'n C. of London Regt.

Army Form C. 2118.

WAR DIARY
or
INTELLIGENCE SUMMARY.
(Erase heading not required.)

Hour, Date, Place	Summary of Events and Information	Remarks and references to Appendices
ST NAZAIRE		
March 23rd 1915.	Battalion Training & Trench warfare. The attack	CGM
March 24th "	Battalion digging in trenches designed in elucidation of attack on B. Sec. A. trenches. (C.O. and party by 13. Sec. A. trenches. Infantry. Wet & cold day.	CGM
March 25th "	Company route marches	CGM
March 26th "	Battalion digging in reserve trenches. Received orders to move to LAPUGNOY. Buses went towards this place in the afternoon	CGM
March 27th "	Battalion marched from ST HILAIRE to LAPUGNOY. Went into billets at to late a place which was an improvement as far as cleanliness went to Sit.	CGM

24th Bn. C./London Reg.t

Army Form C. 2118.

WAR DIARY
INTELLIGENCE SUMMARY.
(Erase heading not required.)

Instructions regarding War Diaries and Intelligence Summaries are contained in F.S. Regs., Part II and the Staff Manual respectively. Title pages will be prepared in manuscript.

Hour, Date, Place	Summary of Events and Information	Remarks and references to Appendices
LAVENTIE		
March 28th 1915	Sunday. Church parade + settling into new billets.	egw.
March 29th "	Battalion digging in morning. Night work (infantry)	egw.
March 30th "	Battalion digging in morning. Formation of Grenadier Platoon (1. N.C.O. + 24 men from each Company under Command of Lt. Saunders)	egw.
March 31st "	Company route marches in morning. Bayonet fighting in afternoon over new bayonet fighting course.	egw.

C.J. Warwick
Colonel C.
24th Bn. London Reg.t

142nd Inf. Bde.
47th Division.

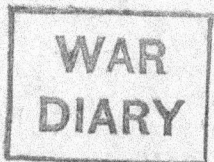

1/24th LONDON REGT.

APRIL

1915

Army Form C. 2118.

2nd Bn. of the Regt

WAR DIARY
-or-
INTELLIGENCE SUMMARY.
(Erase heading not required.)

Hour, Date, Place	Summary of Events and Information	Remarks and references to Appendices
LAPUGNOY		
April 1st 1915.	Digging & bayonet fighting in morning. Digging by night by companies.	afn.
April 2nd "	Good training. Church parade in morning. Digging in afternoon.	afn
April 3rd "	Practice attack from line of trenches against imaginary enemy trench. Knocks of work early as rain came on.	afn
April 4th "	Sunday. Church Parade.	afn
April 5th "	Company route marches. Night digging.	afn
April 6th "	Digging & hab. obstacles.	afn
April 7th "	Digging. Manoeuvre exercise.	afn
April 8th "	Company route marches.	afn

Army Form C. 2118.

24th Bn London Regt.

WAR DIARY
or
INTELLIGENCE SUMMARY.
(Erase heading not required.)

Instructions regarding War Diaries and Intelligence Summaries are contained in F.S. Regs., Part II and the Staff Manual respectively. Title pages will be prepared in manuscript.

Hour, Date, Place	Summary of Events and Information	Remarks and references to Appendices
LAVENTIE.		
April 9th 1915.	Battalion digging "Supers", 3rd class trenches on LABEUVRIERE range.	cpl.
April 10th "	Battalion digging 7½ "otherrank" dugouts.	"
April 11th "	Make Sunday. Church parade on Private Knox Jones made by 6.123 Batn + 6th Balt.	cpl.
	Motor transport Ambulance	cpl
April 12th "	Battalion digging. Hostile aeroplane flew over the village about 6 pm.	cpl.
April 13th "	Company made trenches. hoped in for 1st two movements.	cpl

WAR DIARY or INTELLIGENCE SUMMARY.

Army Form C. 2118.

24th B. C. Hoden Regt.

Hour, Date, Place	Summary of Events and Information	Remarks and references to Appendices
LAPUGNOY		
April 14th 1915	Battalion digging in morning. C.O. & Adjutant visited trenches held by BLACK WATCH near INDIAN Village S. of NEUVE CHAPELLE	9h.
April 15th	Battalion digging in morning. Inspected in afternoon by G.O.C. 1st Army (Sir. D. Haig)	9h.
April 16th	Company route marches & morning — A & B companies night work (digging, occupying trenches, etc)	9h.
April 17th	Digging in morning. Officers & N.C.O's demonstration of attack in trenches. afternoon	9h.
April 18th	Church parade followed by Company and Company 'attacks from recent practice. Battalion warned to proceed next day to the trenches — Mahomed Fay a K trenches.	9h.

Army Form C. 2118.

2nd/5th C. of London Regt

WAR DIARY
or
INTELLIGENCE SUMMARY.
(Erase heading not required.)

Instructions regarding War Diaries and Intelligence Summaries are contained in F. S. Regs., Part II. and the Staff Manual respectively. Title pages will be prepared in manuscript.

Hour, Date, Place	Summary of Events and Information	Remarks and references to Appendices
April 19th 1915	Battalion left LAPUGNOY. Paraded at 1 p.m. and marched via BETHUNE to RICHEBOURG ST VAAST (a hot march) where H.Q. and C & D companies were billeted. A & B companies at 8 p.m. went into the trenches of the 1st Section, Battalion 2nd Welch Regiment respectively to be attached for instruction.	ibm
RICHEBOURG ST VAAST April 20th "	Reserve companies (C&D) + Hindu day resting & tidying up. In vicinity of C company was shelled by 6" howitzers about 2 p.m. No damage. C & D companies fatigues working parties of 150 men each for attachment to 23rd Fd Coy R.E. & Gloucester Regt respectively. Casualties 1 man D company wounded at 8 p.m.	ibm

(73989) W4141-463. 400,000. 9/14. H.&J.Ltd. Forms/C. 2118/10.

Army Form C. 2118.

24th London Regt.

WAR DIARY
or
INTELLIGENCE SUMMARY.
(Erase heading not required.)

Instructions regarding War Diaries and Intelligence Summaries are contained in F.S. Regs., Part II. and the Staff Manual respectively. Title pages will be prepared in manuscript.

Hour, Date, Place	Summary of Events and Information	Remarks and references to Appendices
RICHEBOURG ST VAAST April 21st 1915	RICHEBURG slightly shelled with shrapnel about 9.30 am. No damage. C & D companies in Res Rd. A & B still in Trenches. Working parties from C & D Companies worked on Welch Regt & Gloucester Regt Trenches. Casualties 1 man Killed & 1 wounded in C Company, 1 man wounded in D company.	eye.
April 22nd 1915.	C & D companies in CS all day at night relieved A & B companies respectively taken coming in to vacated billets at RICHEBOURG. Casualties 1 NCO of A company wounded. B, 2 punctures & MS section tent with trenches MK E & D companies respectively.	eye.
April 23rd 1915.	A & B companies in Res Rd. At night C & D found working parties (2 officers, 200 men each) to work up to Ldn: Lowland D with R.E. C & D companies 30th in trenches.	eye.

(73989) W4141—463. 400,000. 9/14. H.&J.Ltd. Forms/C. 2118/10.

Army Form C. 2118.

24th London Regt.

WAR DIARY
INTELLIGENCE SUMMARY.
(Erase heading not required.)

Hour, Date, Place	Summary of Events and Information	Remarks and references to Appendices
April 24th 1915.	H.Qrs, A & B Companies relieved at RICHEBOURG St VAAST by 2 Companies Northampton Regt. Marched to be towed arriving about 5pm. Found two working parties each of 2 officers & 200 men for work under towland Field Coy. R.E. — C & D Companies remained in Trenches and went with Clubs at Rue de L'EPINETTE, Y. Johnson & 38 Middx. and Royal Battalion Fan HAVRE.	CHJ
April 25th "	Battalion in Brigade reserve as above. At night found working party 2 officers 200 men (1 off, 100 men each from A & B Companies) for work under R.E. At II I (C)(d) occupied by 23rd Bn London Regt. One man wounded.	CHJ
April 26th "	Quiet day. Working parties from D, A & B Companies on sector D100-C60	CHJ

WAR DIARY or INTELLIGENCE SUMMARY

Army Form C. 2118.

4th Kings Own Regt.

Hour, Date, Place	Summary of Events and Information	Remarks and references to Appendices
LE TOURET – RUE DE L'EPINETTE		
April 27th 1915	Battn. still in Brigade Reserve. Working parties to trenches of 5 officers + 350 other ranks each night on sect D1 (c) (d). Our HQrs 'B' Coy & HQs still at Draft of 6 men arrived from base.	Coy.
April 28th	Battalion relieved 23rd London Regt. in D1 (c) +(d) at 8.30pm. A, B, C Companies from line & supports. D company local reserve. H.Q. Rouen + 1 man slightly wounded. Considerable sniping during tonight, but there were enemy quiet.	Coy.
April 29th	Quiet day. Companies worked at improving parapet + providing traverses & parados which are particularly weak. 'C' Coy to Batt's Sector. D company provided working party to dig Communication Trench. One man killed, 2 wounded.	Coy.
April 30th	Very quiet day. All night further improvements to parados + traverses occupied by B & C companies. A Company sent out patrols in front of parapet.	Coy.

Army Form C. 2118.

24th London Regt.

WAR DIARY
—or—
INTELLIGENCE SUMMARY.
(Erase heading not required.)

Hour, Date, Place	Summary of Events and Information	Remarks and references to Appendices
April 30th (Continued)	& reported have heavy had allotted a sept to ward our lines. II company completed a communication trench from HQ. to 3rd line breastwork. Two men wounded in the Battalion C9h. less sniping than on any previous night	

C.J Manade
Capt and ?
24t London Regt

142nd Inf. Bde.
47th Division.

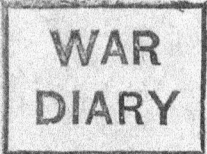

1/24th LONDON REGT.

MAY

1915

Narrative for 25-26 May.
War Diary.
Operation Orders.

WAR DIARY.

Army Form C. 2118.

WAR DIARY
or
INTELLIGENCE SUMMARY.

(Erase heading not required.)

Instructions regarding War Diaries and Intelligence Summaries are contained in F.S. Regs., Part II. and the Staff Manual respectively. Title pages will be prepared in manuscript.

24th May [...]

Hour, Date, Place	Summary of Events and Information	Remarks and references to Appendices
TRENCHES, Section III (c)		
May 1st 1915	Heavy cannonade against "Rue du Bois" & "Port Arthur" made. Battalion stood to arms at 4.30 a.m. but without further casualties. Quiet during rest of the day. Water parties informing Reserve during the night. 2n/Lt Q. Brown seriously wounded on night of April 28th died in hospital at BETHUNE	9/-
May 2nd "	A very quiet day. Very little sniping. 3pm Orders received for Battalion to go into Divisional Reserve at ESSARS on relief on night 3rd/4th.	9/-
May 3rd "	Rather more firing took place from enemy's trenches, which may have shown that we were relieved during the night. Our heavy guns bombarding the enemy's trenches about 8.30 p.m. & did considerable damage to his parapet. The Battalion relieved by 1st 23rd London Regt. (Count[?]) and marched back to ESSARS where divine Divisional	

(73989) W.4141—463. 400,000. 9/14. H.&J.Ltd. Forms/C. 2118/10.

Army Form C. 2118.

WAR DIARY
or
INTELLIGENCE SUMMARY.

Instructions regarding War Diaries and Intelligence Summaries are contained in F.S. Regs. Part II. and the Staff Manual respectively. Title pages will be prepared in manuscript.

Hour, Date, Place	Summary of Events and Information	Remarks and references to Appendices
ESSARS		
May 4th 1915	Battalion in Divisional Reserve. General rest & clean up. B company went to BETHUNE for baths	CJL
May 5th "	Battalion in Divisional Reserve.	CJL
May 6th "	Orders received to relieve 23rd LON. REGT. in DIC(ord) (DEAD COW FARM 2C.ā.) Left ESSARS at 6 p.m. Part of our billets being taken over by the 60th Rifles. Did not finish relieving 23rd Regt. 11.30 p.m.	CJL
May 7th "	Orders received of an infantry attack on enemy's line to-morrow. The 2nd Batt. to hold its present line & cooperate in actual attack by 1st Division in our left. All refs. being made, but an enemy orders countermanded for 24 hours	CJL

Sat May 8th 1915. Battalion in Trenches
Section D I (c) & (d) (DEAD COW FARM).
A, D, C in front line from right to left.
B company in local reserve.
    Received orders that a general attack
was contemplated for the 9th (postponed
from to-day). The LONDON Division to
hold present line of trenches, the 1st
Division attacking immediately on the
left of the 24th Battn (the left Battn
of the Division.)

Sunday May 9th. Battn H.Qs moved from
RUE DU BOIS to dugout at DEAD COW Fm
at 4 a.m. Dressing Station established
at old Battn H.Qrs.] Bombardment
began at 5 p.m and went on till 5.40p.m
Immediately on our left the Northamptons
& 60th Rifles, 2nd BRIGADE, 2nd Divn
attacked at 5.40 p.m, but were stopped
by uncut wire and M.Gs, losing heavily.
The Battalion co-operated by fire and
were under heavy shrapnel fire
for some time.
    Second attack organised for the
afternoon. Bombardment began 3.20p.m
attack by 1st Brigade, 2nd Divn at 4 p.m

2

The Black Watch immediately on our left assaulted about 3.55 pm in a most gallant way, a few of them actually reaching the enemy's trenches, but the attack was finally stopped owing to lack of close support and to the enemy's M.G's. After the attack a company and a half of the 9th LIVERPOOLS (T.F.) were found in our lines. [No further attack attempted this day. Heard that the French south of LA BASSEE had progressed a considerable distance.] Battalion losses Lt. TRUELOVE and Lt. SOLOMON wounded, other ranks 4 killed 44 wounded.

Monday May 10th. Quiet day without incident, battalion remaining in the trenches.

Tuesday, May 11th. Quiet day except for artillery fire. A number of officers of the 7th Division, including Gen. Gough came round Battalion lines & reconnoitred immediate front. In the evening all units of LONDON Div withdrawn except the 24th Batt.

which remained in present position and was temporarily attached to 5th BRIGADE, 2nd DIVISION.

WEDNESDAY, May 12th. In morning heard that Battalion would be relieved by the GLASGOW HIGHLANDERS to night. Handed over to them about midday. Later on this order cancelled, and we were told to hand over to BEDFORDS (7th Div) and Inniskilling Fusiliers (2nd Div). Clearness of orders somewhat complicated by the Yorkshire Regiment (also 7th Div.) trying to take over part of our line. About 7.30 pm told we should not be relieved till further orders. Half an hour later told we should be relieved by BEDFORDS and INNISKILLINGS and that we were to go to BETHUNE. Finally about 8 pm were relieved by BEDFORDS, YORKSHIRES & INNISKILLINGS in about equal parts, and battalion marched to [MONTMORENCY BARRACKS], BETHUNE arriving between 1 am & 2 am.

4

Thursday May 13th. Battalion at MONTMORENCY BARRACKS, BETHUNE. In afternoon heard that Brigade was to take over CUINCHY section of the line by 9 a.m. tomorrow. Orders not out till very late.
Name of London Division changed to 47th Division & that of 6th Lon. INF. BDE to 142nd Inf. Bde.

Friday May 14th. Battalion paraded at 5 a.m. and marched thro' BEUVRY to ANNEQUIN. H.Qs & A & C Companies at latter place, one company at TOURBIERES and one at GLASGOW STREET. The Battalion being in BRIGADE RESERVE.

Saturday May 15th. H.Qs & 2 Companies at ANNEQUIN relieved by 21st Battalion and moved up to join 'D' Company at TOURBIERES & C Company going to CAMBRIN.
Attack by the 1st Army against the AUBERS Ridge began during the night, the 4th Brigade in CUINCHY section however being left in comparative peace —

5

SUNDAY. May 16th. Quiet day. Heard that 1st army's attack had been largely successful in the direction of VIOLAINES.
Received orders to relieve 23rd Battalion to-morrow in Section A1. to-morrow.

MONDAY May 17th. Relieved 23rd Batt in Section A1. beginning at 9 a.m. Relief complete by noon. A ~~day~~ certain amount of bombing from enemy. Lt Fowler & Lt Lodge (Yr Bde Bombing Instructor) wounded by Minenwerfer bomb). Wet day

~~Monday~~ May 18th Co-operated with long range rifle fire with continued attack of 1st Army towards GIVENCHY. A certain amount of rifle grenade fire & bombs from enemy. Casualties 1 killed, one wounded. Wet day.

Wednesday May 19th. Wet day. Very little doing except a little hand grenade firing in the trenches. Received order that the 23rd Batt. would relieve us next morning in the Trenches & that we were to go back into Brigade Reserve at ANNEQUIN.

THURSDAY, May 20th. Battalion relieved commencing 9 a.m by 23rd Battn. Went into billets at ANNEQUIN. Heard in evening that the Brigade was to be relieved by the 1st Division and that we were to be sent to BETHUNE, the 4th Royal Welsh Fusiliers (T.F.) taking our place at ANNEQUIN.

Friday May 21st. Relieved at ANNEQUIN by 4th Royal Welsh Fusiliers at about 11.30 a.m. Just previously told that Battalion was not to go to BETHUNE (our billeting party had already gone to take over the Tobacco Factory at that place), but was to go to WEST GORRE. Marched there by companies, but found that our billets were actually at LE QUESNOY, North of BEUVRY and South of AIRE LA BASSEE Canal.

Saturday May 22nd. Battalion resting. CO, Adjutant & OC Companies went to 142nd Bde Hqs at 8 a.m., and intended attack on enemy's trenches E. of GIVENCHY explained. In afternoon reconnoitred GIVENCHY lines and enemy's line opposite. Heard that intended attack had been postponed 24 hours.

Battalion reserve.   7

Sunday, May 23rd. Quiet day. Attack planned for evening of 24th again postponed 24 hours. Meeting of Company commanders to discuss details of the attack.

Monday, May 24th. Quiet day. Battalion resting. Bomb throwers practised with silvie bombs by Batt. Bomb officer, Lt. Garner-Smith.

Tuesday, May 25th } See attached account
Wednesday May 26th } of operations.
                      see 21st

~~Wednes~~ Thursday May 27th. Battalion moved from reserve dugouts at WINDY Corner, GIVENCHY to north bank of La Bassée Canal [where they bivouacked for a few hours, having dinners there & bathing in the Canal.] Thence they marched via BEUVRY to BETHUNE, [where they were billeted in the TOBACCO FACTORY]. March there took on aspect of a Roman Triumph, as men in great spirits, carrying spoils of war (German helmets, hat badges etc.) [&] inhabitants showed considerable enthusiasm. Gen. Barter commanding 47th Divn met the battalion at BETHUNE & congratulated them on their good work.

Friday May 28th. Still resting. The whole battalion bathed at L'ECOLE DE NATATION in the morning. In the afternoon the Battalion was inspected by Lt. Gen. Sir Charles Monro, Commanding 1st Army Corps, who congratulated battalion on their achievements.

Saturday May 29th. Resting & reorganizing. Narrative of events & recommendations for individual rewards sent in. Casualties reported now as officers 8 (5 killed, 3 wounded). Other ranks 400 (... killed, ... wounded, ... missing).

Sunday May 30th. Resting & reorganizing.

Monday May 31st. Resting & Reorganizing. Route march in morning.

W. Millner
Capt & Act Adjt
24th Batt London Regt
The Queens

NARRATIVE for 25th-26th MAY.

Narrative of Events 25th–26th May
24th Batt. London Regt.

May 25th

6.20 p.m. The Battalion took over the SCOTTISH TRENCH Section of GIVENCHY relieving a company of the 23rd Battalion.

Battalion in following order from front to rear: A, B, C, D Companies; M.G; in a position of readiness in SCOTTISH TRENCH. ½ section 3rd London Field Coy R.E. (T.F.) and a trench mortar battery attached, the latter being stationed in the trenches held by the 18th LONDON REGT on our right.

6.15 p.m. 23rd Battalion reported that they were not certain whether they could be ready to start @ 6.30 p.m., as all their Companies were not in a position. Decided nevertheless that we should start attack at appointed time (6.30 p.m.) owing to danger of interfering with Artillery programme. Reported to 23rd Batt that we were doing so.

6.30 p.m. "A" Company advanced from SCOTTISH TRENCH in a platoon frontage NO I platoon leading. At the same time the 23rd Battalion advanced on our left, the leading platoons of both Battalions

reaching the hostile trench, I 4 to J 7
without great loss.

"B" Company followed at once and ½ "C"
Company were sent up almost immediately in
close support

The remaining ½ "C" Company went forward
about 10 minutes later, and owing to several
applications for reinforcements 2 platoons
of "D" Company were subsequently ordered to
go forward and reinforce the captured trench.
By a mistake the whole of "D" Company
went up at this time, instead of two
platoons.

6.56 p.m O.C. "B" Company reports that
he is unable to advance beyond 1st Objective
I 4, but is consolidating trench captured.
Urgently demanded more bombs, which
were at once sent up.

6.45-9 p.m Captured Trench being consolidated
a severe bomb fight taking place all
the time on the right flank.
Capt. Gill, Lt Morrison, Lt Garner Smith
Lt Chance & Lt Penn Gaskell, killed, and
Capt Nadaud, Capt Wheater & Lt Moberley
wounded during this period.

At least two counter attacks across
the open obliquely against the right of

the line captured (I 4) were repulsed by
rifle fire during this period.

10.15 p.m All four companies now in
captured trench. A request was sent to
Brigade for close support by the 22nd Batt;
more men being also wanted for taking
up ammunition etc to the firing line.

May 26th
    12.30 a.m One Company 22nd Battn, and
Bombers of the Divisional Cyclists Company
arrived, the latter being sent up at once
to I 4, supported by a platoon of
the 20th Battalion detached from a
Company of that Regiment who had
arrived as a working party.
    Their orders were to try & push ~~forward~~
towards I 2.
    Beside the above Company of the
20th Battalion less 1 platoon A Company
of the 22nd Battalion were by now
employed in making communication
trenches - one along sunken road direct
to I 4, another along line of willows
towards same place.
    A party of about 20 Germans were
captured in a newly excavated mine by
Lt Morland. 3rd London Field Coy R.E.

and 2/Lt C. G. Davies 24th Battalion.

Owing to heavy losses in bombers round I.4 due to the Germans being on higher ground than our people, efforts to push along trenches towards I.2 & I.9 were abandoned and henceforward it was rather a question of holding the trench gained in face of heavy bomb attacks and continual sniping from the right flank.

3.25 a.m. Attached situation report (Marked A) sent. The whole of D & 2 platoons of "C" Company withdrawn to Scottish Trench.

4.20 a.m. Owing to continued attentions from enemy bombers, co-operation of more bombers and trench mortars asked for, our first trench mortar battery having been knocked out some little time previously (the report of this happening did not reach me for some hours as the officer in charge had been injured).
Approximate Casualties reported at this time 3 officers killed (Gill, Morrison, Garner Smith) 3 officers wounded (Radcliff, Wheeler, Mobberley) & 2 officers missing (Charles Penn, Gaskell) both subsequently reported killed)

Other ranks 60 killed, 150 wounded.

6.00 a.m. Work in communication trenches had had to be discontinued at daylight. The sunken road one was just sufficiently done to be useful.
The attached situation report (B) sent.

6.60 a.m. Application for further help to evacuate large number of wounded sent to Brigade.

7.20 a.m. Attached situation report (marked "C") sent.

7.30 a.m. Enemy began to shell captured trenches very heavily from an enfilading position on right flank, causing many casualties to ourselves, and the detachments of the 23rd & 21st Battalion holding the positions.

All officers of 23rd Battalion became casualties, and on this being reported I ordered some officer in the front trench to be sent along to look after the surviving men and to tell them to hold on at all costs. Capt Miltner personally went himself and managed to get control of a number of them.

At one time it seemed as though it would be necessary to evacuate the trench and in fact a report ~~had been~~ was sent to the Brigade that this had been done, tho' in reality it was at no time evacuated.

It was only by the personal example of Captain Millner, Figg & Armstrong who remained at their posts and kept the men round them together, that this did not take place.

8.15 a.m Message sent to O.C. Captured trench to widely extend his men along the captured trench, dig themselves in and hang on at all costs. Meanwhile a platoon of "D" Company was pushed up from SCOTTISH TRENCH along the sunken road communication trench (which was defilated from fires from the right) in order to prevent any of the enemy attempting to get into the captured trench from I.4.

11 a.m Captain Millner, Figg and Armstrong and the remainder of their men withdrawn from the captured trench, their places being taken by Lt Kelly's platoon of "D" Company and a section of the 22nd Battalion under

Captain Wooley

11.15 am Attached situation report
(marked 'D') sent

12 noon - 5 pm Captured trench again shelled from right flank but owing to wide extension of the force holding it not many casualties occurred. No attempt was made during this time to recapture the trench either by direct counter attack or by bombing up the trench.

5 - 7 pm Wire from Brigade that the 20th London Regiment would relieve the battalion at 6.30 pm. About this time SCOTTISH TRENCH heavily shelled

8.30 - 10 pm Relief taking place

10.30 pm Battalion relieved and went back to reserve dugouts at
WINDY CORNER

The most noticeable feature of the operations was the retention of the captured trench by a few exhausted and in many cases wounded men after it had been subjected to a very heavy enfilade rifle fire

I should like to draw attention to the good work done by the bombers both of this battalion and of the Divisional Cyclist Company. The battalion bombers went into action 75 strong and came out numbering 14

Also to the battalion stretcher bearers who all thro' the night 25/26 inst worked, often under heavy fire to evacuate the wounded. This work was most efficiently continued during the 26th inst by a platoon of the 19th Battalion London Regt specially sent to help us in this way

The total casualties of the battalion during these 28 hours were 5 officers killed, 3 officers wounded
<u>Other ranks</u> 52 killed, 252 wounded 96 missing.

A.

TO   142ND INF BDE

    26   AAA.

Situation Report AAA line from I4 to point of junction with 23rd consolidated AAA Two platoons 'D' Company at present lining sunken road are being withdrawn to SCOTTISH trench as garrison ample without them AAA Communication trenches connecting SCOTTISH trench with captured trench have been partially constructed and are being improved AAA Officer in charge at I4 reports that their line is somewhat infiladed from direction of I2 AAA He is trying to avoid this by constructing traverses to shield his right flank by covering his parapet and deepening his trench AAA. Attentions from trench howitzers and artillery along "ladder" trench in direction I2 would be appreciated AAA Div. Cyclist bombers supported by one platoon 20th Regt and our right company have gained a few yards south of I4 AAA Great assistance rendered during the night by working parties of 22nd and 29th Battns AAA will send approximate casualty list as soon as possible AAA.

2H LON REGT

3.25 AM (SD) C. G. MAUDE
CAPT + ADJT

B.

10. - 142ND INF BDE.

26 AAA.

SITUATION REPORT Situation somewhat quieter on right flank but are still worried by hostile bombers and snipers just south of I4 who are on high ground commanding our right at the Sunken road AAA We have had about twenty casualties from this source lately AAA Artillery have promised to co-operate towards I2 and mortars will doubtless assist AAA Suggest that rifle grenades used by left of 18th Battn or right of our Battn would be of great use AAA Can suggestion be made to 18th Battn and a supply of these sent to us.

24 LON REGT

6.20 AM

(SD) C.G MAUDE
CAPT & ADJ

C.

TO :-   142ND INF BDE

26.   AAA.

SITUATION REPORT AAA Fairly quiet but vigorous sniping against our right flank at I4 AAA O.C. A Company at this point reports that enemy can be seen working on high ground to his right flank AAA

24 LON REGT

7.20 AM

(SD) C.G MAUDE
CAPT & ADJ

D.

TO:- 142ND INF BDE

26   AAA

Situation Report AAA We are still holding
German trench with a mixed force
of 21ST 22ND & 24TH Battalions AAA
If the guns which enfilade us from the
right flank are kept quiet we shall
probably continue to do so AAA Reference
your BM758 a communication trench
along line of Willows thro' I5 was
constructed last night AAA Another
can only be constructed at night
and I do not think it necessary
in view of those already constructed
AAA It would be better to improve
these latter AAA

24 LON REGT

11.15 AM

(SD) C G MAUDE
CAPT & ADJ

OPERATION ORDERS.

4

PREPARATORY ORDERS
for MAY. 8th 1915.

reference Map ILLIES – VIOLAINES – FESTUBERT 1/10,000

1. **PLAN**. The 24th Battalion will hold its present line of trenches, assisting by fire the advance of the 2nd BRIGADE 1st DIVISION, who ~~starting~~ attacking south through Q2 to P8, will make for a line P4 road junction – LA QUINGUE RUE road junction – M20 road junction.

   Subsequently the battalion may be ordered to advance & relieve an unit of the 2nd Brigade, but definite orders will be issued about this.

2. **CONTROL OF FIRE**. All fire unit commanders will exercise the strictest fire control over their units, so that all danger of men (particularly in section II (d)) firing into the right flank of the advancing 2nd BRIGADE crossing our left front, shall be obviated. A red flag with a white upright bar in centre will be carried on right of 2nd BDE to mark their progress.

3. **Ammunition**. Each N.C.O – man will carry 200 rounds of ammunition.

on them. An additional 200 rounds per man from Trench STORE S.A.A will be in the Trenches, and this only will be used for covering fire purposes. The 200 rounds carried on the man will be intact for a possible advance.

4. SANDBAGS. Each N.C.O & man will carry 2 sandbags.

5. TOOLS. Entrenching tools are to be fitted & carried in the belt.
A proportion of wirecutters & axes will be carried by leading companies.
Should an advance take place every second man in A & D companies will carry a spade slung over his back with spunyarn.

6. RATIONS & WATER.
Every man will carry one day's rations in addition to the Emergency ration.
All water bottles are to be filled.

7. PRECAUTIONS against GAS
Everyone will carry a muffler or cap comforter which in case

poisonous gas is encountered will be damped and tied round the mouth & nose.

Should belts of gas be encountered units should charge quickly thro' them if advancing. If troops are stationary rapid fire ~~also~~ directed at the belt does much to dissipate the gas.

8. <u>DRESS</u>. All ranks will be in

Sweaters & jerseis are to be removed ~~one hour before~~ at and carried in the waterproof sheet

Great coats are not to be worn.

9. <u>GRENADIERS</u>. The grenadier sections of companies will be fully supplied with grenades in case of an advance. They will move with the supports of the company.

10. <u>LADDERS</u>. All available ladders will be brought from DEAD COW FARM to the trenches occupied

by A & D companies where they will be stored under arrangements to be made by O's. C. these companies.

In case of an advance the ladders will be taken forward by the leading lines of these companies, and will be used to bridge ditches & other obstacles.

11. <u>Food</u>. O.C. Companies will arrange for all ranks to obtain a meal including a hot drink 1 hour before the commencement of the bombardment.

A rum ration will be distributed at .

12. <u>References</u>. All reports from O.C. Companies etc. will have reference to the 1/10,000 ILLIES, VIOLAINES, FESTUBERT map, and will refer to <u>numbers</u> & not names of places.

13. <u>PRISONERS</u>. Any prisoners taken will be disarmed, searched & all belongings sent with them (under escort) to Battalion H.Qs.

14. **AID POST**. The Regimental AID POST will be formed at the present Battalion H.Q., RUE DU BOIS.

All ranks should know this and should further be reminded that it is absolutely forbidden for anyone to accompany wounded men to the rear. If unable to walk there, the wounded will be carried by the Regimental Stretcher bearers.

XLVII May 1915

The 6th LON. INF. BDE (less 22nd & 23rd Bns) will support the infantry advance with rifle + M.G. fire

2. INTENTION. The 24th Bn will remain in its present breastworks, distributed as at present and will assist the advance of the 1st Div. commencing at 5.40 a.m.

Subsequently it may be ordered to relieve a part of the 1st Div. along the line P4 — LA QUINQUE RUE — RUE DE MARAIS after these points have been occupied & made good by those troops.

3. DETAIL (a) The Battalion will be in position by 4 a.m.

(b) At 5.40 a.m. vigorous bursts of rapid ~~M.G.~~ fire will be opened by A, D & C Companies ~~at~~ against the enemy, the object being to prevent any withdrawal by him from our front ~~by the enemy~~ to act against the 1st Div. & also to inflict losses on reinforcements he may bring up to oppose the right of that Div., the strictest regard being paid to the fact that the Troops of the 1st Div. will be crossing our front in the assault.

(c) Combined sights will be used, and O.C. Companies will allot definite sectors of the enemy's parapet to each fire unit, ensuring that there is no considerable ~~pa~~ length of parapet unbeaten by fire.

(d) The M.G. will co-operate whenever a suitable occasion or target presents itself.

4. <u>Communication</u>. From 3 a.m to-morrow, all wires are reserved for operation purposes.

5. <u>REPORTS</u>. H.Q's will be at the DUGOUT just North of DEADCOW FARM from 4.15 a.m to-morrow.

6. Orders. No copy of this order is to be carried by officers in the front line. Notes should be taken, all ranks informed & the written order then destroyed. C.P. Mander
Capt. - Adjt

issued at 10.35 pm by orderly to all companies & M.G. offr

142nd Inf. Bde.
47th Division.

WAR DIARY

1/24th LONDON REGT.

JUNE

1915

9

WAR DIARY — JUNE 1915 —

Tuesday   June 1st — Battalion moved from BETHUNE to
           VERQUIN & took over Billets of S.W.B.
Wednesday June 2nd — Resting & reorganizing
Thursday   " 3rd — The Kings Birthday — Royal Salute
           & three cheers given for H.M. on parade.
           Route march by Companies — Instruction of NCO's
           in Bombing — 4 NCO's attend for instruction &
           demonstrations in prevention against [CO with Brigade near NOYELLES area]
           asphyxiating gases at SAILLY — LABOURSE
Friday   June 4th — Companies route march in morning —
           Instruction of NCO's in bombing — all ranks
           drilled in putting on respirators — Commenced
           training new reserve M.G. Section. C.O. & Adjt. visit NOYELLES area
Saturday   June 5th — Companies route march in morning —
           Instruction of NCO's in bombing — CO. visits W3 area
Sunday   June 6th — Divine Service — move to W3 Sector
           and relieving 7th Battn KINGS REGT.
Monday   June 7th — Spasmodic rifle
           fire during night 6/7th. The coron where Battalion
           HQ. situated shelled during morning — A few
           shells sent over again in the afternoon. Quiet
           day
Tuesday.   June 8th. More shelling in the morning — Battn
           H.Q. moved in the evening — Quiet day — C.O. &
           Adjutant 23-d Battalion report they were fired at
           from house in rear of trenches while going up a
           communication trench. More shelling in the evening
           of houses round old H.Q.

Lieuts Poland Turcott & Gauvage arrive from the 2nd Battalion. C.O. to Brigade to discuss improvement of defensive line & construction of strong point in W 3. At 6 pm French guns in our rear send a few shells into the German lines on our front.

Wednesday June 9th – No shelling of neighbourhood of old Battn H.Q. Steps taken for evacuation of all inhabitants (including men attending engines in mine in W 2) further back than the ~~line~~ present boundary line. C.O. makes further examination of line with a view to siting defensive post. Neighbourhood of old Battn H.Q. shelled in late afternoon, perhaps owing to its having been brought into use as a billet.

Thursday June 10th – Quiet day – Relieved by 23 LON REG in W.3 & take over their billets at LES BREBIS. D Coy remains in W 3 attached to 23 LON REG – Relief completed by 11 pm. Col Simpson takes command of the Brigade

Friday June 11th – Resting – Working party of 2 officers 100 N.CO's & men found on night of 11/12

Saturday June 12th – Resting –

Sunday June 13th – Divine Service – voluntary parade –

Monday June 14th – Battalion resting – C.O. & Adjt reconnoitered route to be taken by Company in Brigade reserve in the event of having to reinforce W.3.

Tuesday June 15th – Battalion resting. Issue of Clothing etc.

Wednesday June 16th – Battalion resting. Brigade order state of readiness in case of Emergency as Germans may counter attack from Loos.

11

Thursday June 17th. Relieved 23rd Battn in W.3.

Friday June 18th. Quiet day. Patrols reconnoitred ground in front of trenches in W.3.

Saturday June 19th. Quiet day.

Sunday June 20th
    Relieved at 11 pm by the 19th Bn. London Regt. and marched back to billets at NOEUX LES MINES.

Monday June 21st
    Battalion resting in billets at NOEUX LES MINES.

June 22nd. Battalion resting at NOEUX-LES-MINES.

June 23rd ditto. Refitting & platoon route marches.

June 24th ditto. Major Carr & Capt & Adjt Chlmande reconnoitred routes to MAZINGARBE & positions of assembly there in case Brigade had to concentrate there in support of Sections W or X.

June 25th Battalion resting. Bombing instruction for all N.C.Os under of the Battalion started.

June 26th Platoon route marches & bombing instruction continued.

June 27th. Church parade at 9 a.m. at 6th Lon. Field Ambulance H Qrs. Received orders that we should go up into X2 in relief of 7th Batt. London Regt. tomorrow evening.

13

June 28th. Bombing instruction in morning.
At 5 pm O.C. Companies, and at 9.30 pm companies etc. proceeded to section X2 (H.Q's. Fosse No.7 de BETHUNE) and in conjunction with the 23rd Battn. took over that part of the line from 7th Battn. London Regt. – 2 companies of 23rd Battn. and D company 24th Battn. in front line from right to left; Composite company in local reserve.
Relief completed by midnight. Quiet night, no shelling or firing.

June 29th. Quiet day. Only a little shelling in evening. Enemy's trenches a considerable distance from our line, so little or no rifle fire either by day or night. Major Carr left for England on leave. Col. Lloyd commands in command during his absence.

June 30. Very heavy rain in the morning. Fatigue parties busy cleaning up trenches in the afternoon. Weather quite quiet. Capt. Millner & Rigg returned from leave from England.

Capt tadj't
Commanding
m[t]h Reg. Low Rifle,
"The Queens"

142nd Inf. Bde.
47th Division.

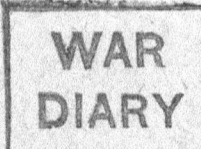

1/24th LONDON REGT.

JULY

1915

Attached:
Operation Order No. 9.

14

July 1st. Fine & quiet day. Heard that the following honours had been conferred on the battalion for the action of May 25/26th.

Capt. L.W. Figg — D.S.O.

No. 149 Coy. Sgt. Maj. H.W. Norris
" 2378 Pte. H.J.W. Allen
" 1592 " W.H. Walters
" 2557 " E. Carr
} D.C.M.

July 2nd. Quiet day. One casualty in early morning, probably due to a stray bullet. In evening Composite Company relieved Capt. Fearon's 23rd Bn. Company in right of X2, Major Parker with D Company remaining in old position on left of X2. — Heard that a draft of 115 men was arriving shortly from the base. The enemy showed a certain liveliness during the night from their sap opposite saps 12 and 12A in our lines.

July 3rd. Quiet day up to 5 p.m. when the enemy shelled our front line (Composite Company) with 'pipsqueaks'

No casualties. The French artillery supporting this part of the line replied and silenced the enemy guns.
Draft mentioned yesterday joined the 1st line transport at HOUCHAIN

July 4th. Quiet Day. 69 of the draft joined the battalion and went into the Trenches, the remainder staying back with the transport at HOUCHAIN.

July 5th. Quiet day. The Battalion ordered to join up the heads of our Saps 12 & 12A. A German saphead suspected of being lying between these points on the line of the proposed new Trench, so it was necessary to take this by assault first.
Orders were issued for this to take place at 10 p.m. (see attached copy of operation orders)
The first attacking party lost direction & were delayed by running into some old barbed wire in front. A bombing

party of the 22nd Batt. however being at once sent out discovered that there was no actual redoubt, tho' traces of recent German work existed. Working parties of the 23rd & 21st Bn. were at once got out & commenced work on the new trench. The Germans, beyond firing a few shots at the beginning of operations, left us severely alone, so that by daylight (about 2 a.m.) a considerable portion of the trench had been completed.

July 6th. Quiet day. Heard that L/Cpl. Keyworth had been awarded the V.C. for gallantry on May 25/26th.

July 7th. Quiet day. Working parties continued digging trench connecting Sabs 12 & 12A.

July 8th. Quiet morning. In afternoon enemy shelled our trenches a little, and about 7 p.m. our battalion reserve billets without however doing any damage

17

July 9th   One or two shells about billets about 8 a.m. Otherwise all quiet.

July 10th   Heard that construction of deep dugouts etc. in trenches were to be pushed on owing to possible German offensive. Command of X2 section taken over by 23rd Battn. All Quiet.

July 11th   All quiet. Work on dugouts etc. proceeding. Heard that Lt. C.G. Davis had been awarded the Military Cross.

July 12th   All quiet. Heard that we were being relieved by 48th (South Midland) Divn tomorrow night, and were going back into Corps reserve.

July 13th   Philosophe heavily shelled in the morning. Heard we were not being relieved by 48th Divn but would go back into Divisional Reserve on the evening of the 14th.

July 14th   Orders received for battalion to be relieved by 17th Battn in X2 and

go back to MAZINGARBE & there take
over billets of 18th Bn London Regt.

H.Q's billet shelled by L.H.V. gun
in the morning.

Handed over to 17th Bn London
Regt. beginning 9 p.m. Wretched
evening blowing & raining hard.
Last Company (Composite Company)
got into billets at MAZINGARBE
at 2 a.m. 15th inst.

July 15th. In billets at MAZINGARBE.
Working party of 130 found
from Composite Company to work
for section W. (Les BREBIS).

July 16th. C.O., Adjutant, Signalling Officer
(Hallett), 3 Company Commanders
(Parker, Armstrong, Pigg) reconnoitred
the trenches of the French Brigade
immediately on the right of the Brigade section
W.3, with a view to supporting
them into a counter-attack from
the direction of Les BREBIS should
necessity arise

Working party of 130 found
from D Company to same place
as yesterday.

19

July 17th. Major Parker, W. Hallett proceeded to ENGLAND on leave. Working party 130 men found from Composite Company.

July 18th. Voluntary Church parade in morning. Working party of 130 men from "D" Company.

July 19th. Working party of 130 men from Composite Company

July 20th. C.O., Adjt. & Company Commanders attended lecture at NŒUX-LES-MINES on bombs. Working party from D Company at same place of same strength

July 21st. All quiet. Working party of 130 from Composite Company. Orders received to take over W3 (MAROC) tomorrow from 6th Bn Sussex Regt.

July 22nd Relieved 6th London in W3. One coy 8th Bn Suffolk Regt. attached for instruction

July 23rd All quiet — work on completing trenches & Keep "D" proceeded with

July 24th — Handed over command of Section 20 to 23rd Battalion — All quiet. Work on line & Keep D proceeded with. Nine new officers arrived from 2nd Battalion. One company 12th Bn H.L.I attached for instruction to the Composite (23/24th) Batt3

July 25th — Shelled in billets of MAROC — (Section W3) eight casualties, the first lost by the battalion since the commencement of the war, while in billets —

July 26th — Shelled at 8.30 a.m. & 1.30 p.m. One Coy. 2nd in Command, M.G.O' & 5 Warrant Officers 12th Battn HLI & 7th Camerons attached for instruction — C.O. & Adjutant sited new advanced H.Q. in W.3. Took over command of W 3 from 23 Lon Regt.

July 27th — Quiet day —

July 28th — Front line shelled. 1 Company 9th Black Watch attached for instruction

July 29th — C.O. & Adjutant inspected Keep D & Line B with Engineer officer — Maroc shelled in morning

July 30th — Quiet day — Heard that we were going into Corps rest in a few days. 2nd Company 9th Black Watch attached for instruction

July 31st — Quiet day — C.O. went round W 3 with Major Wallace, C.O. of the 9th Black Watch who are taking over the sector — Adjutant returns from leave.

C. Maud
Captain ??
24th London Regt.

OPERATION ORDER NO. 9.

Operation Order No 9   Copy
by
Capt. C. G. Meander,
Commanding X2 Subsection.
July 5th 1915.

Reference French maps.

1 PLAN.

The heads of Saps 12 and 12A will be joined up to-night, so as to fill up the gap in the present front line in advance of the OLD FRENCH fire Trench.

This will be done by first seizing the enemy saphead which has intruded into the gap between saps 12 and 12A, and then joining it up with our line.

2 DETAIL.

Lt T. Kelly
6 Bombers
6 Bayonet men
'D' Co
with for Right.

(a) At 10 pm a party as in margin will leave the right horn of sap 12 and will occupy the hostile saphead, if possible, without noise. A double barricade will then be constructed about 50ˣ down the sap in the direction of the enemy, and held at all costs.

(b)

1 N.C.o
6 bombers
6 bayonet men
Composite Coy
24ᵗʰ Jow. Rifles
} This party will be followed as a close support at a distance of about 20 yards by a party as in margin. With these will go a R.E. officer and 4 Sappers one of whom will unwind a tape fastened inside Sap 12. The officer will be responsible for marking out the line of the Trench connecting Sap 12 with the vicinity of the enemy saphead and also subsequently continuing this line to Sap 12 A.

(c) As soon as the saphead
1 N.C.O
2 Sappers
R.E.
} has been seized (signalled by electric lamp) a small party as in margin will leave Sap 12 A and (as in (b) above) connect this point with the vicinity of the captured enemy saphead.

The officer in command will in addition carry a VERREY pistol and 10 rounds ammunition.

(b) O.C. 4th Field Company R.E. will arrange to form a sandbag depôts of 1000 sandbags each in Saps 12 and 12 A.

(c) OC Composite Company 2nd Coy Rifle Bgde will form depôts of extra bombs and rifle ammunition in his sector and will ensure that their whereabouts are known to all ranks

4. Signals

The following signals will be used to communicate between the captured saphead and our present lines.

(a) Electric lamp turned on for 10 seconds, and kept with light pointing towards OLD FRENCH FIRE TRENCH = "We have captured the enemy saphead".

(b) 3 loud blasts on a whistle = "The barricade has been constructed and we are NOT being attacked"

(c) A succession of short flashes with electric lamp = "Running short of ammunition and bombs"

(d) The position of our men holding the saphead centre shown after dawn by a cap held up on a bayonet.

5. Medical

The M.O. will make the necessary arrangements for evacuating the wounded.
Trenches 14 and 14A will be reserved exclusively for this purpose. Stretcher Bearers etc to thoroughly reconnoitre these routes.

6. HQ's

All reports to right Company Commander's dugout from 9.30 pm.

H.Q's
5/7/15   (Sd) C. G. Maude
                          Capt & adjt
Copy No 1   Filed   of 22nd Bn.
       2   N2nd Inf Bde   Som Rgt.
       3   OC 23rd Bn   "The Queens"
       4   " Coy 22nd
       5   " Coy 23rd Bn
       6   — 22nd Bn
       7   O.C. 4th Fd. Coy R.E.
       8   O.C. Rt   ⎫
       9   — Centre   ⎬ Company
       10 — Left   ⎭ x2
       11 Lt. Kelly
       12 M.O.

(g) The Brigade Machine Gun
BDE ⎫ Officer will make dispositions
MG's ⎭ against any hostile counter
attack over the open against the
captured saphead.

(h) The French Artillery will
be ready to co-operate by firing
against the enemy's salient
opposite saps 12 and 12 A.

(i) The Battalion bombers of 24th
RESERVE ⎫ Lon. Rgt. (less those mentioned
BOMBERS ⎭ in (a) and (b) above) and a
party of the 22nd Lon. Rgt,
bombers will be in reserve in
the trench near the right company
H.Q. dugout.

3. Equipment.
(a) Each man in the parties
mentioned in 2(a) & (b) will in addition
to his arms and equipment carry
the following:—
    Rations for 24 hours.
    Filled water bottles
    6 empty sandbags.
    50 extra rounds ammunition

Working Party
from Sap 12A
2 officers &
75 men, 21st
Low. Regt.

Working Party
from Sap 12
2 officers and
75 men, 23rd
Low. Regt.

Immediately these tapes are out two working parties as in margin will leave saps 12 & 12A and will begin connecting these points with the vicinity of the captured saphead.

(i) If the hostile fire is not too heavy by digging a fire trench.

(ii) If the fire is heavy by constructing a series of grouse butts along the line of tape.

1 officer
12 Sappers } R.E.
12 men, 21st
Low. Regt.

(e) A third working party will at 10pm commence to draw a sap from a point X in the old FRENCH FIRE TRENCH between Saps 12 and 12A towards the enemy saphead.

(f) During the operation the Battalion will stand to arms and if necessary assist by fire.

The 22nd Bn, on our right will also be standing to arms.

142nd Inf. Bde.
47th Division.

WAR DIARY

1/24th LONDON REGT.

AUGUST

1915

142nd Bde.
c47th Division.

1/24th LONDON REGIMENT

SEPTEMBER

1 9 1 5

Sept 1st Senior Major + 60 other Ranks to
HOUCHIN for Gas demonstration at 3 pm.
6.45 pm. Battalion moved by Motor bus
to LES BREBIS, Headquarters ek
by Road. Battalion dug on Communication
trenches between LES BREBIS & MAROC
till 2.30 a.m. when it went into billets
at LES BREBIS.

Sept. 2nd Dug on new trench in front of
W3 on night of 2nd/3rd Sept, went
back into billets at LES BREBIS

Sept 3rd Took over 4 Keeps and Control posts
in Section W in afternoon —
at 7 pm started to relieve 23rd Bn
in Brigade Reserve at S.MAROC —
Relief completed by 8.45 pm
Furnished Carrying parties and working
parties for R.E. by whole of Battalion
on night of 3rd/4th

Sept 4th Occasional Enemy shelling in morning
to R&L. of S.MAROC — Furnished Working
parties by whole of Bn. to 2/3 Field Coy R.E's
worked on front line in front of W2 on
night 4/5th —

~~August~~ Sept 5th C.O. met G.O.C. Division
& French General at W1. 9 a.m.
Furnished whole of Bn on working parties
to 4th FIELD Coy R.E.'s to ~~further~~
Support line in front of W.3.

Sept 6th Bn on working parties all night
under R.E's — nothing of importance
occurred — Dummy Trenches dug —

Sept 7 C.O. met Brig-Gen at H.Q. W1
at noon. Battalion on working
parties partly on M.G. emplacements,
partly on C.T. under 3rd Lon. R.E's

Sept 8th CO to G.O.C. Bde at noon —
150 working party on C.T. under R.E's
at 3.0 pm. Remainder of Bn —
50 on M.G. emplacements. 140 on
C.T. under 3rd Field Coy at 4 a.m
on morning of

Sept 9th till 8 a.m. Working parties
at 2.30 pm and 6 pm under R.E's
also on M.G. Emplacements —
Enemy Shells, which had not touched
S. MAROC since our Arrival, began
to arrive in our area — tho' in very
small number —

Sept 10th Working party under R.E.s at
8.30 am and 1.30 pm.

Sept 10th (cont'd)
 Small Party on M.G. Emplacements and
 AID POSTS

Sept 11th Working parties of all Batt: except
 A & C Coys under R.E.'s at 8.30 a.m. &
 2.30 p.m. for 2 3 hour shifts —
 S. MAROC Shelled slightly about 4 p.m.
 Party on M.G. Emplacements during night
 as before —

Sept 12th Working Parties as on 11th. C.O in
 Command of Bde during afternoon, while
 Brigadier at NOEUX LES MINES. Water
 Main nr. C.T. 9 burst by shell & Trench
 partially flooded — Sappers informed &
 Water turned off at Mine.

Sept 13th Working Parties as on 12th

Sept 14th Working Parties as on 13th

Sept 15th Working Parties as on 14th — Billets
 shelled at 10 p.m. for 1/4 hr. No Casualties
 Large Fire noticed in German Lines near
 LENS, burnt all night

32

<u>Sept 16</u> Working Parties as on 15th — 3 or 4
Shells on Billets at 3 pm. No Casualties
Also a few shells during night
<u>Sept 17</u> Several enemy Shells over Billets during
morning. C.O. to Brigadier at 22nd
Bn H.Q. at 11 a.m. Working parties as
yesterday + 1 party to help 23rd Battn
to restore Communication Trenches in W3
<u>Sept 18</u> 9 Officers 32 N.C.O's reported to Staff
Captain at 9 a.m. to rehearse Carrying party
planned for night 18th/19th Sept — This party
consisting of above + 224 other Ranks, carried
out its work which was for W1 & W2, successfully
finishing by 4 a.m. — Less Shelling during day
<u>Sept 19</u> 11.15 a.m. Large Explosion noticed in German
Lines, judged to be at DYNAMITIÈRE, CITÉ
ST LAURENT — Threw up enormous Column
of Yellow Black Smoke, which drifted S. with wind.
— Not much Shelling — Working parties employed
on strengthening own Billets during day
<u>Sept 20</u> Working parties of all Battn during
morning and afternoon, except C Coy which
acted as Carrying party for R.W.F. during night
Sgt Evans gazetted to 2/Lt in this Battn & posted
to D Coy — Shelling much increased — 1 Signaller
killed and 1 wounded while on line work —
Control posts relieved by 47th Div. Cyclist Coy
at 2 pm. Guard from Crossing at LES BREBIS

returning to S. NAROC, caught by a Shell, Cpl and 1 man wounded, 1 man killed. Own Artillery fire during night much heavier

Sept 21 All Battⁿˢ worked on C Trenches nr. LES BREBIS from 5-7 a.m. and from 11 a.m to 1.30 pm. then stopped by SHELLFIRE. C.O. to Bde at NOON. Own Artillery fire continues to get heavier – Very little reply, none at all on our Billets. But a certain amount on Batteries nr. EDUARDS.

Sept 22 Warning rec'd of a demonstration by our Bde in front of us at 8 a.m. Artillery fire very heavy for 5 mins, but no reply came onto us — Our Artillery fire fairly heavy during day. Whole Batt on working party from 8 pm to 2 am during night no Casualties — All greatcoats to LES BREBIS during night.

Sept 23 Heavy Artillery fire on our R. presumably in direction SOUCHEZ, all morning — No enemy shellfire on our Billets — Own Artillery fire not so heavy as yesterday — Found working parties during night of about 300 men — Were warned of a demonstration on 15ᵗʰ DIV. front at 3.55 pm. but no results were noticed here. Received orders from Bde at 7 p.m. to reduce Officers with Battⁿ to 20,

34

<u>Sept 23 (Cont)</u> detailed 2nd Lts ONSEDEN, MAGNUS, P.R. LURCOTT, ASHWORTH + COUSINS to go back to Transport Lines as reserve of Officers —

<u>Sept 24</u> Major CAREY as President, and LT. MERCER as Member, to Bde HQ, for Court Martial 9 a.m. Morning Bombardment less heavy — 1.55 p.m. demonstration on our front at W1 — Heavy bombardment for 11 min. Provoked some reply from Enemy — who sent several shells into our billets during rest of day. At 4 p.m. very heavy cannonade heard to S. in French Area - 4.30 p.m. with heavy rifle fire — Died away about 5.15 p.m.

with B. Dr Grenadier Coy attch'd

<u>Sept 25</u> Moved into position as Div. Reserve in Advanced Second Line in front of Fosse 6, LES BREBIS — Move started 1.20 a.m. Completed 4 a.m. 28th Battⁿ on our left in same line of trenches — Zero notified as 5.50 a.m. when Bombardment started. Could see bank of Smoke and Gas on ridge running N. from MAROC, clearly marking line of our trenches — Wind v. faint, but S.W. Clouds gradually drifted towards German lines. After 6.30 (Time of attack) bombardment continued but gradually decreased during afternoon, and finally died away about 6 p.m. Only 1 enemy shell on or near our trenches during day —

35

<u>Sept 26</u> Still in same trenches till noon.
When ordered to relieve 23rd Bn in W3 —
Having arrived there, directed to send 1 Coy
forward to hold whole of old W3 front line.
Remainder + Green Coy to billets in N MAROC.
This completed by 2·30 pm. D Coy being sent
to hold W3 line — Stragglers from 15th & 21st
Divisions came thro' our lines during all
afternoon & evening — Sent working party
of 200 under Capt MILLNER to work on
C.T. from Sap 3 to DOUBLE CRASSIER at
8 pm. returned safely, no casualties —
Quiet night

<u>Sept 27</u> Quiet during morning and early
afternoon — 3 pm furnished carrying
parties for 3 T.M. Batteries and 3
Wagon loads of various bombs, which were
picked up at FOSSE 5 and taken to LOOS —
Whole of Battⁿ in MAROC was used for this,
and did not return entirely till 11 pm.
Quiet night

<u>Sept 28</u> Billets shelled during morning and
early afternoon — M.O — Capt GIBLIN
R.A.M.C. killed by shell about 11·20 a.m
while in HARROW RD — Substitute Lt
MATHER R.A.M.C. arrived 5 pm.
6 pm Battⁿ moved to outskirts of LOOS,
and relieved 19th & 20th Bns — Holding line

from CHALKPIT M6 a 8.2. on Left to end of Spinney M5 B 8.2 on Right — Left in touch with 9th L'pools — Right in touch with nobody — Worked all night on consolidating Spinney, in very bad condition owing to our shelling when Spinney was taken on 27th. Very wet — Quiet night

Sept 29. Quiet morning: occasional shelling of Loos in morning — Our line in front of Spinney shelled during afternoon, One killed 6 wounded in D Coy — Quiet night — Succeeded in wiring whole of front of Spinney and consolidated so far that D Coy could hold the new line on Enemy side — Also managed to get overcoats for all Battn — Lieut DAVIES joined Battn with remaining 3 M.G's and also had 2 M.G's from 28th Bn making 8 at our disposal — ~~Started~~ ~~line~~

Sept 30. Occasional enemy shellfire over Loos — Bde S.'s. Officer killed 8.15 a.m. Started 2 Bn Dumps for Salved British Arms, equipment etc. No 1 near Chalkpit, No 2 in empty Estaminet at entrance to Garden City — Intermittent shelling of Copse with T.Mortars & 'Pipsqueaks' and Loos with H.E. Quiet night, tho' evidently attack expected — 12 Rockets sent to Copse. Artillery test carried out 12.10 midnight.

C P Saunders
Lieut and Adjt
2nd Vol Regt
"The Queen's"

142nd Inf. Bde.
47th Division.

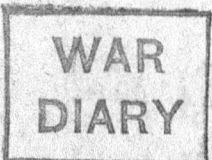

1/24th LONDON REGT.

OCTOBER

1915

From:- O.C. 24th. Battalion London Regt.("The Queens"
To:- D.A.G.
    3rd. Echelon.

Reference your No.140/LXVI dated 15/12/15 please note that the War Diary for October was forwarded to you on or about Nov.2nd.1915.

[Stamp: A.G.'s OFFICE AT THE BASE CENTRAL REGISTRY -4 JAN 1916 C.R. No 140/LXVI]

CAPTAIN & ADJUTANT,
24th (COUNTY OF LONDON) Bn,
THE LONDON REGIMENT,
THE "QUEENS"

26.12.15.

O.C. 1/24th London Regt.
There is no trace of the receipt of the War Diary referred to.
It is requested that a copy may be furnished.

DAAG
for DAG

G.H.Q.
3rd Echelon.
4.1.16.

3.

D.A.G.,
3rd Echelon.

              Herewith copy as requested.

                        Lt. and Adjt.,
                        for O.C.,
10.1.16.   24th Bn., Lon. Regt.,
                      "The Queen's".

24th (COUNTY OF LONDON) BN.
THE LONDON REGT.
ORDERLY ROOM
No.
Date
(THE QUEEN'S)

__Oct 1__ Major Can to Bde Hqrs to meet officers of 68th Regt d'INFANTERIE who then went over our line with O.C. Coys. Afternoon spent in organising relief, salving equipment etc. Relief started 7 p.m. completed 11 p.m. Our Bn. of approx 530 relieved by 2 French Bns of approx 1800 — moved by Companies to Bde rendezvous near MAZINGARBE.

__Oct 2__ Bn moved to VAUDRICOURT at 7 a.m. arriving in billets at 9 a.m. No billets for officers who slept in tents.

__Oct 3__ Moved to billets at FOUQUEREIL arrived 3 pm. Capt. J.W. Pace, Lt Clar, 2nd Lt Drake joined from England. Day occupied in inspections etc. Lt DICK R.A.M.C. reported for duty as M.O. to Bn. vice Lt MATHER returned to Motor Ambulance Column.

__Oct 4__ Remained at FOUQUEREIL — Inspections - refitting etc

Oct 5 Same as Oct. 4 Capt.
MILLNER to England for
6 days leave.

Oct 6 Moved to billets at NOEUX
LES MINES. Started 9.45 a.m
arrived 12 noon.

Oct 7 Formed two working
parties of 49 N.C.O's and
men each. at 8 a.m and
12.30 a.m. resp. Interior
economy etc.

Oct 8 Company training in
morning — baths etc
afternoon. 6 p.m ordered to
stand by on ½ hrs notice —
Heavy cannonade all afternoon
and evening audible in N.E.
direction. State of ½ hr readiness
continued through night.

Oct 9 Till 10 a.m. — at 11.30 a.m.
Bde inspection by G.O.C.
IV th Corps Adjt reviewed
proposed ground for
flagged course in company
with 21st Bn. Adjt, and
Major WEBBER of Div. Staff.

Oct 10 Church parade in
morning followed by
Bn. training — Adjt

Bde Hq in evening - move to
MAZINGARBE trenches arranged

Oct 11 Company training in
morning - our position in
Grenay trenches reconnoitred
by Major CARR. Flagged
course commenced under
Lt. Imelow.

Oct 12 GRENAY line cleaned
by fatigue party in
morning - Bn. moved into
position starting from NOEUX
LES MINES 6.28 p.m. In
position by 9 p.m. Quiet
night.

Oct 13 Ordered to relieve 15th Bn.
in old British front system
of trenches G28.a.8.5 on
right to G22.c.8.6. on left. Bn.
in position by 2 p.m. Line
largely occupied by
artillery, who started heavy
bombardment at noon.
(2nd Lt P.R. Lucott to T.M.
School at ST VENANT)
Bombardment continued
till about 6 p.m. Very
little enemy reply.
Quiet night.

Oct 14 — Still in same line but moved "A" Coy up in evening so as to extend our front to RED FLAG on left, and extended "B" Coy to within 400 yds of LENS ROAD on Right — Quiet day and night — but had to send working party to start C. Trench between Old British and Old German front lines at 1 a.m. under Major CARR. Brigadier visited us in morning.

Oct 15 — Continued Salvage work during day. Whole Battn. worked during night on new communication trench between British front line and Southern Sap in conjunction with 2nd Bn. Quiet day and night.

Oct 16 — Salvage work continued. Same working parties on trench as yesterday during night. Div. Observing officer and 11 men attached. Capt R.C.

ARMSTRONG to Hospital

Oct 17 Salvage work continued during day – working party on new C. Trench during afternoon and evening. Salvage removed at 9 p.m. by A.S.C. wagons. Estd. amount salved – about 500,000 rounds S.A.A. 200 cases assorted Bombs about 600 Rifles and Bayonets – 1 West Bomb-throwing Machine – 200 picks 100 shovels – 2 M.G. tripods – 2 G.S. wagon loads Equipment. Also buried many French dead left since May attacks

Oct 18 Reconnoitred 22nd Bn position in German 1st line. C.O. to Bde at 5 p.m. Our lines occasionally shelled during afternoon – Bn. was relieved by 21st LON. REG at 7.30 p.m and moved to Billets at MAZINGARBE Heavy bombardment and rifle fire audible to ?

left and N. from 5 to 8 p.m.

Oct 19 Bn. went over flagged course, representing HULLUCH during morning and afternoon. G.O.C's 142nd Bde and 47th Div present. Heavy bombardment again from 5 to 8 pm to our NORTH.

Oct 20 Bn. went over flagged course in morning. Supposed spy in French uniform arrested and handed over to A.P.M. about 11 a.m. At 4 pm warned that we were under ½ hrs notice owing to Germans having cut their wire in front of LOOS and their being reported to be massing behind Bois HUGO. At 7.15 pm ½ hrs readiness removed and relief of 22nd Bn. in old German front line from LOOS ROAD REDOUBT proceeded. Completed at 11 p.m. Lt MERCER sent to 141st Bde. Hq as we are at disposal of 141st Bde. Quiet night.

Oct 21. Working parties on PREVITE PASSAGE and new Bde. Hq. in morning — 3 parties each of 75 under R.E's at 65 METRE, N. LOOS AVENUE and LONE TREE redoubts respectively at 6.30 pm. Quiet day and night. Two artillery bombardments were notified as taking place, but nothing was heard of them.

Oct 22 Working party on new Bde. Hq. G.16.b.2.4 in morning — C.O. Major Caw and O.C. Coy's to reconnoitre new line in morning — Took over from 6th Bn. in evening — completed relief at 9 pm Quiet night.

Oct 23 Working party on new Bde. Hq in morning. Lt TOWNSHEND RAMC reported for duty vice GIBBIN but was sent to report to A.D.M.S. Bde. T.M. Battery under 2nd/Lt LURCOTT, and Bde. Sharpshooters arrived and attached to 142nd Bde. Bde. took over from 140th INF. BDE at 9 p.m.

Oct 24 Lt Col. SIMPSON and 20 other ranks to ENGLAND on 7 days leave. Major CARR in command of Bn. Working parties to new Bde. Hq. in morning and on FIRE Stepping HAY ALLEY under Capt MILNER at night. 23 fire steps partially constructed. Quiet night.

Oct 25 Quiet day — working parties on new Bde. Hq and HAY ALLEY as before.

Oct 26 Working party on new Bde Hq in morning — Supervised work of 100 R.A. on fire trench at night. Also found carrying party of 200 for trench grids, which did not materialize owing to TRENCH RAILWAY breaking during morning. Heavy bombardment by our artillery on Enemy front line in front of us at 3 p.m. Result of subsequent retaliation, ONE man wounded, ONE M.G. damaged by shrapnel — Trench gratings arrive in evening — Patrols as previous day.

Oct 8/ Occasional shelling of front line becoming more intense in afternoon. Relieved by 2nd Bn. commencing 6.30 p.m. complete 9 p.m. proceeding to support lines where Bn. finally in position about 2 a.m.

Major Carr to England on leave. Capt Kilner commands Bn.

[signature]
Lieut Col
Cmdg
4th Bn Regt
"The Queens"

down. Quiet day.
Oct 27 Party on Bde Hq. in morning. At 6 p.m. commenced relief of 22nd Bn in B I, completed 9 p.m.
Oct 28 Our artillery bombardment at 5 a.m. fairly severe - little reply. G.O.C. Bde. visited subsection during morning. Very wet, but little shelling. Received some trench gratings per 22nd Bn. during night. "D" Coy carried all rations to front line.
Oct 29 Some H.E. fairly heavy shells near Bn. Hq. at lunch time - asked for artillery support which obtained in full measure - Some shrapnel on front line during day. Had working party of 100 R.E. put at disposal for work on VENDIN ALLEY during night. Patrols out to German wire.
Oct 30 Occasional shelling

142nd Inf. Bde.
47th Division.

WAR DIARY

1/24th LONDON REGT.

NOVEMBER

1915

24th Battn. Border Regt.

November 1915.

Commands to –

Nov. 1st Heavy Rain all day; consequently whole of Trench line falls in. No Dugouts available – Trenches become Waterlogged – Great misery. Lt. Col. Simpson, back from leave, resumes command. – Arrival of Draft, 100 from England to Trenches – They lose their way and arrive about STAND TO –. Occasional Shelling.

Nov. 2 Rain continues – Trenches become more impassable – A Coy removed from 7th Avenue back to 9th Avenue. Draft posted to Companies – Conditions in trenches become worse.

Nov. 3 Rain stops – Shell fire increases – One light Shell wounds Lt. LYSCOTT (Grenadier Officer), kills one Grenadier & wounds another. Sick parade shows noticeable increase, mainly Exposure, Exhaustion & Rheumatism. Carrying party for grids to 22nd Bn.

Nov. 4 Better weather enabled to make progress with clearing Trenches & making Shelters. – No. of Sick in Hospital 49. Relieved 22nd Bn in Bt. Sterling 530 fm.

Nov 4 - Cont'd bent owing to Waterlogged Trenches and slippery ground, and more especially to intervention of large working party, of 141st B.E. in our ONLY Communication Trench — Relief was not completed till 1 a.m. Coys in same order as before, viz.:
A Right B Centre & C Left —
D in Support — Quiet night —
Misty — patrols from 1 - 3 a.m.

Nov. 5 Quiet Day — About 4:30 pm
4 or 5 Heavy BRITISH Shells on own lines — 1 or 2 BLIND — Good shooting on B⁰ H.Q — Missed by 20 yds. Front line of LEFT Coy, One 10 ft behind. One 30 yds behind — Rang up LIAISON Officer who corroborated having heard them go over — Report sent to ADE — No Casualties

About 11:30 pm 2 more heavy British Shells between own & enemy lines in front of Left Company — nearly hitting 2 of our patrols — reported to O⁰⁰ at once by Adjt who was visiting the line at the time — otherwise quiet — Enemy working parties heard

Nov. 6 Misty all day, and very little shelling. Working party on support line. Patrols report same enemy working parties as previous nights. Lt DRAKE return from bomb School otherwise very quiet

Nov 7 Much clearer, consequently more shelling. Good shot for Bn HQ by Medium heavy about 2.30pm. Own bombardment of HULLUCH at 4pm called forth intermittent retaliation for about an hour afterwards. 4 Ot. Coys of 20th Bn arrived about 3.15pm preparatory to taking over. Relief

Do duly commenced at 5.30pm & was completed by 10.30pm. When Battalion moved to MAZINGARBE, completely in billets by 3a.m. on

Nov. 8 Cleaning billets and interior Economy. 2/Lt CRACKNELL reported for duty from 3rd Bn

Nov 9 Col. SIMPSON took command of Bde while G.O.C. Bde on leave - Furnished garrisons for LENS Rd, 65 METRE Pt, N. LOOS Avenue and LONE TREE Redoubts, relieving 22nd Bn. Completed by about 11pm.

Nov 10 Short Company Route Marches and Interior Economy. - Lt MATTHEWS reported for duty from 3rd Battn. 25 men in morning on new Hutments

50

Nov. 11. Interior Economy & cleaning Billets, which had been handed over in filthy condition — Keeps relieved in evening by 21st Bn. all garrisons back by 10.30 pm. No Casualties — Working party of 75 on Front Line Dugouts during night. Marched for 3 hours, did 2 hrs work, and returned — Very wet.

Nov 12. Cleaning billets continued — Heavy Rain all day & night.

Nov. 13 5th Kings Own & N. Lancs of 1st Division took over Billets and Stores — Battn. paraded at 12.10 noon marched to NOEUX Les Mines, Rail to LILLERS, thence to ALLOUAGNE where Battn. went into Billets as Corps Reserve — Arrived 4 pm

Nov 14 Resting and cleaning — Billets found to be left in very good Order by last Troops, said to be Guards

Nov 15. Bn. Route March & Foot inspection Recruits' training started training of Reserve Signallers under 2/Lt MATTHEWS

Nov. 16. Commenced early morning Running & Physical Exercises. Bn Route March. Training of Recruits. ~~Two companies bathed~~

Nov. 17. Bn Route March. Training of Recruits. Two companies bathed at MARLES-LES-MINES.

Nov. 18. Company Training. Training of Recruits & N.C.Os. Two companies bathed. In evening Bn ~~gave~~ concert at Theatre.

Nov. 19. Company Training. Training of Recruits & N.C.Os. Reinforcements (50) arrived. Posted A 14 B 15 C 14 D 7

Nov. 20. Bn Route March, followed by Foot Inspection & Lecture by Platoon Officers on Precautions against frost-bite.

Nov. 21 Bn Church Parade at Theatre.
Nov. 22 Bn on Range at CHAMP DE TIR
Nov. 23 Company Training. Recruits as before
Nov. 24. The Commander-in-Chief inspected the Brigade on field adjoining LOZINGHEM CHATEAU and complimented the Bde on behalf of the Divn for the splendid

work done during the Battle of Loos

Nov. 25. Company Training — Recruits training — Lectures for 2 Companies, football for remainder.
Trench Corkers class started under Sergt- Mestercork. Lewis M.G. section commenced training under 2/LT COLLINS

Nov 26. 120 All Ranks paraded for Gas Demonstration & instruction in Use of Helmets. All officers & men marched through entirely with filled with gas — no casualties. Remainder 1 Bn paraded for Route March. Advanced Squad of Recruits carried out Musketry Test in a pit in LAPUGNOY woods — results satisfactory and recruits passed to Companies.
BATHS for 'A' 'C' & part of 'D' Coys

Nov 27. 'A' & 'B' Coys on range at CHAMP DE TIR.
Company & Recruits Training for Remainder — football in afternoon

Nov. 28. Church Parade at the THEATRE
Nov. 29. Bn Route March. Foot Inspection and Lecture on March Discipline.

Nov. 30. Bn Route March in morning. 60
C.O Inspected Transport loaded,
ready for Div. Route March
in afternoon. Adjutant to Bde
HQ. re preparations for Route
March which had been postponed
24 hrs till 1st Dec.

C.J. Saunders
CAPTAIN & ADJUTANT
24th (COUNTY OF LONDON) Bn.
THE LONDON REGIMENT
THE "QUEEN'S"

142nd Inf. Bde.
47th Division.

WAR DIARY

1/24th LONDON REGT.

DECEMBER

1915

Army Form C. 2118.

WAR DIARY
or
INTELLIGENCE SUMMARY.

(Erase heading not required)

WAR DIARY
of
2nd London Regt "The Queens"
for December 1915

WAR DIARY
or
INTELLIGENCE SUMMARY.

(Erase heading not required.)

Army Form C. 2118.

Place	Date	Hour	Summary of Events and Information	Remarks and references to Appendices
	Dec 1st		Bn paraded at 9 a.m. to join Bde in Div Route March and paraded starting point at BURBURE at 9.27 a.m.; marched via ST HILAIRE (Louis Dolk?) to WITTERNESSE where billetted — arrived there about 2.30 p.m. Supplies, Blankets & Baggage Wagons about 9.30 p.m.	Baggage Capt
	Dec 2nd		Received orders at 1.30 a.m. that 24th, 23rd & 3rd Bns under Lt Col SIMPSON would lead Main Body of Division to pass starting point at ESTREE BLANCHE at 9.56 a.m. Remainder of Bde forming Advance Guard under Brigadier-General LEWIS — Division marching on ESTREE BLANCHE — FER FAY Rd in direction of AUCHEL. Bn paraded 8 a.m. & joined 23rd & 3rd Bns at GUERNES — Column thus formed passing starting point about 2 minutes late. Operations carried about noon — shortly after some confusion was caused owing to 22nd Bn having fallen out for hours halt at point which was the same 24th Bn arrived at	

WAR DIARY
or
INTELLIGENCE SUMMARY.
(Erase heading not required.)

Army Form C. 2118.

Place	Date	Hour	Summary of Events and Information	Remarks and references to Appendices
	Dec 3rd		for their hourly halt of 10 min. March continued afterwards with ¾ hours halt at AVCHEL - finally returned to billets at ALLOUAGNE at 2.15 p.m. 10 men having fallen out on this day and 4 the previous day. - Nearly all on account of foot trouble.	Sgd Col Staff
	Dec 4th		Bn at disposal of C.O.C Company Drill and foot inspection - Lectures Bn wiring Course commenced under Lt MERCER	Sgd Col Staff
	Dec 5th		Company Drill & Musketry - Wiring Course continued. Church Parade: Finals of Bn Boxing Competition in the evening. Wiring Course cont'd : staff to Bde for instruction in writing O. Orders.	Sgd Col Staff
	Dec 6th		Bde Staff tour: Outpost line on Ridge North of R. CLARENCE commenced with Conference at Bde H.Q. at 9 a.m. & concluded with address by Major Gen. BARTER on the ground at 2½ p.m. Coys under Coy. S.M's at drill etc as nearly all officers on tour. Recruits musketry.	Sgd Col Staff
	Dec 7th		Route March in Morning - C.O and Staff to new - LEWIS M.G's	

WAR DIARY
or
INTELLIGENCE SUMMARY.
(Erase heading not required.)

Army Form C. 2118.

Place	Date	Hour	Summary of Events and Information	Remarks and references to Appendices
	Dec 8th		Firing - Afternoon bathing - Bn Concert in Evening. By Cpl sect. Company Drill & Interior Economy. 3 officers on obtaining tour under 13th Major. Bde shooting competition for Sergts at LABEUVRIERE in morning. 24th Teams won 2 shoots out of 3 - Sergts Mess Dinner in evening - C.O. Major CARR, Capt & O.C. Coys attended - notable as being the 1st Bn Sgts Mess Dinner since Mobilization. By Cpl sect.	
	Dec 9th		Outdoor work stopped by rain. Recruits shooting on CHAMP DE TIR in morning. By Capt sect.	
	Dec 10th		C.O., M.G. O's & O.C. Coys to reconnoitre trench line opposite HOHENZOLLERN Redoubt. D2: probably to be taken over by us on 14th/15th inst. By Capt sect.	
	Dec 11th		Final preparations for move. Instructions Billet cleaning etc. Issued	
	Dec 12th		Church Parade - Instructions etc continued. By Cpt sect	
	Dec 13th		as Sunday & Saturday. 2/Lts COUSINS & MAGNUS to Hospital BN	
	Dec 14th		Paraded 7.15 a.m. marched to LILLERS, where Bn worked some trains for	

WAR DIARY or INTELLIGENCE SUMMARY

Army Form C. 2118.

Place	Date	Hour	Summary of Events and Information	Remarks and references to Appendices
	Oct 5		Train entrained at 9.40 a.m. and railed to NOEUX, whence marched to SAILLY LABOURSE, where billeted for night. Bn Grdqrs. Moved at 4 am via PHILOSOPHE to VERMELLES where arrived at 5.30am. Thence to D2 running about HOHENZOLLERN REDOUBT, line extended from A.28.C.5.2 to G.4.D.8.8. Taken over from 11th Argyle & Sutherland Highlanders 15th Division. Trenches very muddy in parts, but generally better than expected - No cover for men in Front line - Two Coys in front line, 1 in Support, 1 in Reserve. In the evening 23rd Bn relieved our R. Front Coy and a portion of Support Coy - Our R. Front Coy returned to Sailly and Reserve Coy began to Lancashire trench, which is roughly as far back from front line as VERMELLES - Owing to C.O. of 23rd Battn being unable to find a HQ he and his Adjt slept with us - Lt Col Simpson being Styled by Bde in command of 23rd & 24th Bns - the intention of the Bde in regard to this move being to have me Coy of each Bn in front line, One in Support, One in Reserve and One in Sailly, they forming the Bde	

1577 Wt.W10791/1773 500,000 1/15 D. D. & L. A.D.S.S./Forms/C. 2118.

WAR DIARY or INTELLIGENCE SUMMARY

Army Form C. 2118.

Place	Date	Hour	Summary of Events and Information	Remarks and references to Appendices
Becks.			Bde Reserve - Arr Reliefs taking place at Bn discretion - and each Bn having only 1 Coy Frontage. Quiet Day. BM Capt. Quiet Day after quiet night. Three subjects under Front boys HQ. Arrangements made to wire round area which were bothered through decision of Corps Divisional Commanders that Dn must be held by 1 Br. So 33rd Front and Support Coys were relieved by our Reserve Coys from SALLY LABOURSE & LANCASHIRE TRENCH - 2nd Bn reverted to its original position as taken over from 11th A & S Highlanders.	
	Sec 17		Relief complete by midnight. Some Enemy MG activity increasing after dark. Enemy Sniping Activity. Sentry killed and periscopes broken in Left Coy. Arrangements completed for making "Box up" round subjects mine - Workings inside face of Guilford St and Savile Row and front of Northampton St. - After dark Enemy MG and Rifle Grenade fire from LITTLE WILLIE. Artillery Assistance on later silenced them for remainder of night. - Enabling us to complete Wiring as arranged, altho' night was not dark. BMCapt.	

WAR DIARY
or
INTELLIGENCE SUMMARY.

Army Form C. 2118.

Place	Date	Hour	Summary of Events and Information	Remarks and references to Appendices
Berles			Resumed Enemy Activity with Sniping, Rifle Grenades, Lister Artillery fire & trench mortars – About 5 casualties. In everything except Artillery Enemy appears to have upper hand in this Sector. By placing Grenade guns in line and Reinforcing Lewis Guns with Maxims, Rifle to subdue this – In afternoon left bay fairly heavily shelled and trench damaged – Our Artillery retaliated – In front of R bay – Germans shewed themselves in obs. were fired on and disappeared – Were seen to wear Grey Caps with Red Bands. This was apparently part of a scheme to entice our men to shew themselves, for as soon as they started firing, Germans fired on them from a flank. They are evidently very told here – Warning received in Evening of intended Gas attack on our left by 3rd Div. for night, also that 99th & 115th Bde were going to those as much under Gibons CRATER (A.27.D.7.0) at dawn on 14th Sep. Wejust Nothing noted of either – Arrangements made for relief by 33rd B. This relief proceeded smoothly was completed by 9am when B was	
Sep 14			distributed as follows.	

WAR DIARY
or
INTELLIGENCE SUMMARY.
(Erase heading not required.)

Army Form C. 2118.

Place	Date	Hour	Summary of Events and Information	Remarks and references to Appendices
	Sept (cont)		A & B Coys. Lancashire Trench C & D. Billets SAILLY LABOURSE Bn HQ " M.G Section	
	Sep 20th		Remainder of day & night without incident Appx [Plan] Quiet any Coys in front line – Coys in SAILLY cleaning up. About 9pm warning was received of possible Enemy attack on Sector C.1 but night passed without incident App [Plan]	
	Sep 21st		Anyesterday – Guides from Trench Coys took 20th Bn Officer round Lancashire Trench Orders not to work on CENTRAL KEEP (G9.b.5.3) however garrison with 2 Platoons Lancashire Trench also to parade a defensive line – but work worked on - Quiet day, night showers App [Plan]	
	Sep 22nd		Such Coys worked on CENTRAL KEEP Lancashire Trench (As British front line in 92) Sent B Coy up to work by day and D Coy by night & below we added A Coy from trench. Certain amount of wiring & clearing was done, No fairly heavily shelled by day & night. Col. Simpson went up to the line at 7pm to take charge	

WAR DIARY
or
INTELLIGENCE SUMMARY.
(Erase heading not required.)

Army Form C. 2118.

Place	Date	Hour	Summary of Events and Information	Remarks and references to Appendices
	Dec 23rd (Cont.)		1 & 2 Coys of 8th Bn Reserve who were working here. Rev 1am. - fairly heavy shelling on CB.1 during night. [Sd] Capt-Capt	
	Dec 24th		Bde was relieved in line by 14th Bde at dawn. Our Trench Coy 1/20th Bn, Bde Reserve in LABOURSE 1/15th Bn - B concentrated at Verquin at noon & went into Billets as Div Reserve. [Sd] Capt-Capt.	
	Dec 25th		Moved to SAILLY took over billets vacated by 19th Bn arrived 7.15am. Report that suspected mine had been blown up at 7am were current - Some little shelling of SAILLY as we arrived - Otherwise quiet day. Br Capt-Capt. Church Parades in morning. C.O. visited Billets to wish troops "Merry Christmas" at dinner - C.O. to Bn at 3pm. Bn moved to billets at VERQUIN at 9pm. [Sd] Capt Capt.	
	Dec 26th		C.O. & O.C. Coys reconnaitred C.1 in morning - Preparations for move. [Sd] Capt Capt.	
	Dec 27		Bn guided by Coys starting 3.30am. Guides met at VERNELLES Church at 7am. took over C.1 in QUARRIES Subsection from 7 J on Regt. Relief complete about 9am. Frontage of Bn from DEVON LANE C.I.D.A.9.3 on RIGHT to GOEBEN ALLEY C.H.B.8.6 on LEFT. Our Right being in touch with Left of 1st DIVISION - Trenches very bad evidently much neglected by previous	

WAR DIARY
or
INTELLIGENCE SUMMARY.
(Erase heading not required.)

Army Form C. 2118.

Instructions regarding War Diaries and Intelligence Summaries are contained in F.S. Regs., Part II. and the Staff Manual respectively. Title pages will be prepared in manuscript.

Hour, Date, Place	Summary of Events and Information	Remarks and references to Appendices
December 27 (Cont.)	scarce. Natives in many places from 1 to 2 ft deep - very little shelter for men. A & B Coys R.I.L. have successively C by in Support in old German Front line, & Div Reserve in O.B. 4 & 5. Day passed quietly, some shelling in afternoon of Support line. Efforts made to rehabilitate lines - covering early but out there. Sap in bank of B. Coy in course for working parts under R.E.'s who are making a new front line in front of our present Front. Enemy Rifle fire at night very noticeable. Rather more shelling than yesterday, situation generally normal - covering parties at night as before all when working party had limited posts but out to hold this New line during night - which was quiet. Patrolling etc. continues.	G.O.C. Lt. Coy Left
December 29th	Support & Reserve Coys relieved RIGHT & LEFT FRONT Coys respectively by Lists Gns & ans. Rather heavy shelling of O.G.I. as A Coy entered it. No serious damage - G.O.C. Bde accompanies by a Brigadier of 16th Div. was known lines in morning - None or tendal continues. Also shelling - Generally quiet.	G.O.C. Lt. Coy Left

WAR DIARY
or
INTELLIGENCE SUMMARY.
(Erase heading not required.)

Army Form C. 2118.

Instructions regarding War Diaries and Intelligence Summaries are contained in F.S. Regs., Part II and the Staff Manual respectively. Title pages will be prepared in manuscript.

Hour, Date, Place	Summary of Events and Information	Remarks and references to Appendices
December 30th 14.	1 Officer and 6.0. Ranks from GRAND FLEET arrived during morning for duties in front line — Heavy Shelling of HAIRPIN in our left during morning — C.O. reports of FLEET went round FRONT LINE during afternoon at + Dolan — 2 MINES were exploded by enemy in HAIRPIN at same time. Heavy Shellfire opened in Front & Support Lines — Also Rifle & Machine Gun and Trench Mortars fire — Major PARKER Comn? ordered C?y had in view the bombers of the and felt already advanced that should it happen the B Coy from the support on a direct RAPID FIRE on enemy front line and bomb of HAIRPIN meantime Dow LEFT Coy Stood to with Bayonets fixed. Thus — C Coy would enfilade GERMAN Front line in front of QUARRIES also bring fire to bear on the head of HAIRPIN. Owing to a rise in ground between D Coy line and the GERMAN — no direct fire would be brought to bear — When the mine exploded, above dispositions were carried out within a few seconds, and we opened heavy RAPID	[sketch map showing BRITISH LINE, GERMAN LINE, HAIRPIN, QUARRIES, CHAPEL, STAFFORD LANE, FOSSE WAY, OLD GERMAN FRONT LINE, O.G.1, with A, B, C marked] A to B — L Coy B to C — R Coy

WAR DIARY
or
INTELLIGENCE SUMMARY.
(Erase heading not required.)

Army Form C. 2118.

Instructions regarding War Diaries and Intelligence Summaries are contained in F. S. Regs., Part II and the Staff Manual respectively. Title pages will be prepared in manuscript.

Hour, Date, Place	Summary of Events and Information	Remarks and references to Appendices
December 30th (cont)	Rifle fire as arranged almost immediately. A Coy in Support in O.G.I moved up two Coys E WAY and reinforced short line. This was completed by about 5am. As all telephone communication ceased from 4.35pm. O.C. Coys had to work on assumptions in case of attack which thought to be taking place - Having learnt by Runner of 'A' Coys move, B Coy in Reserve in O.B.1. (some way behind Btn H.Q.) was moved up to O.B.1. west of 2 Platoon on Rd FOSSEWAY & 2 on LEFT. About 5.30pm the fire died down to a desultory shelling of Support Lines - It was evident that an Infantry attack was not intended and though Coys were left in their advanced positions all night which included manning the partially dug line to our front - Arrangements were made tel withdrawing them to their original positions on Dec Capt Baff day passed fairly	
December 31st	quietly - GRAND FLEET contingent left. Hung officials the Operations HQ Trenches - Notified that 21st Bn would relieve us, arrangements were made for Relief at dawn tomorrow, 1st Jan 1916. Heavy MINENWERFER FIRE	

Army Form C. 2118.

WAR DIARY
or
INTELLIGENCE SUMMARY.
(Erase heading not required.)

Hour, Date, Place	Summary of Events and Information	Remarks and references to Appendices
December 3rd 15 G.H.	Aerial Torpedoes on O.G.1 between 8 to 10 p.m. No Casualties during operation of 30th inst — faint tr tr tr fallen 1. Casualties 1 3+ wounded — Enemy reported sounds of Drilling under our lines — Tunnelling Expert who came + listened confirmed this. LEFT Coy also reported similar sounds under them.	

Mhmm. Ltd.
Capt 2nd Bn Loy Reg.

49

24 London Regt.
Jan 1916
Ypl X

Army Form C. 2118.

WAR DIARY
or
INTELLIGENCE SUMMARY.
(Erase heading not required.)

Instructions regarding War Diaries and Intelligence Summaries are contained in F.S. Regs., Part II and the Staff Manual respectively. Title pages will be prepared in manuscript.

Hour, Date, Place	Summary of Events and Information	Remarks and references to Appendices
January 1st 1916	21st Bn relieved us on C.1 at dawn. Relief complete 6 a.m. when Bn moved into Bn Sectors after 8 days in front line.	
	2 Coys in Bully Grenay (A,B)	
	2 Coys M. Guns in VERMELLES (C+D)	
	Quiet day. D Coy bathed.	
January 2nd 1916	Quiet day. Coys cleaning, resting and bathing. Officers of 3rd & 4th Bns DISMOUNTED DIVISION reconnoitred positions preparatory to taking over.	
January 3rd 1916	Quiet Day. Here advised of an artillery bombardment to start at 12.30 a.m. It - no sound of it was heard. Preparation for move in progress.	
January 4th 1916	Relieved by 4th Battn 2nd Dismounted Bde. Relief started 4.30 a.m. completed by 6.30 a.m. Bn moved by Companies to VERQUIN - found 7th Battn. still occupying our billeting area - had to wait 7 hours before we could take over.	
	E. CLARE sent to HABARCQ.	
January 5th 1916	Bn moved to LES BREBIS. Sent at 4.30 p.m. arrive at 6.30 p.m. Billets quickly found. Only snow fell out on march.	

WAR DIARY
or
INTELLIGENCE SUMMARY.
(Erase heading not required.)

Army Form C. 2118.

Instructions regarding War Diaries and Intelligence Summaries are contained in F.S. Regs., Part II. and the Staff Manual respectively. Title pages will be prepared in manuscript.

Hour, Date, Place	Summary of Events and Information	Remarks and references to Appendices
January 6th/16	Companies engaged in trench economy. A few shells fell near the mine.	
January 7/16	CO and Company Officers reconnoitre line held by 15th Bn Subsector 16	
January 8th/16	At night Bn relieves 15th Bn in Subsector G - from W. end of Double CRASSIER to M.C.6, M.3. A Coy on LEFT, B Coy in Centre, along N. CRASSIER, C Coy on RIGHT, at N. end of DOUBLE CRASSIER, D Coy in Reserve, in OG line. Some bombing during relief.	
January 9th/16	Right Coy complain of RIFLE GRENADES falling between the CRASSIERS also of Shells from Readers Command being sent along the gap between the CRASSIERS. No wire erected in line new in Reserve during No [?] 20 reply possible. Support + B[?] stated at varying intervals during the morning. After some delay managed to get effective artillery reply.	

Army Form C. 2118.

WAR DIARY
or
INTELLIGENCE SUMMARY.
(Erase heading not required.)

Instructions regarding War Diaries and Intelligence Summaries are contained in F.S. Regs., Part II. and the Staff Manual respectively. Title pages will be prepared in manuscript.

Hour, Date, Place	Summary of Events and Information	Remarks and references to Appendices
January 10th 1916	Night quiet. Morning was a repetition of previous morning. Again no rifle grenades to reply with and some delay in getting artillery retaliation. At 7pm relieved by 2nd Bn Notts & Derby Regt. Support - two Companies in S. MAROC, "A" in N. MAROC, 2 in old British line.	
January 11th 1916	Reconnoitring Parties for Subsection D - M+C,H,3,6 S. MAROC and AIRFOW ROAD N.5.F.16 shelled by heavy H.E. and shrapnel. CAPT BARBER, K.E.H. attached for the R.E. instruction in duties of Adjutant.	
January 12th 1916	Relieved 2nd Bn in Subsection D. Dispositions 3 Coy on RIGHT B centre, "A" left. 6 by SUPPORT. Found line very short of S.A.A. - started refilling at once - Front line very poor Entire - enfiladed from Fosse 11 and CITE ST ELIE - trenches - during and traverses commenced.	
January 13th 1916	Centre by shelled intermittently during morning by light high velocity guns - traverses and parapet slightly damaged - two slight casualties. Two field guns retaliated in trench in M.S.C. firing but ineffective got howitzers in	

WAR DIARY
or
INTELLIGENCE SUMMARY.
(Erase heading not required.)

Army Form C. 2118.

Hour, Date, Place	Summary of Events and Information	Remarks and references to Appendices
January 13th 16 (con)	to FOSSE 11 and CITÉ ST PIERRE - enemy shelling ceased: Sounds of mining reported from Left Coy at M.5.a.3.3. No work possible by day, as any movement draws shell fire.	
January 14th 16	Trench improvements continued during night, but at 8:30am enemy shelling again started, causing fresh damage. Answering with artillery to retaliate with Feb guns and howitzers at once. Sounds of mining still heard and mining experts attend.	
January 15th 16	Same as previous day - enemy started shelling our centre, but our retaliation proved immediately effective - field guns firing on enemy front line in N.5.a. and howitzers on FOSSE 11 and CITÉ ST PIERRE. At night a Company of 7th Bn relieved our Left Company, which was assigned a position in BOYAU DE SUD as Reserve. This change was necessary owing to a readjustment of Sectors, making the NARIC Sector end at M.5.a.33. The BOYAU is merely a communication trench with no shelter of any sort. The Company there was employed on trench work all night.	

WAR DIARY
or
INTELLIGENCE SUMMARY.

(Erase heading not required.)

Army Form C. 2118.

Hour, Date, Place	Summary of Events and Information	Remarks and references to Appendices

January 16th 1916. After a quiet night, B Company now on the "left", was again shelled but retaliation again braced too much for the enemy. At night the Bn was relieved by the 1st Bde, the Bn being relieved by the 20th Bn. Relief started 6 P.M. and was completed by 8.10 P.M. The Bn proceeded by Companies to billets in LES BREBIS as Brigade Reserve — details to support the 141st Bde in case of attack at one hour's notice.

January 17th 1916. Practically all the Bn employed on working parties on a new road in course of construction between NOEUX and LES BREBIS. Court-Martial work becoming very disquieting. The cases of men sleeping at sentry posts seem to be becoming frequent.

LT.COL. SIMPSON leaves for ENGLAND on leave. MAJOR G.A. BUXTON CARR takes over command of the Bn.

January 18th 1916. Bn employed in bathing and interior economy. CAPT CLARK goes to hospital.

January 19th 1916. Reconnoitring Party for LOOS SECTION.

Army Form C. 2118.

WAR DIARY
or
INTELLIGENCE SUMMARY.
(Erase heading not required.)

Instructions regarding War Diaries and Intelligence Summaries are contained in F.S. Regs., Part II. and the Staff Manual respectively. Title pages will be prepared in manuscript.

Hour, Date, Place	Summary of Events and Information	Remarks and references to Appendices
January 20th 16	Bn relieved the 6th Bn in 8th Subsection. None attack faced at the COPSE, in CENTRE Subsection. "C" Coy in TRAIT D'UNION, G35 c detailed to support CENTRE, B Coy in O.G. Line to support LEFT, "A" Coy in N. MAROC to support RIGHT. "D" Coy in N. MAROC moves to ENCLOSURE every night. On relief ammunition found no S.A.A Reserve with any of the Companies and no Bombs.	
January 21st 1916	Quiet night - "C" Coy starts to make TRAIT D'UNION a defensive LINE. S.A.A. Dumps established.	
January 22nd 1916	A & B Companies worked by night in clearing O.B.L. to be occupied by Reserve Battn in case of attack. Day quiet	
January 23rd 1916.	At night R.E. announced our counter mine at the "Knuckle" of the COPSE would be ready to explode at 2AM. "B" Company detailed as carrying party for bombs, sandbags and the like. 35 men of "D" Company sent to citizen in LOOS as Reserve Carrying party. "A" Company	

WAR DIARY
or
INTELLIGENCE SUMMARY.
(Erase heading not required.)

Army Form C. 2118.

Hour, Date, Place	Summary of Events and Information	Remarks and references to Appendices
January 23rd 1916	Detailed to be in O.G. Line by 2am as a Second Reserve Party. At 1.57 am our Mine was exploded and from all reports inflicted considerable damage to the enemy mine. The enemy showed no inclination to retaliate but caused some casualties by sniping. At 4am everything going well, "A" Company dismissed to their billets. Day quiet.	
January 24th 1916.	At night "A" Company supplied a working party to assist 31st in consolidating crater of the mine. Two casualties suffered through rifle grenades. By day Co. of Company Officers reconnoitred the line and at 6pm Bn. relieved the 31st in CENTRE. "A" on the right C on the LEFT front line. "B" Coy in REGENT ST. with one platoon of "D" Coy — a second line of defence in case the COPSE is lost. "D" Coy the ENCLOSURE as Reserve.	
January 25th 1916.	Having found the line very deficient of S.A.A. and Grenades, occupied "D" by all night in carrying up fresh supplies. "A" Company were harried continuously by trench mortars and rifle grenades, could get no	

WAR DIARY
or
INTELLIGENCE SUMMARY.
(Erase heading not required.)

Army Form C. 2118.

Hour, Date, Place	Summary of Events and Information	Remarks and references to Appendices
January 25th '16 (Contd)	effective reply from our T.M.B. and lack of rifle grenades seriously felt. Casualties - 2 killed & 9 wounded. Day quiet generally - B Coy shelled for some time during afternoon by heavy H.E. Casualties - 1 killed 6 wounded all slightly.	
January 26th '16	During night "A" Company again complained of trench mortars, but our T.M.B. replied & enemy firing ceased, probably due to fact that enemy were working in their trench. Continuous sniping from SNIPERS HOUSE which lies on road just beyond RIGHT end of COPSE - it is heavily fortified and shelling appears to have no effect on it. Morning quiet - at 1.45 p.m. the enemy started a heavy bombardment with H.E. and shrapnel of our communication trenches and REGENT ST. especially the latter. The 27th is the Kaisers birthday and in view of the attack made at YPRES last year to celebrate that event, a warning had been received to be ready for a similar occurrence on this front, on	

Army Form C. 2118.

WAR DIARY
or
INTELLIGENCE SUMMARY.
(Erase heading not required.)

Instructions regarding War Diaries and Intelligence Summaries are contained in F. S. Regs., Part II. and the Staff Manual respectively. Title pages will be prepared in manuscript.

Hour, Date, Place	Summary of Events and Information	Remarks and references to Appendices
January 26th '16 (cont)	which the enemy had devoted great running activity. For some time there was some anxiety whether this bombardment was the prelude to an attack, but at 3.30 PM the bombardment died away, though our heavy field artillery still continued retaliating. REGENT had been filled in in many places; the Cy H.Q. being blown in on the officers who luckily escaped, Lt COUSINS emerging with severely bruised leg. The FRONT line had suffered slightly one man of "A" Coy being the only casualty — he was buried in a blown in dug-out and could not be extricated. In the evening "B" Coy and "C", "D" Coy and "A" exchanged positions. One Company of the 31st Bn sent up to ENCLOSURE to reinforce, and 3 sections moved up along the line — 25 of 31st Bn sent to help clear REGENT ST + 25 to work on trench by cook. 31st joins us in HQ dug out	
January 27th '16	Working parties reported to be suffering from trench mortars rifle grenades, due to fact that the trench is in	

WAR DIARY
or
INTELLIGENCE SUMMARY.

Army Form C. 2118.

Hour, Date, Place	Summary of Events and Information	Remarks and references to Appendices

January 27th (Cont) that 11 casualties caused by German mortar but many have completely filled in. Subsequent reports established of a working party of 25 all of 2nd Bn. The work was proceeded with and the trenches to a large extent cleared.

In the morning enemy opened a heavy bombardment of REGENT St and communication trenches, lasting from 11.30 a.m. to 1.15 p.m., again doing much damage and destroying several dug-outs - also a portion of front line on RIGHT of COPSE but no casualties.

By night working parties were arranged for - at 4.30 p.m. - violent rifle and machine gun fire heard on the left - II bns reported enemy attack Pont 17A 1000 yds S of HULLUCH but artillery fire kept enemy from leaving his trenches. All quiet on our front and a working party proceeded - 50 of 2nd Bn to RIGHT of COPSE, 50 to REGENT ST also 50 men of 1st HANTS, as at present REGENT ST is hardly defensible, and is the only second line to which we could retire in the event of the COPSE being mined and

Instructions regarding War Diaries and Intelligence
Summaries are contained in F.S. Regs., Part II
and the Staff Manual respectively. Title pages
will be prepared in manuscript.

WAR DIARY
or
INTELLIGENCE SUMMARY

(Erase heading not required.)

Army Form C. 2118.

Hour, Date, Place	Summary of Events and Information	Remarks and references to Appendices
January 27th /16 (cont'd)	and stormed. Enemy trench mortars again busy, and very harassing, causing several casualties.	
January 28th /16	At 8 A.m. Enemy opened heavy bombardment with guns of all calibres up to 6" on REGENT ST, ENCLOSURE, and communication trenches. Locomotory shells and incendiary shells were also reported. All telephonic communication destroyed. At 11.15 A.m. bombardment ceased. REGENT ST. reported badly damaged and communication trenches filled in. Accuracy of enemy's shooting again noticeable, but our reply was extremely good. In the afternoon bombardment was resumed with less intensity. No casualties reported. NIGHT - Quiet - 14th Bn. relieve 14th & 19th Bns. relieve 21st. Relief starts 7 P.m. and ends	
January 29th /16	at 5 A.m. Bn. remains in Bde. Reserve to 11th Bde. A.B. in advanced position in N. MAROC with 2 Lewis guns, remr. of Bn. in billets at LES BREBIS at 2 hours notice. C' + D' on working parties all day. LT. COL. SIMPSON assumes Command.	

Army Form C. 2118.

WAR DIARY
or
INTELLIGENCE SUMMARY.

(Erase heading not required.)

Instructions regarding War Diaries and Intelligence Summaries are contained in F. S. Regs., Part II. and the Staff Manual respectively. Title pages will be prepared in manuscript.

Hour, Date, Place	Summary of Events and Information	Remarks and references to Appendices
January 30th 16	C & D on Working Parties all day.	
January 31st 16	C & D on Working Parties all day.	

GHQ
47

24 London Regt

Feb. 1916

Vol XI

WAR DIARY
or
INTELLIGENCE SUMMARY.
(Erase heading not required.)

Army Form C. 2118.

Instructions regarding War Diaries and Intelligence Summaries are contained in F.S. Regs., Part II. and the Staff Manual respectively. Title pages will be prepared in manuscript.

Hour, Date, Place	Summary of Events and Information	Remarks and references to Appendices
February 1st 1916	1.20 p.m. 13th relieves 140th Bn in MAROC Section. — 2nd Bn relieves 6th Bn in LEFT Subsection. "C" in Right, "D" in Left; "A" & "B" in O.G. Line in Support. — "A" sends 2 Platoons to CORDIALE AVENUE as Armoured Support in the LEFT. Relief started 7 p.m. — completed 9 p.m.	
February 2nd 1916	Night quiet. Occupied in repairing trenches and refitting S.A.A. Dump. Day unusually quiet — only very intermittent Shelling.	
February 3rd 1916	Night quiet — except for slight retaliation by gun enfilading ON LEFT, causing 2 casualties in return for our artillery activity. CARFAX Rd debouch and approach to some extent, the trench is hostilely situated, being enfiladed and enfiladed for its entire length. At 7:30 A.M. 14 "Minnenwerfer" bombs and just over RIGHT FRONT LINE; fired from DOUBLE CRASSIER. At 8 A.M. enemy started intermittent Shelling of communication trenches until 5:9 p.m. — ceased at 11.30 A.M. Remainder of day quiet. At 6.30 P.M. 23rd Bn relieved the Bn. 8.30 P.M. Relief complete. Bn moves into 13th Bn Support "C" Coy in O.B. 3 with 1 Lewis Gun at disposal of O.C. LEFT Subsection. "D" Coy with 1 Lewis Gun at disposal of O.C. centre Subsection, in N. MAROC. Remainder of Bn in S. MAROC.	
February 4th 1916	Quiet day — little Shelling.	

WAR DIARY
or
INTELLIGENCE SUMMARY

(Erase heading not required.)

Army Form C. 2118.

Hour, Date, Place	Summary of Events and Information	Remarks and references to Appendices
February 5th 1916	Quiet day - some heavy shells fell in S. MAROC. At 6.15 pm the Bn relieved the 10th in the CENTRE Subsection MAROC Section. Disposition: "A" Coy on LEFT, "C" Coy in CENTRE, "B" Coy in RIGHT - "D" by in Support, "D" Coy in Reserve. Relief complete. Lt. Col. SIMPSON leaves for Gunnery Course at AIRE. MAJOR PARKER takes command. Night quiet generally - 3 grenades wounded by a bomb, thought to come from an enemy 'bombthrower'.	
February 6th 1916	Quiet day - Some intermittent shelling by 4.5" of SEVENTH AVENUE causing some damage to trenches. At night employed Company of 33rd Bn "at our disposal on work in clearing DUG OUT ROW & O.B.1. against threats, to be executed in case of attack.	
February 7th 1916	Night quiet. In the afternoon enemy opened fire with wooden guns from direction of FOSSE 11 - immediately silenced by our artillery. Some rifle grenades were thrown over by enemy during evening.	
February 8th 1916	Night quiet - working parties of R.E. Dublin Fusiliers and 23rd Bn all employed in forming a second line of strong points & moved over a few to small defenses miles would be attached to N.E. corner of COPSE at 1 AM. Heavy bombardment heard all day from direction of Trench line.	

WAR DIARY
or
INTELLIGENCE SUMMARY.
(Erase heading not required.)

Army Form C. 2118.

Instructions regarding War Diaries and Intelligence Summaries are contained in F.S. Regs., Part II. and the Staff Manual respectively. Title pages will be prepared in manuscript.

Hour, Date, Place	Summary of Events and Information	Remarks and references to Appendices
February 9th 16	4.5 AM field guns opened rabid fire, presumably to cover the explosion of mine. Enemy opposite our left sent up several "golden rain" rockets, at 4.30 AM - two smaller bombs were thrown out from enemy line & 3 red rockets sent up. Artillery brought lives on smoke, but apparently it was not a screen for any enemy action. - Day very quiet. 6.15 PM. 19th Bn commences Relief. - 9.00 PM. Relief complete. Bn moves to LES BREBIS, becoming Bn in Reserve at disposal of G.O.C. MARoc SECTION.	
February 10th 16	2 Companies on working Parties - all "Stakes". "Practice gas attack" scheme received from Bde. Arrangements for leaving Companies etc in event of sudden alarms completed. MAJOR CARR returns from LEAVE and takes command of Bn.	
February 11th 16	O for 2 Bns on working parties - street and billet cleaning started. "Gas Alert" received 1.30 PM. Lt Col. Simpson returns and resumes command of Bn.	
February 12th 16	2 Companies on working parties. "Gas Alert" cancelled.	

WAR DIARY
or
INTELLIGENCE SUMMARY.
(Erase heading not required.)

Army Form C. 2118.

Hour, Date, Place	Summary of Events and Information	Remarks and references to Appendices
February 13th 16	"GAS ALERT" received 8.50 a.m. Working parties of 100 men all day. 9.30 p.m. - practice Gas attack - relieved - all Bn reported complete by 10.5 p.m. Companies paraded in fairly quick time - O.C. Companies had to inspect every man before reporting complete & this naturally took some time in the dark.	
February 14th 16	16 2ND Bn moves into Army Reserve. 31st Bn to RAIMBERT. Bn paraded 12.15 p.m. - entrained at NOEUX-LES-MINES at 3.15 p.m. - arrived LILLERS 3.40 p.m. - handed over P.H Smoke Helmets to D.A.D.O.S. - and marched to RAIMBERT arriving there 6.30 p.m. - All officers Billets - Men goth - went Billets good on the whole, some indifferent - all greatly scattered at RAIMBERT.	
February 15th 16	All moves to permanent area - 31st Bn to ALLOUAGNE.	
February 16th 16	10.50 a.m. in motor gale towards tram - Arrived ALLOUAGNE 12.10 p.m. - all Cops in their old billets.	
February 17th 16	Companies employed in cleaning up and administration.	
February 18th 16	Co. inspected Companies, 11.30 a.m., and Transport 3 p.m. Company Training started but little could be done owing to continued rain. WORKING PARTY. 50 men at MINX.	

WAR DIARY
or
INTELLIGENCE SUMMARY.
(Erase heading not required.)

Army Form C. 2118.

Instructions regarding War Diaries and Intelligence Summaries are contained in F. S. Regs., Part II and the Staff Manual respectively. Title pages will be prepared in manuscript.

Hour, Date, Place	Summary of Events and Information	Remarks and references to Appendices
February 19th 16	Early morning Physical Exercises - Company training - Lectures to all officers by Major Genl - Cdg Divn. WORKING PARTY, 1 officer, 50 men at BRAY FOSSE.	
February 20th 16	Church Parade at the Theatre. WORKING PARTY, 4 officers, 150 men at HESDIGNEUL FLYING GROUND.	
February 21st 16	Company training continued. Lectures by G.O.C. 142nd Inf. Bde. to all officers. Orders received to move to BRAY MANOEUVRE AREA.	
February 22nd 16	Bn. moved to BRAY area. Bn. Staff 750 m. firs owning WOODS Gr./Ky. R. Btn. Preliminary orders to act as LEFT FLANK GUARD OUCHY-AU-BOIS. 1st Bn. became Advanced Guard, with 1 Troop K.E.H. 2 Sns 22nd Bn. became Advanced Guard, with 23rd Bn details. 1 Coy to act and 1 Platoon Divl Cyclists - 23rd Bn details. 1 Coy to act as Rear Guard. Orders received for all Mounted Officers to proceed to HILL 140, NW of ERNY ST JULIEN meeting MAJOR GEN Cdg Divn under MAJOR CARR, arriving OUT POST LINE meeting MAJOR GEN Cdg Divn at 2.30 pm. Bn proceeded to billets in BRAY under MAJOR CARR, arriving 3.30 pm. Heavy snow fell all day.	
February 23rd 16	6 on brigade practise ATTACK SCHEME. Starting from N of H in RECLINGHEM. Combined attack enemy holding line COVECQUES - HILL 140.	

Army Form C. 2118.

WAR DIARY
or
INTELLIGENCE SUMMARY.
(Erase heading not required.)

Instructions regarding War Diaries and Intelligence Summaries are contained in F. S. Regs., Part II and the Staff Manual respectively. Title pages will be prepared in manuscript.

Hour, Date, Place	Summary of Events and Information	Remarks and references to Appendices
February 24th 16	Battalion Training	
February 25th 16	Brigade "	
February 26th 16	Battalion "	
February 27th 16	Brigade "	
February 28th 16	Battalion "	
February 29th 16	Batt. parade at 8.15am and marched back to ALLOUAGNE via LIGNY-LEZ-AIRE, AUCHY-AU-BOIS and AUCHEL.	

M Minjun
Lt Col Commanding
9th 15th Bn London Regt
(The Queen's)

Officer in charge
Adjutant General's
  Office at the Base

Seventh War Diary
for month ending MARCH 31st 1916.

C J Saunders
for   CAPTAIN & ADJUTANT,
O.C. 24th (COUNTY OF LONDON) Bn,
      THE LONDON REGIMENT,
      THE "QUEENS."

1/24 London Regt
———————————
    Vol XII

Army Form C. 2118.

WAR DIARY
or
INTELLIGENCE SUMMARY.
(Erase heading not required.)

Instructions regarding War Diaries and Intelligence Summaries are contained in F.S. Regs., Part II and the Staff Manual respectively. Title pages will be prepared in manuscript.

Hour, Date, Place	Summary of Events and Information	Remarks and references to Appendices
Nov 1st 1916	Batn. bathed and day devoted to interior economy. Lecture by G.O.C Divn. for all Officers.	
Nov 2nd 1916	Company Training - Lectures	
Nov 3rd 1916	Company Training - Lecture by Lt Col Simpson to all officers of Brigade on Artillery.	
Nov 4th 1916	Company Training - at night firs at Batn H.Q. - battalion turned out but was soon dismissed, fire having been already extinguished.	
Nov 5th 1916	Church Parade	
Nov 6th 1916	Company Training. Lecture by Major Hunt on Machine Guns	
Nov 7th 1916	10th Sn S.H. Bde being placed at disposal of 2nd Divn, 24th Bn move to CORONS FOSSE 10 near PETIT SAINS. Started 8.30 AM - arrived 3 PM.	
Nov 8th 1916	Whole Bn. on working party at night.	
Nov 9th 1916	Whole Bn on working party at night	
Nov 10th 1916	200 men on working party - remainder employed in cleaning Bn area.	
Nov 11th 1916	Grenadier training under C.O. - Company Officers reconnoitred ground for practise defence scheme of villages	

WAR DIARY or INTELLIGENCE SUMMARY.

Army Form C. 2118.

(Erase heading not required.)

Instructions regarding War Diaries and Intelligence Summaries are contained in F.S. Regs., Part II. and the Staff Manual respectively. Title pages will be prepared in manuscript.

Hour, Date, Place	Summary of Events and Information	Remarks and references to Appendices
March 11th (Cortin)	Lt Col Simson leaves to take command of Bde. Major G.A.D. Carr takes over command	
March 12th 16	Whole Bn on day working parties	
March 13th 16	Working parties, day 50 MEN - night 200 MEN.	
March 14th 16	Whole Bn on day working parties - No parties were detailed whilst working	
March 15th 16	Whole Bn area thoroughly cleaned. Billeting parties leave for VERDREL - Billeting party of 11th D.L.I. arrives to take over	
March 16th 16	17th Bn relieves 33rd Bn in RIGHT SECTOR OF CORPS frontage - frontage from BOYAU DE-L'ER-SATZ, S.15.a.3.2. to SOUCHEZ River. 14.21st 34 Bde moves into Divl Reserve. VERDREL. Start 9.15 A.M. - arrives 11+5 AM.	
March 17th 16	Company training - Lectures to Section Platoon Sergeants by Major PARKER on new frontage and general dispositions	
March 18th 16	1st Plat. Grenadiers practice Bomb throwing with live grenades.	
March 19th 16	2nd Plat. Grenadiers practice Bomb throwing with live grenades. General Cleaning of area carried out. "GAS ALERT" message received 8 A.M.	

(73989) W.4141—463. 400,000. 9/14. H.&J.Ltd. Forms/C. 2118/10.

WAR DIARY or INTELLIGENCE SUMMARY

Army Form C. 2118.

Hour, Date, Place	Summary of Events and Information	Remarks and references to Appendices
March 30th 16	42nd Inf Bde moves to take over position of Support Bde. 2th Bn moves to Bouvigny Huts (R.25.d) Working party 5 officers and 350 men by night to CABARET ROUGE	
March 31st 16	24th Bn move to relieve 15 Bn at garrison of LORETTE RIDGE. Relay starts 7.30 p.m. – completed 9.15 p.m. Dispositions – C, A, B, for front line defence D in Reserve. Line of Defence runs along base of SE slopes of Ridge. Right Company (C) along road X.12.a.5.0, to X.13.a.2.9.1. Centre and Left in a semi-circular line from X.5.d.7.0.6 X.6.d.0.5. Reserve Coy – 2 Platoons on S Slope X.4.d.8.3, X.5.c.d.7.8 – in event of attack moving to line N of SUCRERIE, holding ABLAIN – ST – NAZAIRE – SOUCHEZ road. 2 Platoons on N. Slope in R, 34, c, in event of attack moving to support left front line company. Bn H.Q. in ABLAIN – ST NAZAIRE X.10, c, 3, 1. Lt. Col. Simpson returns from Bde and takes over command of Bn.	

Army Form C. 2118.

WAR DIARY
or
INTELLIGENCE SUMMARY.
(Erase heading not required.)

Instructions regarding War Diaries and Intelligence Summaries are contained in F. S. Regs., Part II and the Staff Manual respectively. Title pages will be prepared in manuscript.

Hour, Date, Place	Summary of Events and Information	Remarks and references to Appendices
March 22nd 16	Slight shelling of ABLAIN ST NAZAIRE during morning – Contour cleaning and improving trenches.	
March 23rd 16	Snow fell during night and continued – quiet day – work on trenches continued.	
March 24th 16	Further snow during night – Quiet day – O.C. Bn visited the line. MAJOR G.A.B. CARR goes to take temporary command of 20th Lan Regt – MAJOR PARKER taking over his duties as 2nd in command.	
March 25th 16	Heavy fall of snow during night – in state of bright day. Very little artillery activity.	
March 26th 16	Rain and sleet during night – working work on trenches difficult – Day quiet.	
March 27th 16	Heavy rain interfered with work in trenches during night. Day quiet. At 7.30 P.M. 118 Bn. commenced Relief – completed 10.15 P.M. 142nd 9th Bde moves into Front Line – 21st Bn in Reserve, one Company (C) attached to 25th Bn in Subsection A. Disposition – 2 Companies (B, D) and M.G. Section in dug outs at CARENCY. 1 Company (A) and Grenadiers at VILLERS-AU-BOIS. HQ at VILLERS-AU-BOIS temporarily.	

WAR DIARY
or
INTELLIGENCE SUMMARY.
(Erase heading not required.)

Army Form C. 2118.

Instructions regarding War Diaries and Intelligence Summaries are contained in F. S. Regs., Part II and the Staff Manual respectively. Title pages will be prepared in manuscript.

Hour, Date, Place	Summary of Events and Information	Remarks and references to Appendices
From 28th 16	Working parties A Coy 50, B Coy 50, B Coy 50 for 23rd Bn — B Coy 100 for 22nd Bn.	
March 29th 16	Reconnaissance of lines of approach to front line. Working Parties A Coy 75, D Coy 75, for 23rd Bn. B Coy 100 for 22nd Bn	
March 30th 16	Reconnoitring officers from Res. Bns conducted by Capt Kelly— Working parties as previously.	
March 31st 16	Reconnaissance by Officers of Res. Bns. Working parties as before.	

W. M. Milton
Lt. Col.
Commanding
24th Bn. Lon. Regt.

47/142

1/24 London Regt

Vol XIII

April
1916

WAR DIARY
or
INTELLIGENCE SUMMARY.
(Erase heading not required.)

Army Form C. 2118.

Instructions regarding War Diaries and Intelligence Summaries are contained in F.S. Regs., Part II. and the Staff Manual respectively. Title pages will be prepared in manuscript.

Hour, Date, Place	Summary of Events and Information	Remarks and references to Appendices
April 1st 16	141st Inf Bde commences to relieve 142nd Inf Bde. 24th Bn less 1 Coy relieved by 9th Bn moves to VERDREL.	
April 2nd 16	400 men in working party. 9 a.m. - 3 p.m. at Gouy SERVINS. 24th Bn being relieved by 21st Bn moves to FRESNICOURT. Travelling Detachment rejoin hrs Working Parties on Yesterday - Capt & Adjt C.T. SAUNDERS returns to Bn for duty, after being attd for instruction.	
April 3rd 16	to II Corps 160 + 7 Inf Brown. 200 men - working party at Gouy SERVINS in morning, 100 men working party near R.W.F. at night in Sabot Filler VILLERS-au-BOIS	
April 5th 16	200 men working party at Gouy in morning Whilst Bath & c. engaged at MUSKETRY practice near Ranchicourt during afternoon. It was visited by G.O.C. IV Corps.	
April 6th 16	morning Working Party as before. G.O.C. 1st Army, IV Corps, 47th Division, and 141st Inf Bde. Sir inspected Bn, while at MUSKETRY Practice in Range as yesterday. Sir CHAS MUNRO expressed his satisfaction.	

WAR DIARY
or
INTELLIGENCE SUMMARY.
(Erase heading not required.)

Army Form C. 2118.

Instructions regarding War Diaries and Intelligence Summaries are contained in F. S. Regs., Part II and the Staff Manual respectively. Title pages will be prepared in manuscript.

Hour, Date, Place	Summary of Events and Information	Remarks and references to Appendices
April 7th 16	Coy working parts as yesterday - Remainder of Batt at MUSKETRY practice. Lecture & firing instruction for Officers.	
April 8th 16	Batt. rode from Reserve to Support - 9th Br relieving 23rd Br in BOUVIGNY HUTS. B.25.d. Relief commenced 3pm finished 6pm. 65 O Ranks & men LT FOWLER all left permanent working party on BATAILLE line.	
April 9th 16	Quiet day. 100 O ranks working party under LT GAMAGE worked on LORETTE Defences at night under 23rd Battn - Lt. Col. N.G. SIMPSON bade farewell to the Battn on parade on occasion of leaving to take up post as Chief Instructor Army Inf. School.	
April 10th 16	Lt. Col. SIMPSON left 6am C.O. (Major P. ??) & Adj. inspected assembly position in case of attack, mainly SUNKEN ROAD at E. Edge of BOUVIGNY WOOD during morning. Night working party as usual. 1.30 am Bombardment by 23rd Div Artly commenced on French opposite CALONNE Defence and by 47th Div Arty gun	

(73989) W4141—463. 400,000. 9/14. H.&J.Ltd. Forms/C. 2118/10.

WAR DIARY
or
INTELLIGENCE SUMMARY.

(Erase heading not required.)

Army Form C. 2118.

Hour, Date, Place	Summary of Events and Information	Remarks and references to Appendices
April 10th 16 (con)	AMPLE. No retaliation was noticed from our ones. Men working party aerial Batt. turned out at 7am at practice alarm. Ready to reinforce Bn - Punisher bomb thrown to goal being fast to asph bomb was empty.	
April 11th 16	Quiet day - usual working party.	
April 12th 16	C.O. reconnoitred Subsection "B" - returned about 9.30pm having been held up IN STEEL TRS.	
April 13th 16	On being relieved in BOUVIGNY HUTS by 20th Bn moved back to GOUY SERVINS for 1 nights more comforts. by 1pm. Relieving 22nd Bn who went into line at 6pm.	
April 14th 16	On arrival of 18th Bn moved to VILLERS au BOIS arriving at 1.30 pm. Relieving 6th Bn - on arrival of 17th Bn moved at 7.30pm to Tr. see 700, line at "B" 1. March Refs 36.1 3W 20.00 , S.F. 0.93 & S.F. 3.5.2. Reach 1st Bn trans by 11pm. Quiet night - work landed on trenches	

WAR DIARY
or
INTELLIGENCE SUMMARY.
(Erase heading not required.)

Army Form C. 2118.

Hour, Date, Place	Summary of Events and Information	Remarks and references to Appendices
Abt 5/16	Quiet morning - Our T.M. Battery started registering on enemy front line. Claimed destruction of enemy trench Sent - R. of (Gray?) TM and shell fire retaliation on our line all afternoon. Left guns fired and took down mm mortar slates - Cavalry in sight - from Guns dug up later No way to be improved. Nothing found all night or really long. Much in our own trench by 50 mm (long?)	
Aug 6/16	25a Bn - Pioneers Coy Quiet day till 9 P.M. when our TM started working. Three cutting in German salient S.S.D. 9.100 - Teuton fill and constant shower of all calibre TM Our TM down KE to write instructions - also Bush fire fight between our sap 5+6 and Boyes newer front trench. Our total casualties 7 wounded - Many has - Lt Brinson on our Right strung 3 mines At midnight - Ricks Willey activity in conference. Lt McKay on in. Gas horn heard to sound at 1 am	

WAR DIARY
or
INTELLIGENCE SUMMARY.

(Erase heading not required.)

Army Form C. 2118.

Hour, Date, Place	Summary of Events and Information	Remarks and references to Appendices
April 16 (cont)	...wind was S.W. for... no... hand over this claim owing to GAS SHELLS - high wind during night	
April 17/16	Quiet till 10 pm when heavy T.M.B. fires to cut wire ahead of company sap. there rounds were fired, and immediately a heavy minenwerfer T. Morten and Medium H.E. fire opened on our Reserve and Support lines - the enemy fired till near 1 o'clock. We obtained Artillery support with Morters. Our T.M.'s silenced Minenwerfer positions - Our Casualties 3 killed in S. bay, 1 wounded - much damage to trench - Remainder of day Quiet, usual work Carried on at dusk. At 10 pm L/C MOSELEY + Pte long on on R/ll of fire were suddenly fired on by M. Gun - Key got back safely but bands of fire "once" apparently at OPPY ROUGE + caused casualties in others units this is F.M.G. We worked on our front line. We have been in... the ability of fire of this Gun was exactly the same as own VICKERS GUN - a captured British Gun is suspected.	

WAR DIARY
or
INTELLIGENCE SUMMARY

Army Form C. 2118.

Hour, Date, Place	Summary of Events and Information	Remarks and references to Appendices
April 17th (cont)	3/Lt Robin in [?] on LEFT discovered that a German communication trench joining from our SAP 6,5 German trench line. Patrols kept out owing to [?] of our men standing at their ends.	
June 18/16	Quiet day, not our line. Our command went out line in afternoon. Brigadier also about 11am. Now continued Artillery retaliation had on German MG fire about 11pm (?). M returned from leave.	
April 19/16	Quiet morning, afternoon till about 2.30pm when LM Battery on our right fired rounds on Saucisse Crevasse 21st St. — Immediate retaliation made for us was heavy detonation by 1 morters in our Right Subsector line and HE. Also fire on Ruins line from direction ANGRES — Very damaging — no casualties. Heavy mortars Attachment to corps too weak. Party arranged for 6.30pm. 5 hits were made on Pimple 1 on sap + 5 on front trench. Sack of Sap — very little retaliation.	

WAR DIARY
or
INTELLIGENCE SUMMARY.
(Erase heading not required.)

Army Form C. 2118.

Instructions regarding War Diaries and Intelligence Summaries are contained in F. S. Regs., Part II. and the Staff Manual respectively. Title pages will be prepared in manuscript.

Hour, Date, Place	Summary of Events and Information	Remarks and references to Appendices
April 9th (cont)	10.30 pm – 1st Inf Bde on our Right blew big mine – Stonewall retaliation small. 1095 pm – Barrage of Shrapnel on Zouave Lns and across ZOUAVE VALLEY heaviest on our Right flank IN LEFT 3	
	10.50 pm – Died away	
	10.55 pm – Recommenced with more vigour	
	11.05 pm – Died away slowly	
	Remainder of night quiet.	
April 10th	3.15 am – Enemy working party fire on opposite our Centre. 1 man seen to fall. Party dispersed	
	7 am – Enemy hy battery observed in PIMPLE	
	5.30 pm – 14th Inf Bde Bde take position	
	6.35 pm – Scan 2 if mine exploded on our Right	
	6.40 pm – Shrapnel Barrage on ZOUAVE VALLEY about 1000 yds to our right	
	6.45 pm – Such to inform Bde – Bn Hooked wk coming @ message re Stokes bombs. Stokes fire Contacted with WG Lns in addition	
	6.30 pm – Artillery have no information	

WAR DIARY or INTELLIGENCE SUMMARY.

(Erase heading not required.)

Army Form C. 2118.

Hour, Date, Place	Summary of Events and Information	Remarks and references to Appendices
April 20th 16 (Sun)	6.55 pm. Shelling with Gas Shell being impossible for some reason or other. Probably wind set. 7.10 pm. Shell fire dies away. All quiet. 7.55 pm. Spoke to Bde. They know nothing. Batt. returned N 19 A Sn. Bn. Regt. at 11 pm and M	
April 21st 16	Marched to ESTREE CAUCHIE (Wolz at ESTREE CAUCHIE by 9am) Middle of Path in	
April 22nd 16	Battalion resting and generally cleaning up	
April 23rd 16	To Bde Commander - left Bn. on 11.30. Wilson Exchange to Battalion in the afternoon	
April 24th 16	Bn. prepares for instruction by the C.O. at 9 am for the instruction by the Major-General Brig + 7 Bn. Gen. M. tomorrow	
April 25th 16	Bn. Paraded at 9am and inspected by G.O.C. 7th Division where it was addressed by him in support at Govt Servens	
April 26th 16	Bn. relieved 7th York in trenches PINISNIL SOUCHE E. Relief complete by 3 pm. Sgt. Maj. Lethridge Y.M. Heavy Lymmonitic Staff met Bn. on arrival to being Lymmonitic Staff meeting for ten days	

Army Form C. 2118.

WAR DIARY
or
INTELLIGENCE SUMMARY.
(Erase heading not required.)

Instructions regarding War Diaries and Intelligence Summaries are contained in F. S. Regs., Part II and the Staff Manual respectively. Title pages will be prepared in manuscript.

Hour, Date, Place	Summary of Events and Information	Remarks and references to Appendices
April 7th 16	Battalion formed a number of fatigue parties N.C.O.'s per company daily. DAIZIEL and Pte MER under Sgt. Roy Inst. Stock off for instruction	
April 28th 16	Found 300 men for mining fatigue. Futher instruction in Rynedes training of subaltern officers & N.C.O.'s	
April 29th 16	Fatigues found as yesterday. 6 other Lay. L.J. Saunders returned from hospital, having been away since 24th Nov.	
April 30th 16 SUNDAY	Church Parade. Working parties of usual about 6.30pm heavy bombardment heard in direction of the outpost line & not about 9 pm heard descriptive rifle firing came that strange were in our ROSINGAU TRENCH — our right.	

W. Wain Parker
Major
24th R.W.F.

2/4 London Regt
WE/14
142

WAR DIARY or INTELLIGENCE SUMMARY

Army Form C. 2118.

(Erase heading not required.)

Hour, Date, Place	Summary of Events and Information	Remarks and references to Appendices
May 1st-16.	Quiet day - Whole Battn engaged on various working parties including a night party at CABARET ROUGE under 2/Lt PALMER - 15 Diphtheria contacts discovered and isolated.	
May 2nd-16	Relieved by 20th Bn at GOUY during morning - Thereupon Bn moved to VILLERS relieving 15th Bn. 142nd 2nd Bde took over front line at 5·30 p.m. and we relieved 6th Bn in subsection "B" (see entry for April 14th) - Found the line much altered owing to new craters on the left having been formed - The 6th Bn had had many casualties owing to mines exploded on April 30th. Estimated at 80 killed, 60 wounded. Relief proceeded smoothly, being complete at 12·45 a.m on May 3rd. At 8·30 p.m. heavy bombardment on the right of our line. Subsequently heard it was a mine sprung to our right in 25th Divisional front.	
May 3rd-16.	Preparations made in morning for explosion of 3 heavy mines at S.15.A.23.80. - S.15.A.23.93. and S.9.c.25.25, the latter particularly concerning us being in Nomansland opposite the front of our junction with Right Battalion the 24th London. C.O. made final arrangements with O.C.	

Army Form C. 2118.

WAR DIARY
or
INTELLIGENCE SUMMARY.
(Erase heading not required.)

Instructions regarding War Diaries and Intelligence Summaries are contained in F. S. Regs., Part II. and the Staff Manual respectively. Title pages will be prepared in manuscript.

Hour, Date, Place	Summary of Events and Information	Remarks and references to Appendices
May 3rd 16 (dd)	Coys and O.C. 31st London and	
2.30 pm	O. Order issued	
4.40 pm	D Coy report all clear: B & C dis	
4.47 pm	3 mine shocks felt. – Artillery opened simultaneously	
4.55 pm	Hostile shrapnel & medium H.E. beginning to fall near Bn H.Qs	
4.59 pm	Message heard on phone from 31st Bn to Bde reporting that mines went up very successfully. Right crater 20 to 30 yards in diameter. Centre crater 40 or 50 yds distant from German front line and 30 to 40 yds in diameter. This is at end of our sap. 31st front line reported unmanaged.	
5.5 pm	A Coy report large proportion of heavy shells falling in their line and BLIND. unconfirmed report that CRATER opposite right Coy. is opposite head of BRISSON –	
5.15 pm	Bde informed and B Coy asked for details	
5.10 pm	Bde line Dis. message not sent. Thereforward occasional M.G. Fire; shrapnel and H.E over ZOUAVE VALLEY	
5.47 pm	Artillery Cfts.	
5.50 pm	D Coy report front line reoccupied.	
6.10 pm	All Coys. Dis.	

WAR DIARY
or
INTELLIGENCE SUMMARY.
(Erase heading not required.)

Army Form C. 2118.

Instructions regarding War Diaries and Intelligence Summaries are contained in F.S. Regs., Part II and the Staff Manual respectively. Title pages will be prepared in manuscript.

Hour, Date, Place	Summary of Events and Information	Remarks and references to Appendices
May 3rd (Contd). 6.40 pm	Pigeon message sent to Bde.	
8.00 pm	Runners return from Centre, and left Coy. also. Lewis Guns and report. Normal positions resumed about 6 pm. Total damage slight. Casualties 1 Rifles (by sniper). 3 wounded. Lewis Guns fired about 3000 rounds. also covered advance of 31st Bn on right CRATER. No attempt to molest us on existing Craters.	
8.30 pm	Communication restored to Bde and Coy. Remainder of night quiet. Heard that 31st Bn have consolidated all Craters occupy but lips. Brigadier visited Bn Hq about 1 am.	
May 4th 16	Quiet day. G.O.C. 47th Division called at Bn HQ about 10.30 am. Mine expected on our front this evening. Every precaution taken to withdraw our troops and consolidate possible Craters.	
7.58 pm	Mine shock felt - observer on Lorette says large mine on right of Division - all quiet -	
May 5th 16	Quiet day till 7.15 pm when combined artillery and T.M demonstration began	

WAR DIARY
or
INTELLIGENCE SUMMARY
(Erase heading not required.)

Army Form C. 2118.

Hour, Date, Place	Summary of Events and Information	Remarks and references to Appendices
May 5th (Contd.)	against enemy front line opposite. Divisional front. Retaliation against us soon became very intense, especially on ZOUAVE Valley and Reserve Line - All wires cut except to Bde 7.30pm.	
7.45 pm	Time planned for cessation bombardment fierce. Bde enquire whether mine had exploded on our front, as reported by 2nd Div. - Nothing known.	
8.00 pm	Arty report enemy attack against 25th DIVISION.	
8.30 pm	Fire dying down - Bde tell us infantry attack nearly a bombing affray between saps.	
9.00 pm	Normal - work commenced under R.E. on Craters. Fair progress made. - Work continued during night, assisted by party from 22nd London - Support line strengthened.	
May 6.10	Quiet till about 3pm when enemy minenwerfers became active against whole front. - Howitzer and field gun retaliation was immediate and vigorous. Suspicion is aroused by "fact" that for first time in this town he was firing on front line of Right Coy. This may point to a mine explosion there later on - Quiet night - usual working parties, fair progress made.	

WAR DIARY
or
INTELLIGENCE SUMMARY.
(Erase heading not required.)

Army Form C. 2118.

Hour, Date, Place	Summary of Events and Information	Remarks and references to Appendices
May 7th 16	Much quieter day. Slight minenwerfer activity in afternoon, but artillery retaliation apparently stamped this out after 2 rounds. Usual procedure is now that directly observing officer on LORETTE sees "Mini" bomb drop in our lines. (a) 18 pdrs shrapnel PIMPLE (b) How's shell "Mini" positions and then report that they have fired. Quiet night, much work done on CRATERS.	
May 8th 16.	Till evening much quieter day. Some "Mini" activity about 2 pm. silenced even more quickly than yesterday — warned that mine would go up in 25th. Div. area this evening at P sector S.22.c.20.05. Guides for 18th Bn put off 2 hours. Explosion due at 8.10pm.	
8.7pm	Mine shock felt.	
8.18pm	XVII Corps Arty open fire slowly.	
8.25pm	All quiet again	
11.59pm	Relief by 18th for Regt complete.	
May 9th 16	Moved to MAISNIL BOUCHÉ to Reserve billets arriving there between 3 and 4 am. Remainder of day spent in rest and bathing.	

Army Form C. 2118.

WAR DIARY
or
INTELLIGENCE SUMMARY.
(Erase heading not required.)

Instructions regarding War Diaries and Intelligence Summaries are contained in F.S. Regs., Part II. and the Staff Manual respectively. Title pages will be prepared in manuscript.

Hour, Date, Place	Summary of Events and Information	Remarks and references to Appendices
May 10th.16	Companies at disposal — 100 men working party under Capt CLARK at night — Major Parker had to supervise Bde party owing to complaints that infantry working parties did not work.	
May 11th.16	Musketry on range. — Remainder of Battn Physical training — 11am lecture on gas by Divisional Gas officer — Afternoon NCOs to view demonstration of Gas fans at Govy. Cpl. SCAMMELL accidentally gassed. Inoculation continued	
May 12th.16	Coy bombers on bombing practice — Remainder continue Physical Training — C.O. and O.C. D Coy. reconnoitre line during night prior to taking over on 14th inst. Very little change since last tour reported.	
May 13th.16	Much rain consequently little work — Cleaning area by fatigue party.	
May 14th.16	Church Parade — Bn relieves 18th Bn in Centre Subsection — Relief started 7.15pm — Complete 11.30pm	
May 15th.16	Day quiet — Bde inform us that 25th Div on the right would explode 5 mines at 8.30pm. Mine shocks were felt at that time and mutual artillery	

WAR DIARY
or
INTELLIGENCE SUMMARY.
(Erase heading not required.)

Army Form C. 2118.

Instructions regarding War Diaries and Intelligence Summaries are contained in F.S. Regs., Part II and the Staff Manual respectively. Title pages will be prepared in manuscript.

Hour, Date, Place	Summary of Events and Information	Remarks and references to Appendices
May 15th 16	duel followed — enemy only kept a desultory barrage on our area. By 9.30 pm all was quiet, and good progress made with work. 100 men of 32nd Bn provided working party.	
May 16th 16	Day very quiet. Bde propose 32nd Bn should provide 50 men to stay in the line, and 50 to come up nightly — this was accordingly arranged. At 10 pm enemy aeroplanes came over and dropped bombs on CARENCY; BROADBRIDGE CRATER was subjected to harassing M.G. fire coming from the left and in reverse. Communicated with 22nd Bn on left, and arranged artillery retaliation — this proved at once effective.	
May 17th 16	Day again quiet — at 8.30 pm apparently an enemy bombing attack on 25th Divn, with brisk artillery activity. Enemy reported sapping forward on NEWCUT CRATER, to a point which would command our front line. Found it impossible to obtain adequate R.E. assistance or material for proper consolidation of CRATERS, and construction of much needed dug-outs in the area.	

Army Form C. 2118.

WAR DIARY
or
INTELLIGENCE SUMMARY.
(Erase heading not required.)

Instructions regarding War Diaries and Intelligence Summaries are contained in F. S. Regs., Part II. and the Staff Manual respectively. Title pages will be prepared in manuscript.

Hour, Date, Place	Summary of Events and Information	Remarks and references to Appendices
May 18th 16	Day quiet generally – Some minenwerfer activity by enemy. He endeavoured to blow in enemy sap on NEWCUT CRATER, but T.M.Bs. failed to get the range. At night enemy reported extending sap in NEWCUT CRATER – Our Stokes T.M.B. again endeavoured to destroy this but failed to get a single hit.	
May 19th 16	At 6 a.m. enemy started heavy minenwerfer fire; artillery retaliated on PIMPLE and suspected minenwerfer position without apparent effect, until 1.30 pm, when our heavy howitzers successfully intervened. Front line by NEWCUT CRATER badly damaged also BRISSON. All men available employed during night in clearing same. At night, considerable activity was heard on the Right Brigade of Division on that flank, informs us that it is on the front of Division on his right where some bombs were being thrown.	
May 20th 16	At 7 a.m. enemy minenwerfer again active – artillery and medium T.M.B. retaliated. Again observed that our artillery firing on PIMPLE had not its previous salutary effect. Enemy are evidently using O.Ps in CRATERS for	

Army Form C. 2118.

WAR DIARY
or
INTELLIGENCE SUMMARY.
(Erase heading not required.)

Instructions regarding War Diaries and Intelligence Summaries are contained in F.S. Regs., Part II. and the Staff Manual respectively. Title pages will be prepared in manuscript.

Hour, Date, Place	Summary of Events and Information	Remarks and references to Appendices
May 20 (contd)	Observation of minenwerfer fire.	
12:15 pm	Visited by Major MOMBA of 176th Tunnelling Coy. to inform us enemy are mining activity S·W of NEWCUT CRATER, but no immediate danger. He suspects enemy have been using interior of this CRATER for this purpose. This explains enemy's minenwerfer activity on our O.P.s on this CRATER.	
4:10 pm	Brigade inform us there will be an artillery demonstration on our right at 4:36 P.M.	
4:36 pm	Nothing happens — all quiet	
6 pm	Still quiet.	
11 pm	17th Bn Lon. Regt starts to relieve us.	
May 31st		
1·15 am	Relief Complete. Bn moves to MAISNIL BOUCHÉ	
3·30 am	Bn arrives MAISNIL BOUCHÉ	
	PETIT SERVINS. Shelled during morning transport of our Bn in Bde suffered casualties from midday onwards. Sounds of intense bombardment on our front were heard.	
5·40 pm	Received message from Bde to be in readiness to move at ½ hours notice.	

WAR DIARY
or
INTELLIGENCE SUMMARY.
(Erase heading not required.)

Army Form C. 2118.

Hour, Date, Place	Summary of Events and Information	Remarks and references to Appendices
6.5 pm.	Reported to Bde. "Bn in readiness."	
7.30 pm.	Received message from Bde. to be ready to move at once, on receipt of orders, & take up position on W edge of BOIS de la HAIE.	
7.53 pm.	Reported "ready to move."	
8.30 pm.	Verbal message from Bde. "MOVE" confirmed by written message. Bn moves - by companies to BOIS de la HAIE, leaving cookers, packs etc, at MAISNIL BOUCHÉ.	
8.55 pm.	Last company clear. - 2/Lt N. TAYLOR. reports to Bde at lodge of CHATEAU de-la-HAIE.	
10 pm.	Bn in position. - Lt Col. G.A.B. CARR arrives and takes over Command.	
10.15 pm	Arrival of 31st Bn.	
10.35 pm.	2/Lt N. TAYLOR. brings orders from Bde to move to VILLERS at once, handing over present position to 97th Bde which had been brought up by motor-lorries. CAPT NADAUD and 2/Lt N. TAYLOR remain to guide them to position.	
11.35 pm	Bn at VILLERS - learn that 2nd Bn has moved to MAISTRE LINE - 21st Divn with us in VILLERS - 32nd on TOART RIDGE.	

Army Form C. 2118.

WAR DIARY
or
INTELLIGENCE SUMMARY.
(Erase heading not required.)

Instructions regarding War Diaries and Intelligence Summaries are contained in F.S. Regs., Part II. and the Staff Manual respectively. Title pages will be prepared in manuscript.

Hour, Date, Place	Summary of Events and Information	Remarks and references to Appendices
May 21st (Cont)	Make S.A.A. up to 300 rounds pr. man, and 10 bombs pr. bomber.	
11.45pm	31st Bn moves to MAISTRE LINE - 23rd to BAJOLLE LINE.	
May 22nd		
12.20 Am	G.O.C. Bde and Brigade Major arrive - inform us that the situation is obscure - apparently 8th Bn. had lost front line - 30th Bn. had lost part of their line, but subsequently regained it - 25th Divn had been driven some way back on the right flank - counter attack was going to take place at 1 Am.	
1.25 Am.	Violent artillery activity.	
2.50 Am.	G.O.C. Bde returns to Bde Advanced H.Q. Bde warn us to have 2 companies ready to move to MAISTRE LINE.	
3.30 Am	During day - Bn at VILLERS. In afternoon Lt Col Carr. goes up to Advs H.Q. of 140th and 141st Bde at CABARET ROUGE with G.O.C. 142nd Bde Returning reports we are to counterattack at 1.30 Am, and retake line lost by 8th Bn, the 21st Battalion attacking on own left and 99th Bde on our right.	
6.15pm	Bde message arrives - "No attack" that night, but Bn is to relieve 15th Bn in BERTHONNAL SECTION as arranged.	

Army Form C. 2118.

WAR DIARY
or
INTELLIGENCE SUMMARY.
(Erase heading not required.)

Instructions regarding War Diaries and Intelligence Summaries are contained in F.S. Regs., Part II and the Staff Manual respectively. Title pages will be prepared in manuscript.

Hour, Date, Place	Summary of Events and Information	Remarks and references to Appendices
May 22nd (cont.) 7:30pm	and carry on with preparation for the attack. Bn leaves VILLERS - delayed by heavy barrage on CABARET ROAD - dense tear shell gas encountered causing some casualties	
May 23rd 1:10am	Relief of 15th Bn. complete during relief enemy opened heavy artillery barrage on ZOUAVE VALLEY, evidently anticipating an attack. Day spent in locating SAA and bomb dumps, and clearing up the line - many dead were found, and 28 wounded of the 8th and 15th Bns were in the AID Post - all these were evacuated to F.A. during the day by volunteers from the Coy. and some R.A.M.C. Preparation for the attack pushed forward. Decided to keep A on LEFT and C on RIGHT of line as a garrison. A Coy to go over in support if necessary - B to attack on LEFT, D on RIGHT coupled with bombing attacks to clear the flanks	

WAR DIARY
or
INTELLIGENCE SUMMARY.
(Erase heading not required.)

Army Form C. 2118.

May 23rd (Contd.) SKETCH showing position on night May 22/23.

[Hand-drawn sketch map with the following labels:]
- GERMAN / BRITISH (arrows)
- OLD BRITISH FRONT LINE (2)
- OLD BRITISH SUPPORT LINE
- BLUE BILL (Russell)
- B Coy. / A Coy.
- D Coy. / C Coy.
- LINE DUG NIGHT 24/5 by R. BERNS
- 99th Bde.
- INTERNATIONAL
- GRAN BY STREET
- Bn H.Q.
- UPPER RIDGE
- 24th Bn.
- AID POST
- ERSATZ
- PARTLY DUG LINE
- 21st Bn.

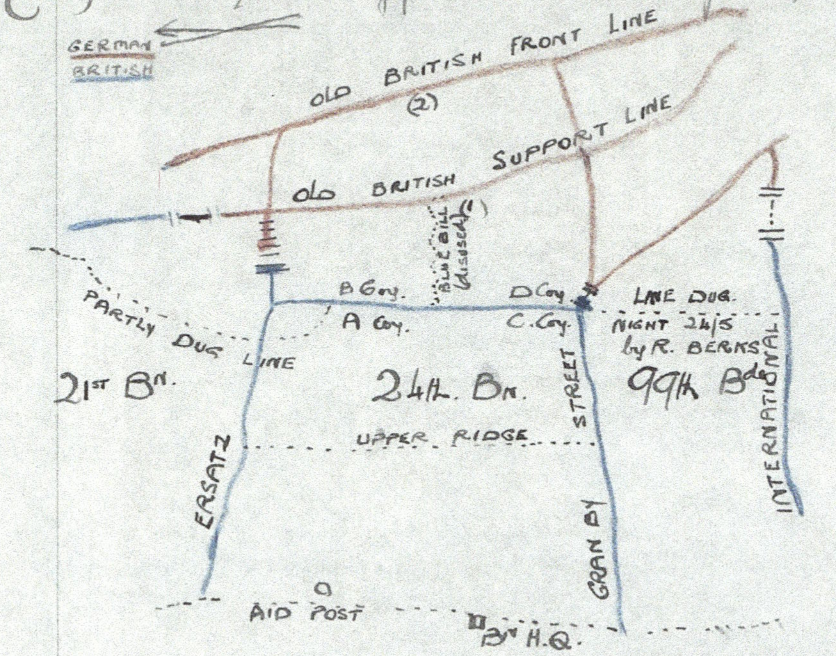

We are ordered to retake the old support line and if possible to push on to the old front line, 21st Bn & 99th Bde. conforming to the same plan. Our present position is precarious there is only one line and our right flank is in the air. The 15th Bn had attempted to counter attack on the previous evening but meeting with Infilade M.G. fire & heavy shelling

WAR DIARY
or
INTELLIGENCE SUMMARY
(Erase heading not required.)

Army Form C. 2118.

Hour, Date, Place	Summary of Events and Information	Remarks and references to Appendices

Maj Douglas had lost 2 Companies and gained nothing. The General Attack is ordered for 8.25pm, but the following facts have to be reckoned with:

(a) 99th Bde have no line to attack from, and have to start lower down the ridge.

(b) It is useless to launch an attack over the open until the bombers have cleared the flank trenches.

The following detachments are placed at our disposal for carrying etc.

(1) 2 Companies (about 110 Men) of 22nd Bn for carrying etc.
(2) Bombers of 33rd Bn under Lt BULGIN + 4 Lewis guns + Sections of same Bn.
(3) 80 Men of 4th R.inf. for consolidation.
(4) Section of R.E. for wiring etc.

Decided:-
When attack opened, to launch bombing attacks down both flanks, and as soon as sufficient progress had been made to launch infantry attack over the open, if possible joining up with the 99th Bde.

8.3pm. Enemy opens violent barrage on ZOUAVE VALLEY.
8.20pm. Barrage slackening.
8.25pm. Barrage of extreme violence, our front line suffering considerable casualties already

Army Form C. 2118.

WAR DIARY
or
INTELLIGENCE SUMMARY.
(Erase heading not required.)

Instructions regarding War Diaries and Intelligence Summaries are contained in F.S. Regs., Part II and the Staff Manual respectively. Title pages will be prepared in manuscript.

Hour, Date, Place	Summary of Events and Information	Remarks and references to Appendices
8.40 pm.	Message from 99th Bde. that they were standing fast, and not going to attempt advance.	
8.45 pm.	Major Parker, from Advanced H.Q., reports that first wave has gone over, but advance held up by the fact that our bombers, in spite of 3 gallant attempts, had failed to carry the enemy saps on the flanks. Ordered attack to stand fast.	
8.50 8.52 8.54 } pm.	Capt Kelly's reports, confirming above.	
8.58 pm.	2/Lt BASEDEN confirms above.	
9 to 9.30 pm.	CAPT KELLY, CAPT TRUELOVE, CAPT CLARK, 2/Lt ROBIN at Bn H.Q. wounded.	
9.20 pm.	Enemy shelling decreasing - ours still very active. Since 8 p.m. we have been out of touch with Bde. - since we came into the line we have had no direct liaison with the artillery, the ranging of which was in some cases most inaccurate.	
9.40 pm.	Sent off Situation Report to Bde by 2 runners - this arrived safely.	
9.45 pm.	Enemy shelling seems to have ceased.	
10.30 pm.	Our artillery active, replied to by enemy with sudden intense outbursts.	

Army Form C. 2118.

WAR DIARY
or
INTELLIGENCE SUMMARY.
(Erase heading not required.)

Instructions regarding War Diaries and Intelligence
Summaries are contained in F.S. Regs., Part II.
and the Staff Manual respectively. Title pages
will be prepared in manuscript.

Hour, Date, Place	Summary of Events and Information	Remarks and references to Appendices
May 20 (Contd) May 21st '16 1.10 am	Barrages on the ZOUAVE VALLEY. Informed by O.C. 4th R.W.F. party, who had got into touch with 99th Bde., that 22nd Fusiliers would attack at 1.30am and endeavour to link up with our right flank. Sent up 20 of 22nd Bn. to relieve any of our men who were suffering from the strain - instructed Lt. MOBBERLEY who had taken command of the line and reorganised with great skill and courage, to stand fast if this attack should come off, and give all assistance possible to the attack	
12.5 am	Heavy shells falling at intervals on ZOUAVE VALLEY.	
3 am to 7 am	22nd Bn. gradually relieving our men in front line. Day quiet though our artillery were constantly active. Artillery Liaison officer swore during morning - without any wire - he made constant efforts to establish communication and finally managed to get one wire laid - first enemy shell that fell in the valley cut this	

WAR DIARY
or
INTELLIGENCE SUMMARY.

(Erase heading not required.)

Army Form C. 2118.

Instructions regarding War Diaries and Intelligence Summaries are contained in F.S. Regs., Part II and the Staff Manual respectively. Title pages will be prepared in manuscript.

Hour, Date, Place	Summary of Events and Information	Remarks and references to Appendices
May 24th (cont)	Though constantly repaired, communication was never maintained. Artillery Officer investigates shells falling behind our line.	
7pm.	Message from Bde. re possibility of Relief by R. BERKS - got into touch with them. Find that 13th Bn has relieved 12th Bn during last night.	
8pm.	Relief cancelled.	
11.15pm.	Received warning order that 6th Bde would relieve us on night 25/26.	
May 25th '16		
7am.	24th Bn. (B & D Coys) relieves men of 22nd Bn. in the line. A & B Coys. in upper ridge - 22nd B"Coy. 23rd L.G.S. and bombers in Reserve by Bn H.Q.	
10.50am.	Artillery report considerable enemy movement behind MOMBER CRATER.	
11.15am.	Reconnoitring officers of Kings Liverpool arrive.	
2.pm.	Col. Cavr. goes to confer with Col. Matthews re relief. Nothing definite settled - apparently it has not been decided whether 6th Bde. or 99th Bde. will take over.	
MIDNIGHT.	Our line. Relief. Kings Liverpool reported arrived at 23rd Bn.	

WAR DIARY or INTELLIGENCE SUMMARY.

(Erase heading not required.)

Army Form C. 2118.

Hour, Date, Place	Summary of Events and Information	Remarks and references to Appendices
May 26th.		
12:30 am	Coy of 1st Sork Staffs relieves our front line - Lates 1 L.G. relieves our B.	
2 am	1st Kings L.R. sends 1 Coy to be in support.	
2:20 am	Relief complete. Enemy M.G. fired on us during journey out. causing 1 casualty.	
4:45 am	Arrived at VILLERS. Receives orders to move to BEUGIN at 2pm.	
2pm	Move to BEUGIN	
6:45 pm	Arrive at BEUGIN. Major PARKER goes on leave.	
May 27th '16	Men resting and cleaning. General refitting	
May 28th '16	Church Parade - Inspection of 142nd Inf Bde by G.O.C. First Army, at which the Bde was warmly congratulated on its conduct during the recent operations. Draft of 44 men arrives with 3 Officers Lt A.L. PALMER - 2/Lts. BUSHELL and LONGLEY.	
May 29th '16	Training started under Company officers. Lt-Col CARR attends First Army Enquiry into recent operations. Draft of 11 men arrives Division is at 4 hours notice	

Army Form C. 2118.

WAR DIARY
or
INTELLIGENCE SUMMARY
(Erase heading not required.)

Instructions regarding War Diaries and Intelligence Summaries are contained in F.S. Regs., Part II. and the Staff Manual respectively. Title pages will be prepared in manuscript.

Hour, Date, Place	Summary of Events and Information	Remarks and references to Appendices
May 30th 16	Company Training Physical Drill, Bayonet fighting - 10 officers arrive from HAVRE - 2/Lts FULLER, ANSELL AE. BROCK, CATTELL, WATTS, BURROUGHS, ROBINSON, WALKER, AMBLER and LIVERMORE. Also Draft of 23 Men.	
May 31st 16	Company training continued	

Clewis Linton
Lt-Col.
Cdg. 24th Lon Regt.
"The Queen's"

47

— 1/24 London Regt
Vol 15

WAR DIARY
or
INTELLIGENCE SUMMARY.
(Erase heading not required.)

Army Form C. 2118.

Hour, Date, Place	Summary of Events and Information	Remarks and references to Appendices
June 1st 1916	Battalion moves to FOSSE se la CLARENCE, near DIVION - starts 3 am - arrives 125 am - Bn H.Q. at LA CAUCHIETTE	
June 2nd	Company training, Bayonet fighting - Riding Instruction for Officers	
June 3rd	Church Parade for Brigade at DIVION 10 am - Rev. Instruction of Officers under Capt. Holliday. Bombers proceed to DIVION 2/Lt Bushell, Fuller, Watts, Hey under instructors of R.E.	
June 4th	3 day Course Riding Instructor under Transport Officer for Officers Company training, Bayonet Exercises	
June 5th	The B.G.C. lectured to all newly joined officers in the Brigade at Det. Bn. 1/4 Rl Riding Instructor for Officers. Company Training, Bayonet Fighting, Bayonet	
June 6th	Riding & Physical Exercises for Officers Company Training, Bayonet fighting & Riding Instruction Company Bombers under 2/Lt Bussden Pte Hart awarded the Military Medal, attached to Bn Signals.	
June 7th	Riding Instruction under T.O. for Officers Baths at OURTON. B.G.C. inspected Bn. Transport and	

Army Form C. 2118.

WAR DIARY
or
INTELLIGENCE SUMMARY.
(Erase heading not required.)

Instructions regarding War Diaries and Intelligence Summaries are contained in F.S. Regs., Part II. and the Staff Manual respectively. Title pages will be prepared in manuscript.

Hour, Date, Place	Summary of Events and Information	Remarks and references to Appendices
June 7th (contd)	expressed his satisfaction. Musketry in range at OURTON. No long rifles in Battn. withdrawn.	
June 8th	Riding Instruction for Officers. Battalion out for the day — Training carried out at T.b.a. 6.6. "Battalion Drill", extended order drill. Bayonet Exercises.	
June 9th	Four Officers to Res-3day Course. Battn formed a convoy out at 1.35.C.S.S. Class order Drill, Extended order drill, Bayonet Exercises — Lt Col G.A.Burton Gave lectures to all subalterns. Lt. Col. Law attended Courtmartial at 2nd Inf. H.Q. Witness in the Major Stuart (Berks Regt) case Riding Instruction for Officers.	
June 10th	Company Training "Bayonet Exercises - Capt WHEATER, 2/Lts VANDYK, KIRKUP, MARTIN & HEATHCOTE & SANDERS joined the Battalion	
June 11th	Church Parade at OURTON	
June 12th	Company Training — Lt Col G.A.Burton Gave lectures on new file.	11.30 a.m. 28th 94th Bde reconnoitres

Army Form C. 2118.

WAR DIARY
or
INTELLIGENCE SUMMARY.
(Erase heading not required.)

Instructions regarding War Diaries and Intelligence Summaries are contained in F. S. Regs., Part II. and the Staff Manual respectively. Title pages will be prepared in manuscript.

Hour, Date, Place	Summary of Events and Information	Remarks and references to Appendices
June 13th.	Batt. moves to COUPIGNY - Division having taken over NOULETTE Sector - 123rd Inf Bde in Divl Reserve.	
June 14th.	Working party of two under Major Parker, burying cable at BULLY GRENAY	
June 15th.	Working party 100 as before - Permanent Working Party 75 men goes to BOUVIGNY BOYEFFLES under Capt WHEATER	
June 16th.	Bn cleaning up billets - working party of 75 men by night. During this period rear line has been thoroughly reconnoitred by Company Offrs.	
June 17th.	123rd Inf Bde relieves 141st Inf Bde in front line - in ANGRES Sector - 24th Bn relieving 19th Bn in ANGRES II (LEFT) Relief completed 6.45 pm - Guides arranged to take routes for "Secret Carrying Party" Dispositions - A B + C Coys in front line from RIGHT to LEFT - each with one Platoon in SUPPORT in PYRENEES - D.Coy and 2 sections of Bombers in RESERVE - 1 Section	

WAR DIARY or INTELLIGENCE SUMMARY

Army Form C. 2118.

Hour, Date, Place	Summary of Events and Information	Remarks and references to Appendices
June 17th (cont)	of Bombers on BULLY CRATER. Lewis Guns, all 4 in support lines – Major Parker remained behind to take over command of 18th Lon. Regt. Capt. MILNER in charge of Bde School, COUPIGNY. Company of 2nd R.M.L.I. are attached to us in the line for instruction.	
June 18th	Everything very quiet – in evening Capt WHEATER reports he has been informed by Tunnelling Officer that a mine is likely to be exploded by the enemy on his Company front. Investigation shows this improbable, but necessary measures to deal with it taken. Special Carrying Party cancelled for tonight – Patrols out all night.	
June 19th	Everything quiet – some slight T.M. and rifle grenade activity. Intelligence work pushed on in abundance with Bde Order. Company of HANKE Bn relieves Company of 2nd R.M.L.I. Special Carrying Party again cancelled. Patrols out all night.	

WAR DIARY
or
INTELLIGENCE SUMMARY.
(Erase heading not required.)

Army Form C. 2118.

Hour, Date, Place	Summary of Events and Information	Remarks and references to Appendices
June 20th '16	Still quiet - T.M and rifle grenade activity on hot side. Patrols out all night. "Steeves" carrying party continued.	
June 21st	Very quiet - 4 pm. Relief by 17th Bn started - owing to one of their Companies not waiting for guides, relief was not complete till 8.5 pm - 21st Bn move to BOUVIGNY	
June 22nd	BOYEFFLES - "Steeves" Carrying Party, 300 men by night.	
June 23rd	"Steeves" Carrying Party, 180 men at night	
June 24th	Bn resting	
June 25th	Bn relieves 15th Bn in NOULETTE WOOD. Relief starts 10 pm - completed 10.45 pm. One Company attached to provide numerous control posts & other duties. Our Artillery continuously active.	
June 26th	Our artillery activity continues. Working party 100. Men at night - Some violent thunderstorms.	
June 27th	Much heavy rain fell throughout the day and night. Artillery continue steady activity by day. 141st Inf/Bde.	

WAR DIARY
or
INTELLIGENCE SUMMARY.
(Erase heading not required.)

Army Form C. 2118.

Instructions regarding War Diaries and Intelligence Summaries are contained in F. S. Regs., Part II. and the Staff Manual respectively. Title pages will be prepared in manuscript.

Hour, Date, Place	Summary of Events and Information	Remarks and references to Appendices
June 27th (cont)	Raid on enemy trenches at night	
11.45 pm	Our Artillery commenced heavy bombardment as to be used at intervals during operations.	
2 Am (28th)	All quiet	
2.30 am	Bn. informs us Battalion (less 1 Company), which had been standing to in huts to stand down - remaining Coy to stand down at 3 A.M.	
June 28th '16 1.30 A.M.	Bde inform us raid has been very successful - 120 enemy being accounted for. Our own casualties stand about 20	
1 p.m.	Bde inform us raid by 8th H.L.I. further north has also been successful. 40 prisoners and 2 M.G's being taken. Bn engaged in carrying bombs throughout the morning.	
June 29th	Special Carrying Parties for trenches morning and afternoon. Leading Party at night.	

Army Form C. 2118.

WAR DIARY
or
INTELLIGENCE SUMMARY.
(Erase heading not required.)

Instructions regarding War Diaries and Intelligence Summaries are contained in F. S. Regs., Part II. and the Staff Manual respectively. Title pages will be prepared in manuscript.

Hour, Date, Place	Summary of Events and Information	Remarks and references to Appendices
June 30th	"Special burning parties for "empties" during the morning – Loading Party at night. Relieved by 6th Bn Lon Regt.	

C. B. Jourdain
Lt. Col. C.O. 2/4th Bn Lon Regt.
"The Queen's"

142nd Brigade.
47th Division.

1/24th BATTALION

LONDON REGIMENT

JULY 1916

Headquarters,
~~47th Division~~
142 Inf Bde.

Herewith please receive WAR DIARY for JULY 1916.

[signature]

Lieut & Adjt for C.C.
24th Bn Lon Regt.
"The Queen's"

[stamp: 1 Aug 1916, ORDERLY ROOM, THE LONDON, No. 631, (THE QUEEN'S)]

Army Form C. 2118.

1/24th Batt. London Regt.

WAR DIARY
or
INTELLIGENCE SUMMARY
(Erase heading not required.)

Hour, Date, Place	Summary of Events and Information	Remarks and references to Appendices
July 1st 1916.	Bn at BOUVIGNY BOYEFFLES. Special Carrying Parties 100 Men by day, for empty 'ROGERS'.	Vol 16
July 2nd 1916.	Special Carrying Party 100 Men by day. Carrying Party of 200 for T.M. Ammunition at night - 15 Signallers & 20 Transport had to be included in this party.	
July 3rd 1916.	Bn relieves 17th Bn. as SUPPORT Bn to ANGRES Section. Dispositions: 'A' Coy in MECHANICS at disposal of LEFT Bn (22nd Bn) - 'D' Coy in SPINNEY TRENCH at disposal of RIGHT Bn: 'C' Coy in MECHANICS at disposal of 1142nd Bde. 'B' Coy in CORONS D'AIX and CAP DE PONT: R.G.S. and Bombers scattered – until 22nd Bn relieves NELSON Bn on LEFT; 1 L. Gun and 2 Sections of BOMBERS are lent to them - Bn H.Q. BULLY GRENAY. Draft of 103 Men, with Lt. COUSINS, arrives at RAILHEAD, and are quartered in CONVENT, HERSIN. During night, 141st Inf Bde. raid enemy's trenches - Bn "Stands to" from 1.30 A.M. to 3 A.M. Raid executed by 15th Bn reported successful.	

Army Form C. 2118.

WAR DIARY
or
INTELLIGENCE SUMMARY.
(Erase heading not required.)

Instructions regarding War Diaries and Intelligence Summaries are contained in F.S. Regs., Part II. and the Staff Manual respectively. Title pages will be prepared in manuscript.

Hour, Date, Place	Summary of Events and Information	Remarks and references to Appendices
July 4th.	Very quiet - Bombers are placed at disposal of B.B.O. 100 Men of new draft are brought up and equally distributed.	
5pm.	Urgent orders received to find guides for "special" carrying parties from COLONEL'S HOUSE. ROUTE absolutely unknown to this Bn. Bn. H.Q. supply a Trench Nav. D'Coy ordered to find guides and in spite of lack of time for proper reconnaissance carried through their duties successfully. Control Posts for ROUTES also found.	
July 5th.	Everything very quiet. Carrying Party for T.M. Ammunition. 100 Men during the morning. At night, Guides, Control Posts, and "assistants" for Special R.E. found as before.	
July 6th.	Still very quiet - Carrying Party, 100 Men for T.M. Ammunition in morning. Control Posts, guides etc for "Special" Parties arranged, for new routes cancelled at the last minute.	

Army Form C. 2118.

WAR DIARY
or
INTELLIGENCE SUMMARY.
(Erase heading not required.)

Instructions regarding War Diaries and Intelligence Summaries are contained in F.S. Regs., Part II. and the Staff Manual respectively. Title pages will be prepared in manuscript.

Hour, Date, Place	Summary of Events and Information	Remarks and references to Appendices
July 7th.	Still quiet - some shelling of Bully GRENAY. Carrying Party 180 Men, for T.M. Ammunition in morning. Have now absorbed all draft of 193. At night provided 160 Men for "Special" Carrying Parties - 60 men. ordered for pushing trucks (later reduced to 30. Having only 220 men (2 Companies) at disposal have to employ men who arrived in the morning - Torrential rain fell during night - men very exhausted - trenches congested. But all work was performed.	
July 8th.	Still quiet - 20 Men found for Carrying Party during morning; 2nd Bn. are under orders to carry out 2 raids in M.26.c. during night.	
11·15pm	Bn. HQ. moves to Btn HQ.	
11·55pm	Artillery Bombardment commences.	
July 9th. 12·30am	Artillery ceases.	
1am.	First Raid reported successful - enemy trenches entered and dug-outs bombed.	
1·35am.	Renewed Artillery Bombardment - Gas + Smoke released.	

WAR DIARY
or
INTELLIGENCE SUMMARY.

(Erase heading not required.)

Army Form C. 2118.

Hour, Date, Place	Summary of Events and Information	Remarks and references to Appendices
2.40 A.m.	All quiet. - 2nd raid apparently unsuccessful, men being unable to see owing to smoke and gas cloud.	
3.5 A.m.	Bn. H.Q. returns to former position. Bn. relieves 2nd Bn in ANGRES II. Relief starts 2.30 p.m. - completed 4.30 pm. Company of HOOD Bn attached for instruction. Patrols sent out at night.	
July 10th	Quiet day - some slight enemy trench mortar activity speedily silenced by our T.M.Bs. Patrols out at night - wiring parties of enemy observed, with strong covering parties.	
July 11th	Quiet day - our trench mortars very active. Patrols out at night - 2/Lt W.C.H. Palmer wounded in an encounter with a German, whom he killed with a dagger. - Wiring front line started.	
July 12th	Very quiet - Our T.M.Bs cutting enemy wire - Lewis Guns firing on gaps at night - Patrols report enemy endeavouring to repair his wire. Wiring of PYRENEES.	

Army Form C. 2118.

WAR DIARY
or
INTELLIGENCE SUMMARY.
(Erase heading not required.)

Instructions regarding War Diaries and Intelligence Summaries are contained in F. S. Regs., Part II. and the Staff Manual respectively. Title pages will be prepared in manuscript.

Hour, Date, Place	Summary of Events and Information	Remarks and references to Appendices
July 13th.	Very quiet – Our T.M. Bs continue cutting enemy wire. Lewis Guns of 1st R.M.L.I. relieve our L.G.S., who stay in the line. Patrols out at night – Lewis Guns firing on gaps in German wire.	
July 15th.	Very quiet – TMBs continue wire cutting.	
2.30pm	Relief by 1st R.M.L.I. starts – completed 6 p.m. Bn. moves to billets in HERSIN. Interior Economy.	
July 16th.	47th Divn relieves 2nd Divn in CARENCY & BERTHONVAL Section. 142 Inf Bde. takes over CARENCY SECTION, 24/k in RESERVE at VILLERS-AU-BOIS, relieving 2nd SOUTH STAFFS.	
July 17th.	Working party, 100 men at night, on BAVIARE TRENCH, from HOSPITAL CORNER to 130 Trench	
July 18th.	Training of Company Bombers under Bombing Officer. Working party at night, 100 men as before – carrying party of 75 men at IRON POST. X.12.a.1.1.	

Army Form C. 2118.

WAR DIARY
or
INTELLIGENCE SUMMARY.
(Erase heading not required.)

Instructions regarding War Diaries and Intelligence Summaries are contained in F.S. Regs., Part II. and the Staff Manual respectively. Title pages will be prepared in manuscript.

Hour, Date, Place	Summary of Events and Information	Remarks and references to Appendices
July 19th.	Training of Company Bombers - Lewis Gunners - Company Training.	
July 20th.	Training of Company Bombers - Lewis Gunners etc - Company Training. Working Parties 50 by day: 50 by night: Carrying Party 50 by night. Training of Specialists & Reserve Specialists continues.	
July 21st	Training of Specialists as before. Working Parties as before.	
July 22nd.	Training of Specialists as before. Working parties as before. Inspection of Draft by Brigadier General.	
July 23rd.	Capt C.J. SAUNDERS. returned from attachment to 141st Inf Bde & took up duties of Adjt - Lt GAMAGE proceeding to Div. School. Working Party on BAVIAKE Trench in morning - Otherwise Company Training - Reconnaissance of CARENCY II by C.O. & O.C. Coys	
July 24th	Relieved 22nd Lon Regt in CARENCY II. First Company left VILLERS at 8.30 pm. Relief complete 1.10 am July 25th	

Army Form C. 2118.

WAR DIARY
or
INTELLIGENCE SUMMARY.
(Erase heading not required.)

Instructions regarding War Diaries and Intelligence Summaries are contained in F.S. Regs., Part II and the Staff Manual respectively. Title pages will be prepared in manuscript.

Hour, Date, Place	Summary of Events and Information	Remarks and references to Appendices
July 25th.	Quiet night and morning till 1pm when Mine shock felt. No action. Enemy heard working on wire opposite Centre Picquet.	
	Our Dispositions	
	Right Coy. holding craters . . . . . . A.	
	BANKSIDE and R. Picquet. Centre Coy. . . . B.	
	Left and Centre Picquet . Left . . . . D.	
	Quarries . . . . RESERVE . C.	
	Parties from "C" & "B" Bns. Composite Bde arrived to reconnoitre preparatory to RELIEF.	
	"C" Bn from present N. Boundary to ROBINEAU.	
	"B" Bn thence inclusive to ARNAU.	
July 26th.	Quiet Night	
5.40 am.	One of our snipers shot one of enemy who exposed himself through loophole	
9am.	Enemy tried to fraternise opposite Right Coy. - Officer and 4 or 5 men being seen. - Began by showing Board with "GOOD MORNING" printed on it. This continued till about 1pm. when our efforts to obtain identifications being finished, we closed the	

(73989) W.4141—463. 400,000. 9/14. H.&J.Ltd. Forms/C. 2118/10.

Army Form C. 2118.

WAR DIARY
or
INTELLIGENCE SUMMARY.
(Erase heading not required.)

Instructions regarding War Diaries and Intelligence Summaries are contained in F.S. Regs., Part II and the Staff Manual respectively. Title pages will be prepared in manuscript.

Hour, Date, Place	Summary of Events and Information	Remarks and references to Appendices
July 26th (contd)	Conversation and fired a shot. Enemy seemed to be Prussian and Hessian. Also apparently aware we were LONDON REGT.	
July 27th.	Quiet night - joining up of Right and Centre Picquet continued - also wiring of BANKSIDE. Cratery Saps repaired. Orders recd for relief this night and march tomorrow to DIEVAL in Corps RESERVE AREA. Relief duly complete by 2 A.m. morning of When Battalion moved to GOUY SERVINS - paraded again at 1.30 p.m. to join B'de on march to DIEVAL. Day very hot and men very tired owing to lack of sleep and recent move from trenches, with the result that very large numbers fell out. Battalion arrived DIEVAL 6 p.m.	
July 29th.	G.O.C. First Army inspected ourselves and 22nd Bn at 4 p.m. - Several Officers including Lt GAMAGE rejoined from PERNES, whither CAPT NADAUD and another officer were sent. Orders recd for march to GOUY en TERNOIS early tomorrow	

Army Form C. 2118.

WAR DIARY
or
INTELLIGENCE SUMMARY.
(Erase heading not required.)

Instructions regarding War Diaries and Intelligence Summaries are contained in F.S. Regs., Part II and the Staff Manual respectively. Title pages will be prepared in manuscript.

Hour, Date, Place	Summary of Events and Information	Remarks and references to Appendices
July 30th '16	Bn moves 5.30 A.M. arrives at GOUY-EN-TERNOIS, 9.45 A.M. Only 1 man fell out during the march.	
July 31st '16	Orders received to be ready to move 7 or 8 p.m. or 4 A.M. August 1st. Companies engaged in Interior Economy. Lecture by C.O. to all Officers. Orders received to be ready to move 4 A.M. Aug 1st - these orders subsequently cancelled - Bn. ordered to be ready by 7 p.m. August 1st. Capt SAUNDERS leaves for duty with Division	

C.J. Smith
Lieut-Col. Cmdg.,
7th Bn. Rn. Regt.,
"The Queens"

142nd Brigade.
47th Division.

1/24th BATTALION

LONDON RGEIMENT

AUGUST 1 9 1 6

Headquarters,
142nd Inf'ᵈᵉ Bde —

Herewith please receive WAR DIARY for
August 1916.

[signature]

Lieut & Adjt. for O.C.
24th Bⁿ Lon Regt
"The Queens"

[stamp: 24th (COUNTY OF LONDON) Bn. THE LONDON REGT. ORDERLY ROOM 28/9/16 (THE QUEEN'S) £450]

1/24th **on Regt**

Vol 17

Army Form C. 2118.

WAR DIARY
or
INTELLIGENCE SUMMARY.
(Erase heading not required.)

Instructions regarding War Diaries and Intelligence Summaries are contained in F.S. Regs., Part II and the Staff Manual respectively. Title pages will be prepared in manuscript.

Hour, Date, Place	Summary of Events and Information	Remarks and references to Appendices
Aug 1st 16	Bⁿ moved to MEZEROLLES. Started 6:35 A.M. Arrived 9:15 a.m. Bⁿ resting and bathing in river	
Aug 2nd		
Aug 3rd	Company Training - Bathing	
Aug 4th	Bⁿ moved to MAIZICOURT. Started 5:15 a.m. Arrived 9:15 a.m.	
Aug 5th	Bⁿ moved to NEUVILLE. Started 5:30 a.m. Arrived 9:30 a.m. Bⁿ in xxx in ABBEVILLE Young Area	
Aug 6th	Company Training - Close Order Drill and Ceremonial. Brigade Church Parade.	
Aug 7th	Company Training - Extended Order Drill - Platoon in the attack.	
Aug 8th	Company Training - Company in the Attack. 3rd Inniskillens for breakfast and at night concentrated after leaving and again assumed forward formation. Bⁿ Scheme - Bⁿ as advanced Guard to a Brigade.	
Aug 9th	Subsequently taking up line of Outposts Bⁿs their Attack Scheme - Bⁿ breakfasts in to fields. Relieve.	
Aug 10th	3 a.m - 12 p.m - Bⁿ assault - 3.1 p.m Support, 9 a.m. 7th Div carcases as desired. Allies no practice to C.O.C + 7th Div carcases as desired. Owing to damage to crops Bⁿ Training continued - Outpost line repeated. Bⁿ practised in Artillery formation.	

WAR DIARY
or
INTELLIGENCE SUMMARY.
(Erase heading not required.)

Army Form C. 2118.

Hour, Date, Place	Summary of Events and Information	Remarks and references to Appendices
August 11th 16	B[n] moved to NEVILLY L'HOPITAL. Company Training in evening	
Aug 12th	Company Training by day. Digging trial and a trench at night	
Aug 13th	B[n] Church Parade	
Aug 14th	Brigade Attack Practice – 24th B[n] acting as B[n] in Support	
Aug 15th	G.O.C. 47th Div[n] was present. B[n] practice attack before G.O.C. 47th Div[n] who subsequently addressed an address to the B[n] expressing himself well pleased with what he had seen.	
Aug 16th	Draft of 50 o.r. arrived. Brigade Attack Practice – 24th B[n] acting as B[n] in Support. Being through this assaulting B[n] and being a fixture. The G.O.C. 10[?] Corps and G.C. 47th Div[n] Attended. The practice was a great success.	
Aug 17th Aug 18th	B[n] Practice Wood fighting in CRECY WOOD. Company in attack practice – at night B[n] Orientals content attack practice. Machine manœuvrers to occupy Cuis – Violent rain fell and drenched water in bivouac. B[n] returned to billets at 5 a.m.	
Aug 19th	B[n] resting. Draft of 20 o.r. arrive.	

Army Form C. 2118.

WAR DIARY
or
INTELLIGENCE SUMMARY.
(Erase heading not required.)

Instructions regarding War Diaries and Intelligence Summaries are contained in F.S. Regs., Part II and the Staff Manual respectively. Title pages will be prepared in manuscript.

Hour, Date, Place	Summary of Events and Information	Remarks and references to Appendices
Aug 20th	4 a.m. Company Training. Bn moves to BELLANCOURT. Start 3.15 p.m. — This is about 14 m another Bn en route.	
Aug 21st	Arrived 7.30 p.m. — 8 miles. Bn moves to VIGNACOURT. 15 miles. Start 6.55 a.m. — halt up by another Bn en route, for 1½ hours. Arrive 2.30 p.m.	
Aug 22nd	Bn moves to PERREGOT — 7½ miles. Start 6.40 p.m. Arrive 11 p.m. — some delay in getting in to village owing to all the villages crowded with troops and transport.	
Aug 23rd	Bn moves to BEUVENCOURT — 5½ miles. Start 10.40 a.m. Arrive 12.40 p.m. Baths — men in river Port.	
Aug 24th	Company Training	
Aug 25th	Bn and Company Training — digging practice	
Aug 26th	Bn and Company Training — digging practice	
Aug 27th	Capt. MILLER joins Bn and assumes duties of 2nd in command.	
Aug 28th	Bn Church Parade; cancelled owing to heavy rains.	
Aug 29th	Bn Training — digging — musketry for recruits	
Aug 30th	Company Training — digging — musketry for recruits	
Aug 31st	Bn Attack Practice — digging — musketry for recruits. Company Training — digging — musketry for recruits.	

Geo S Ruthven
Lt. Col. Cmdg.
1/3rd Bn Lon. Regt. "The Queen's"

Head Quarters
142nd Inf. Bde.

142/47

Herewith War Diary for the
month of September 1916, please.

LChama 9c

Lieut. & Adjt.
for O.C. 1/24 Lon Regt
"The Queens"

Army Form C. 2118.

WAR DIARY
or
INTELLIGENCE SUMMARY.
(Erase heading not required.)

Instructions regarding War Diaries and Intelligence Summaries are contained in F.S. Regs., Part II. and the Staff Manual respectively. Title pages will be prepared in manuscript.

Hour, Date, Place	Summary of Events and Information	Remarks and references to Appendices
HIGH WOOD		
September 1st	Battalion attack practice – digging – musketry for recruits.	
2nd	Brigade attack practice – digging – musketry for recruits.	
3rd	Brigade Church Parade – Musketry.	
4	Company training – Musketry – Digging	
5	Battalion training – Musketry – Digging	
6	Company training – Musketry – Digging	
7	Battalion training – Musketry – Digging	
8	Company training – Musketry – Digging	
9	Company training – Interior Economy	
10	Battalion moves into forward Area starts 7.30 am. and arrived BECORT WOOD 5 PM Orders received to be ready to move at 2.30 am.	
11	Battalion relieve 1st NORTH HANTS in HIGH WOOD Sector, starting from BECURT WOOD 3 am and arriving in line 8 am. Dispositions:– 'D' Coy RIGHT FRONT 'C' Coy LEFT FRONT in QUEENS TRENCH – 'B' Coy in SUPPORT in BLACK WATCH TR. 'A' Coy and Bombers in Reserve in MILL STREET. During afternoon the enemy bombarded BLACK WATCH TRENCH intermittently – 2 Platoons of 'B' Coy were withdrawn to MARTLE TRENCH. 2/Lieut. Y TAYLOR wounded.	

Forms/C. 2118/10.
(73989) W4141–463. 400,000. 9/14. H.&J.Ltd.

Army Form C. 2118.

WAR DIARY
INTELLIGENCE SUMMARY.
(Erase heading not required.)

Instructions regarding War Diaries and Intelligence Summaries are contained in F. S. Regs., Part II. and the Staff Manual respectively. Title pages will be prepared in manuscript.

Hour, Date, Place	Summary of Events and Information	Remarks and references to Appendices
September 11th	At 9.30 pm enemy opened heavy bombardment of SUPPORT Area — evidently expected an attack. LT. MOBBERLEY and party of 8 men killed in BLACK WATCH TR. Bombardment eased at 10.10 pm then artillery bombardment has been continuous	
12th	Withdrew two remaining Platoons of "B" Coy. to ARGYLE TR. Day quiet on the whole, our artillery keeping up steady fire day and night	
13th	10 am – 2 pm 3 Heavy Howitzer batteries bombarded enemy front line in HIGH WOOD. We clear our front line as far as possible leaving 1 Platoon and Lewis Guns of Black Company only. 2/Lieut MARTIN Killed	
	Received verbal warning from Brigadier that the Battalion will be relieved by 2 Bns of 141 Inf Bde tomorrow. Our artillery continue bombardment	
14th	Bombardment continues — enemy artillery comparatively quiet. During afternoon relieved by 141st Inf. Bde. 21st Br. by 140 Bde. Preparatory to the attack.	

Army Form C. 2118.

WAR DIARY
of
INTELLIGENCE SUMMARY.
(Erase heading not required.)

Instructions regarding War Diaries and Intelligence Summaries are contained in F.S. Regs., Part II. and the Staff Manual respectively. Title pages will be prepared in manuscript.

Hour, Date, Place	Summary of Events and Information	Remarks and references to Appendices
September 14th	Battalion moves back to QUADRANGLE - arriving 9.30 pm. Gunned equipment of men in full fighting order.	
15th	ZERO for attack is 6.20 am. - 47th Division is attacking HIGH WOOD, 141st Bde on LEFT, 140th Bde on RIGHT - 50th Div on LEFT and NEW ZEALAND on RIGHT of 47th Division. "TANKS" or landcruisers are employed for the first time. These were not altogether successful on our part of the line, both getting stuck nr HIGH WOOD.	
6.20 am	Bn moves to MAMETZ WOOD	
7.30 am	Bn in position at MAMETZ WOOD	
1.7 PM	Received orders to move to MILL STREET. Bn. has been placed at disposal of 141 Bde. 2nd Bn at disposal of 140 Bde - Lt Col CARR reports to 141 Bde for orders.	
2.30 pm	Bn in MILL STREET	
3.45 pm	Lt Col CARR returns with orders that Battalion is to attack and take 2nd and if possible 3rd objective of 141 Bde. Bde have informed him	
	(1) that 141 Bde has been held up in taking 1st objective	
	(2) that 50th Division had taken its 3rd objective	
	(3) that 21st Bn would be attacking on right of us. both attacks being separate	
	Lt Col CARR had endeavoured to synchronise our attack with that of 21st Bn but could not as two different

WAR DIARY
INTELLIGENCE SUMMARY.
(Erase heading not required.)

Army Form C. 2118.

Hour, Date, Place	Summary of Events and Information	Remarks and references to Appendices
September 15 3.45 pm	The C.O. had also been informed that probably no Germans would be encountered in our advance. Events proved (1) that 50th Divn had only taken 1st objective (2) that the ground was held by enemy strong points	
4.30 pm	Bn advanced in artillery formation from Main St. to form up upon line of 1st objective — Capt Figg D.S.O. instructed to give orders to advance as soon as Bn should be in position — dispositions D.A.D.C. from right to left. Bn. 9/8 moves to front of SUTHERLAND TRENCH where 4 Bn. HQrs of 146 Bde were already assembled. Bn. H/Q then to remain in touch adjoining, which was heavily shelled throughout the operations.	
7.5 pm	No news received that attack had started — visited assembly line and found "C & B" Companies waiting for orders from Capt Figg to advance. Troops of 50th Divn seen advancing on left — proved to be Divl. I. going to attack 2nd objective.	
7.30 pm	Ordered B & C Companies to start at once owing to 50th Divn advance — "A" & "D" Coys. which had apparently gone on some 100 yds. were picked up on the way. Reports of enemy massing for counterattack were	

Army Form C. 2118.

WAR DIARY
or
INTELLIGENCE SUMMARY.
(Erase heading not required.)

Instructions regarding War Diaries and Intelligence Summaries are contained in F.S. Regs., Part II. and the Staff Manual respectively. Title pages will be prepared in manuscript.

Hour, Date, Place	Summary of Events and Information	Remarks and references to Appendices
September 15th 7.30 pm	Received from artillery, just as the advance started - ordered Capt WHEATER and 2/Lieut LONGLEY, if this were so, to meet them half way and disperse them.	
7.45 pm	Message received that Troops Commander ordered an advance to 3rd objective.	
9.10 pm	2/Lt LONGLEY reports back to Bn H.Q. that Bn has advanced some 800 yards or more and had found that both flanks were in the air, that they had been enfiladed from the left by heavy M.G. fire, and had been compelled to fall back and dig in some 200 yards in front of first objective. Ordered him to consolidate there and endeavour to get in touch with troops on the flanks, and to clear our old C.T. back to 1st. objective.	
10 pm	Reported situation to 141 Bde.	
10.20 pm	Patrol sent out by Lt. BASEDEN reports that our Bn. are in touch with 5th. Bn. on their left. Both were digging in on line shown on sketch - - - - - . Reported this to 141 Bde.	
11 pm	The heavy shelling which had been in progress throughout operations began to subside, but continued intermittently throughout the night	

WAR DIARY
INTELLIGENCE SUMMARY.
(Erase heading not required.)

Army Form C. 2118.

Instructions regarding War Diaries and Intelligence Summaries are contained in F.S. Regs., Part II. and the Staff Manual respectively. Title pages will be prepared in manuscript.

Hour, Date, Place	Summary of Events and Information	Remarks and references to Appendices
September 16th 12.30 am	Received report through 22nd Bn. from 2/Lt. SHIELDS who had been wounded. "D" Company had apparently lost touch with rest of Bn. and only 14 men of this Coy were present.	
5.45 am	L.O. visits line — reports it well consolidated.	
7.30 am	Received notes from Bde. that 22nd and 23rd Bns. were going to attack 2nd and 3rd objectives — nothing was heard of this attack.	
11.30 am	Capt. FIGG reports 265 O.R. available for duty.	
12.15 pm	Capt. FIGG reports officers wounded WHEATER CLARK, SHIELDS YARDYK BUSHELL missing BROCK, LIVERMORE.	
12.40 pm	B.G.C. 141 Bde visits Bn. H.Q. and enquires if my Bn. Can go forward and take 2nd and 3rd objectives: C.O. informs him he considers it impossible having regard to exhaustion of men — that they had held front line for 4 days previous to the attack made heavy shelling and had since done an attack and were still holding the front line under continuous bombardment. Withdrew "C" Company to Reserve Line.	
7.45 pm	Col. NORMAN 17th Bn. informed me that he had received orders from 141 Bde. that 24th Bn. is to relieve that Bde at pnt. — Bn. strength 270, 141st Bde about 900. Inform him that we have had no orders and cannot relieve until we receive written orders to do so. B.M. 141 Bde. spoke to C.O. on phone and was informed of the above.	

WAR DIARY
OF
INTELLIGENCE SUMMARY.
(Erase heading not required.)

Army Form C. 2118.

Instructions regarding War Diaries and Intelligence Summaries are contained in F.S. Regs., Part II. and the Staff Manual respectively. Title pages will be prepared in manuscript.

Hour, Date, Place	Summary of Events and Information	Remarks and references to Appendices
September 17th 11.30 P.M.	At our disposal under MAJOR HARGREAVES - Bn. strength estimated at 220. 50th Divn were to do similar attack on our left - 22nd Bn on RIGHT; endeavoured to synchronise with 50th Divn - discovered they had done their attack in the afternoon and were not attempting another. At conference decided to attack in 2 WAVES, ABD in 1st Wave 23rd Bn and C in 2nd - Capt. FIGG on right to direct marching on a compass bearing of 66°(Magn.) from N. corner of HIGH WOOD. LT. & ADJT NEWTON (23rd Bn) who had been over the ground on the right flank the day before volunteered to go out and fix a tape at 4 tents - this to succeed in doing and proved of great value. We have been informed that both the STARFISH and COUCH DROP are held by us their being on right of 22nd objective. ZERO fixed for 3.45 a.m. MAJOR HARGREAVES made to find company of 23rd Bn - rang up Bde. - Bde consents to ZERO at 4.45 a.m. we must attack then whether 23rd Bn had arrived or not. Further T.M.Bs on R.E. have reported as directed in orders 1 Section of 13 M.G. Coy had reported under LT IVORY - duled him to remain with his two guns at N. corner of HIGH WOOD sending forward 4 men with the assault, these men to bring back word as soon as line is consolidated and suitable positions found.	

Army Form C. 2118.

WAR DIARY
of
INTELLIGENCE SUMMARY.
(Erase heading not required.)

Instructions regarding War Diaries and Intelligence Summaries are contained in F. S. Regs., Part II. and the Staff Manual respectively. Title pages will be prepared in manuscript.

Hour, Date, Place		Summary of Events and Information	Remarks and references to Appendices
September 17th	1.30 am	Received 111nd Bde message that enemy counter attack expected at 2 or 3 am. — warned front line.	
	3.50 am	Received orders from 142 Bde to relieve 141 Bde — informed Col. Norman who replied that he had not yet received orders to carry on with relief — apparently report of enemy counter attack had caused a change of orders.	
	7.10 am	C. Coy. 24 Bn. takes over line held by Bns. of 141 Bde. Informed Bde. of our strength and of the exhaustion of the men. Warning order received that 47th Divn. intended further attack on large scale on the 18th.	
	4–7 PM	Heavy bombardment of our line — many casualties. counter attack expected. Subsequently found that this was due to an attack by 50th Divn. on 2nd objective.	
	7.15 PM	Received order that 142 Bde would be engaged on night operations tonight — ZERO 2.30 am. 141 Bde would take over our line, so as to free Bde for this purpose.	
	8 PM	2 Companies 18th Bn. reported arrived to take over in front line.	
	11.30 PM	Relief completed. Rations to be issued and made — men refreshed. Bn. is to attack and take part of (1) STARFISH TRENCH (2) CRISLE LINE and PRUE TRENCH — right of final objective being at QUATRE VENTS — Company of 23rd (Ind.) Ahead

WAR DIARY or INTELLIGENCE SUMMARY

Army Form C. 2118.

Hour, Date, Place	Summary of Events and Information	Remarks and references to Appendices
September 16. 4.45 am	Assault started – 23rd Bn. arrived in time. Pitch dark night, pouring rain – ground in front a mass of mud dotted with shell holes.	
5.30 am onwards	2/Lt. LONGKEY and several runners report that STARFISH LINE had been seized in spite of heavy M.G. fire from an enemy strong point on the LEFT, and some artillery bombardment. When daylight came the enemy showed plenty of bombing attacks supported by M.G. fire and had driven us back along the trench to the EMBANKMENT where we had taken up a defensive position and went holding the enemy back. Capt. FOO meanwhile had recommitted to the RIGHT, as far as the STARFISH, and found no one except a few men of the 6t. for in the STARFISH. He withdrew two men and placed them in the STARFISH as a garrison, the line staff being a lot too crowded previously. Urgent messages received at Bn. HQ to send up bombs with great difficulty a party from the 23rd was finally got together and sent up under an R.E. guide. Col. NORMAN 17th Bn. offered all the bombers he could muster and provided a party of 6. Unfortunately neither party managed to find its way. Lt. BASEDEN reports at HQ wounded and states we are holding on still, some of the men being the shell holes covering the trench.	

WAR DIARY or INTELLIGENCE SUMMARY.

(Erase heading not required.)

Army Form C. 2118.

Instructions regarding War Diaries and Intelligence Summaries are contained in F.S. Regs., Part II. and the Staff Manual respectively. Title pages will be prepared in manuscript.

Hour, Date, Place		Summary of Events and Information	Remarks and references to Appendices
September 18	8.30 am onwards	The 22nd Bn. on our right were not to be seen - it transpired that they had lost their way, and failed to reach objective (?)	
	4.45 pm	Received news that 22nd. Bn. would relieve us - they were to make a bombing attack from the STARFISH along the STARFISH LINE. This was carried out unsuccessfully	
	9.30 pm	Bn. HQ. moved to MILL STREET - all stragglers etc collected - orders sent by with hot tea.	
September 19	3.10 am	CAPT FIGG reports back with the remainder of the Battalion - very exhausted and covered in mud. Men have been unable to eat their rations owing to mud, and water had been scarce.	
	2.30 pm	Received order that Bde would be relieved by 2nd. Bde.	
	4.10 pm	2nd. Munster Fusiliers relieve Bn. in MILL STREET. Bn. moves back to bivouac at BLACK WOOD - arrives at	
	10 pm	More rain - men in shelters, officers in tents 2/Lt. ALLISON reports for duty. Bn. Strength 370 O.R.	
September 20th	2.45 pm	21st & 23rd Bns move to MINDEN COURT - 24th Bn to move tomorrow.	
	6.30 pm	Bde inform us 22nd and 24th Bns will move by lorry this night	
	7.45 pm	Order cancelled as far as concerns 22nd Bn.	

Army Form C. 2118.

WAR DIARY
INTELLIGENCE SUMMARY.
(Erase heading not required.)

Instructions regarding War Diaries and Intelligence Summaries are contained in F.S. Regs., Part II. and the Staff Manual respectively. Title pages will be prepared in manuscript.

Hour, Date, Place	Summary of Events and Information	Remarks and references to Appendices
September 20. 8.30pm	No lorries having arrived as ordered, commandeered every lorry going to MILLENCOURT.	
11.45 pm	Last man up for in lorry.	
September 21. 12.50 am	Bn. H.Q. at MILLENCOURT. Found draft of 266 O.R. under 2/Lt. Y. KELLY awaiting there. Bn. resting and cleaning.	
September 22	Interior economy - Inspection of draft by G.O.C. 142nd Inf. Bde.	
September 23	Interior economy - Training of draft under Major MILLER. Draft of 21 O.Rs arrives. Major General Brig. Gen. visits H.Q. to congratulate Bn. and discuss recent operations.	
September 24th	Bde. Church Parade - address by Major General congratulating Bde. on recent operations.	
September 25th	Company in attack practice. Draft of 120 arrives with 2/Lt. BUSBY.	
September 26th	Training - Company in attack	
September 27th	Training - Company and Battalion in attack	
September 28th	142 Bde. moves to Support Bde. area - Bn. Bn. to BECOURT WOOD.	

Army Form C. 2118.

WAR DIARY
INTELLIGENCE SUMMARY.
(Erase heading not required.)

Instructions regarding War Diaries and Intelligence Summaries are contained in F.S. Regs., Part II. and the Staff Manual respectively. Title pages will be prepared in manuscript.

Hour, Date, Place	Summary of Events and Information	Remarks and references to Appendices
September 29th.	Having been informed that 142 Bde were to attack EAUCOURT L'ABBAYE proceeded to reconnoitre line — were informed by Bde. that 141 Bde. were going to do the attack this Bde. being in support.	
September 30th.	All men equipped in fighting order. Transport moved forward to S.25.b. on the GERMAN road. C.O. & Company Officers reconnoitre front line and approaches to EAUCOURT L'ABBAYE	

O.R. Austin (?) OC.
Lieut Col 1/24th
1/24 London Regt.
"The Queen's"

SKETCH to illustrate OPERATIONS 15-18 Sept 1916.
(NOT TO SCALE)

Map labels:
- TO FLERS
- THE FLERS LINE
- DROP ALLEY
- THE COUGH DROP
- 3RD OBJECTIVE
- PRUE TRENCH
- CABLE OR PIPE LINE
- ENEMY STRONG POINT
- 2ND OBJECTIVE
- EMBANKMENT
- THE STARFISH
- STARFISH LINE
- 50TH DIV.
- 47TH DIV.
- NZ DIV.
- Divⁿ B^{dy}
- 750 yds
- Dug by 50 Divⁿ
- Dug by 24 Bⁿ
- 1ST OBJECTIVE (CONSOLIDATED)
- SWITCH LINE
- HIGH WOOD
- BRITISH FRONT LINE

22.9.16.

142/47

1/24th Bn London Regt.

Vol 16

Army Form C. 2118.

WAR DIARY or INTELLIGENCE SUMMARY.

(Erase heading not required.)

Instructions regarding War Diaries and Intelligence Summaries are contained in F.S. Regs., Part II and the Staff Manual respectively. Title pages will be prepared in manuscript.

Hour, Date, Place	Summary of Events and Information	Remarks and references to Appendices

October 1st

10.30am — Battalion moved from BECOURT WOOD to FIFE St. and CHESTER St. move completed by 2.15 p.m.

3pm — Received orders from the Bde. that Battalion comes under 141 Bde. at 6pm & are to move to PIT 70 & 1m2 and C.0.15 about 6. B.A.C. 141 Bde. at BLACK WOOD. 6pm Combined to B.A.C. 141 Bde. that Battalion was moving off to SWITCH LINE — no other at present.

October 2nd

2am — Reported to B.A.C. 141 Bde. who are now that Battalion was moving to OLD BRITISH FRONT LINE and to be in position by 4am under 23rd Lon Regt. must in a short and places ange chink on attached to FLERS LINE.

3am — OC. new Company Commander and are ordered to move at 3.40am.
3.40am — Battalion made for SWITCH LINE.
5am — The Battalion arrived at SWITCH FRONT LINE and found that the 23rd Lon Regt. who had not yet made their attack on the 1st and 19th Lon Regt as well as could not do so until 9am. It was impossible to place whole Battalion in the Line — one B Company was in the Bombers managed to get into the right of the line and the FLERS LINE and some B Company was in the Communication trench. Air Raeymath completely A Company [illegible] the O.B.L. and their ranks [illegible] to B Company 6am — ending they and the movement casualties [illegible]

7am — on being evacuated to DUMP ALLEY

2nd Lieut. R. D. GOMAS seriously wounded Capt. KELLYAND [illegible] K.I.A.

Army Form C. 2118.

WAR DIARY
or
INTELLIGENCE SUMMARY.
(Erase heading not required.)

Hour, Date, Place	Summary of Events and Information	Remarks and references to Appendices
October 1st Tnte		
11am	Formed Bn HQ at Sap from PROUST	
10.30pm	2Lt Williams evacuated from Depot and relieved duties of Adjutant	
October 2nd		
3.45am	2nd Lt. Boyd arrived Depot over command of D Coy	
	A at 2.30 Brigade ¾o Order from 141 Bde that details of 141 Bde & 2 London Regt having returned cancelled O.B.1 2nd Lon Regt were to reoccupy mile of this.	
10.60am	Orders received from 142 Brigade that 191 came again under that Brigade and were to relieve part of O.B.1 and part of NERVE TRENCH order issued accordingly one 15th HQ notice to STARFISH LINE	
October 4th		
9am	B.Q.C. LEWIS called at Bn HQ. C Company withdrawn to STARFISH LINE 2nd Lt. ANSELL returned from Depot	
October 6th	2nd Lts. KIRKUP and BAILEY wounded	
	Carrying parts + officers and 200 ORs others knelt Tramway West of HIGH WOOD at 5.30pm	
	2 Lt. Hey wounded	
5.30pm	Rens B Companies orders to	
	142 Brigade Orders and occupied BOAST TRENCH in rear of STARFISH LINE	
	ARQ	
October 6th	2Lt WALKER reported from Depot and took over command	
	Company Officers reconnoitred EN COURT LAG RUE Obstacles Order received from 142 Brigade relieving two Companies to make BOAST TRENCH and receive position and O.B.1 move at dawn 15th Order issued accordingly.	
October 7th		
6.30am	Revs D Companies vacated BOAST TRENCH and moved	
	O.B.1	

Army Form C. 2118.

WAR DIARY
or
INTELLIGENCE SUMMARY.
(Erase heading not required.)

Instructions regarding War Diaries and Intelligence Summaries are contained in F.S. Regs., Part II. and the Staff Manual respectively. Title pages will be prepared in manuscript.

Hour, Date, Place		Summary of Events and Information	Remarks and references to Appendices
October 8th Ervik	10am	Company Officers reconnoitred EAUCOURT L'ABBAYE. area by the Brigade.	
	1.45pm	Received warning orders received by the Brigade to move	
	8pm	to attack and to attack the outposts. 872 in Reserve.	
October 9th	6am	Received Operation Orders.	
	9am	2nd Lt. Busby Acting Lieut with 23rd Bn. Post and accurate information and time they were nearing FLERS LINE	
	11am	Lt. Busby returned with Map showing companies of 2nd Lon Regt. in FLERS LINE. L.21 B 2nd & 3rd got obvious notify they all were moving and to keep Runner at their HQ to bring back message.	
	9pm	Received orders that two Companies by day would be FLERS LINE came in and rear of same Bn.	
		A and D Companies in position in EAUCOURT L'ABBAYE	
		B Company moved from PRUE TRENCH to FLERS LINE and	
	9:30pm	C Company to PRUE TRENCH relieved by 21st and 23rd LON POST	
October 10th		C.O. and Officers of North African Infantry reconnoitre	
	10pm	line for relief. Relief completed. Bn. marched to QUDRRVILLE	
October 11th	3pm	Bn. relieved by 9th SCOTTISH RIFLES and marched to LAVIEVILLE	
October 11th		Interior Economy. Absence of C.O. met Brigadier.	
October 12th	10am	Inspection of 142nd Brigade by Corps Commander. Conference at Brigade Hd. with G.O.C. Division.	

Army Form C. 2118.

WAR DIARY or INTELLIGENCE SUMMARY.
(Erase heading not required.)

1/24 London Regt Oct 1916

564
81

Instructions regarding War Diaries and Intelligence Summaries are contained in F.S. Regs., Part II and the Staff Manual respectively. Title pages will be prepared in manuscript.

Hour, Date, Place	Summary of Events and Information	Remarks and references to Appendices
October 13th	Transferred by motor to BELLANCOURT	
October 14th	billet of army	
October 15th. 10 am	Battalion marched to ALBERT entrained 3 pm Arrived at LONGPRES. LES CORPS SAINTS. Detrained and marched to Billetin BELLANCOURT.	
October 16th. 10 pm	Entrained at PONT REMY	
October 17th. 1 am	Reached GODEWAERSDE detrained and marched to ABEELE and occupied Billets there	
October 18th. 9.30 am	Received orders to reconnoitre Hill 60 Reconnaissance C.O. Company Commanders, Bombing Officer and L.G. Officer took bus to YPRES saw O.C. 21 Australian Infantry & made arrangements for relief. Officers reconnoitred the line & arranged to send up Billeting party tonight for GLENCORSE BURY POSE.	
	B.M. "C" Australian Brigade arranged his Divisional relief beforehand so that I am then from Brigadier	
	Sherwood Forest Life for her to Brig	
October 19th. 3 pm	Battalion marched to opening entrance to YPRES and relieved 21 Australian Infantry in front line Hill 60 Ypres Relief completed by 12 midnight	
	Disposition C. Right C. Bngs. B. left A. Bengt in LARCH WOOD. A Company formed Special front line under 2 Lt - BOTEE	
October 20th	C.O. sent down front line 1-9am saw him in command Tunnelling Scene the causes Damage acum Tram. B.G.C visited front line	

Army Form C. 2118.

WAR DIARY
or
INTELLIGENCE SUMMARY.
(Erase heading not required.)

Instructions regarding War Diaries and Intelligence Summaries are contained in F.S. Regrs., Part II. and the Staff Manual respectively. Title pages will be prepared in manuscript.

Hour, Date, Place	Summary of Events and Information	Remarks and references to Appendices
October 21st.	In camp.	
October 22nd.	C.O. went round front line 9-11 am. Capt HIBBROUD Lieut BROWN POLL and PERRY inspected no mans land.	
October 23rd.	Officer 23rd Bn reconnaissance. Details of Relief.	
October 24th.	Bt. H.Q. and MARSHALL MACKENZY knocked down, wounded, removed 5.20-8 pm. G.O.C. Division 13 G.C. 149 Inf Bde visited front line.	
October 25th.	Thirteen men missing. Relief by 19th Lon Regt completed by 11 pm. Battalion moved to HALIFAX CAMP.	
October 26th.	Visit by Div. Gas Officer to Officers and N.C.O.s on Bn Respirator — Eupiene training and gas.	
October 27th.	8 pm. Lecture in Canny. Bn. Respirator — training and use of Box Respirator and gas.	
October 28th.	6 pm. Early Lecture in Canny. Inspection and use of Box Respirator and gas.	
October 29th.	Training — use of Box Respirator and gas. C.O. visited Front line depts. Chest Parade. 3 pm. Bn HQ and 2 Companies moved to BELGIAN CHATEAU. C Company in new lines at YPRES-YPRES RAILWAY DUGOUTS. B Company in ASYLUM. D Company in RAILWAY DUGOUTS.	161

Army Form C. 2118.

WAR DIARY
or
INTELLIGENCE SUMMARY.
(Erase heading not required.)

Instructions regarding War Diaries and Intelligence Summaries are contained in F.S. Regs., Part II and the Staff Manual respectively. Title pages will be prepared in manuscript.

Hour, Date, Place	Summary of Events and Information	Remarks and references to Appendices
October 30th	In the line Conway. 2 Lt Carter Buff's and 2 Lt Jones RWF reporting for duty. Carrying Party 1 officer and 80 men. Trenching & Wiring Party 6 men on Railway off 30 men.	566
October 31st	In the line Conway. 2 Lt G./Sgt Williams visited Embankment at Railway. Dugouts and trenches. Two carrying parties for tunnelling. 1 officer and 40 men. 1 officer and 25 men.	

31/10/16.

Geo. ? Bunton ?dt.
Lieut. ?S? ?
1/24 Bn London Regt
The Queen's

(73989) W4141—463. 400,000. 9/14. H.&J.Ltd. Forms/C. 2118/10.

WAR DIARY
or
INTELLIGENCE SUMMARY.
(Erase heading not required.)

Army Form C. 2118.

1st Batt. London Regt Vol 20

Hour, Date, Place	Summary of Events and Information	Remarks and references to Appendices
November 1st, 1916	Battalion at CHATEAU BELGE near YPRES (H33.b.6) Relieving companies of 20th Railway Dugouts west Pol. Lanen (Regt.) Ely in support of 1/2nd Lon Regt. in front line H13.60. Lieut. E. Sophy Williams G.S.O excepted on air duties in England. He returned to England by air plane.	
November 2nd.	L.O. made no Railway Dugouts (H21 C.2.9) and made arrangements for next relief.	
November 3rd.	Col. Kemble 25th Lon Regt arranged reconnaissance in view of next relief.	
November 4th H.L.6	A.D.M.S. inspected billeting area around CHATEAU BELGE T.A. LODGE Lower Pavilion & ordered to get Army two dispensary (Believed [illegible]) in front line. Wol. Vin left at Railway Dugouts. A. Coy [illegible] Lanen at disposal of 2/100 London Regt. in N.19 (H28.d.90) after Relief at Valbaden Farm (H43. C.9.9.).	
November 5th	Quiet Day.	
November 6th.	Reminder Working Parties. 6 front line problems are carrying parties to R.E.S. [illegible] Promise [illegible] and Company Commander if can realise penetrability in the out-night (as for army 6 Lt. Col Pyle of 1/London Regt.) Lt. Col Carrol or cutting of Supply of R.M.C. Lt. Col assumes command Lance Cpl. G.B. Snowden of R.M.G. awarded the Military Medal. Lt. H.C. Mitchell + Lt. C.W. Turner evacuated sick.	

WAR DIARY
or
INTELLIGENCE SUMMARY
(Erase heading not required.)

Army Form C. 2118.

Instructions regarding War Diaries and Intelligence Summaries are contained in F.S. Regs., Part II. and the Staff Manual respectively. Title pages will be prepared in manuscript.

Hour, Date, Place	Summary of Events and Information	Remarks and references to Appendices
November 7th	Sanitary Officer inspected area Cape Hel, Commanding Off London Regt & Coy Commander reconnoitred area	
November 8th	Relieved at O.C. Inn. Regt at 5pm and moved to Devonshire Lines and Burrs Room. Lt. H. Gofer (K.W. (ret)) & Lt. L.G. Morris (late R.S.) unaccompanied for duty	
November 9th	Rn. resting. B.A.C. inspected camp area	
November 10th	Company training & Intercommy H.O. Parade on leave.	
November 11th	Rn. resting. Platoon training. 2/Lt. J. Underwood (Royal West Kent Regt) reports for duty. Capt. T.H. Jordan R.A.M.C. reports for duty as M.O. during absence of Capt. Townsend.	
November 12th	Cultal parade. Inoculation of medicals by Major Cowl Spring & G.O.C. Division to review men of unit unable to expect a representative of the countrys to his left Tetl Lewis & B.G.C. on leave the principle relieves Col William there from leave.	
November 13th	10.30 a.m. Commanders, General Jordan inspected Br. lines & Companies training, accompanied by B.G.C. during afternoon. In attention B.G.C. walks round Res. pts has felt that generally keen in good fettle. Major J. Marks Lewis commanded on leave reports for duty.	

(73989) W4141—463. 400,000. 9/14. H.&J.Ltd. Forms/C. 2118/10.

WAR DIARY
or
INTELLIGENCE SUMMARY.
(Erase heading not required.)

Army Form C. 2118.

Instructions regarding War Diaries and Intelligence Summaries are contained in F.S. Regs., Part II and the Staff Manual respectively. Title pages will be prepared in manuscript.

Hour, Date, Place	Summary of Events and Information	Remarks and references to Appendices
November 14th	G.O.C. Division, B.G.C, A.D.M.S. & Staff photographed. Bn. Rugby & Association teams. Demonstration by R.E. of the use of explosives in the construction of Trenches.	
November 15th	Company training. Inner platoon games. 60 acres at Duidam	
November 16th	G.O Coy Commanders reports for this Bn & Bn Section. Company training to include training in gas	
November 17th	There were Officer reconnoitre front line. Junior Officers & N.C.O.s in charge. Company training. All N.C.O.s & men confined to duty. Rest Parties returning have to England. N.C.O. withdrawn preces to ZUYT PEENE or Infantry Brigade.	
November 18th	Majr. Willmerations, Co's Conference and B.G.C. Reference 19 London Reg's in front half Bluff. Buff relief 19 London Reg. It fell to the officers parties of men to reconnaissance a few reconnaissance patrol.	
November 19th	B.H. prepared out return T.M. returned afternoon	
November 20th	R. A. Group commander (Col Murray) also officers from the weather impact damaged by T.M. He kindly repaired successfully remaining badly very few lives and infantry front line of hostile available to be Bde. Battalion reports for duty	

Army Form C. 2118.

WAR DIARY
or
INTELLIGENCE SUMMARY.
(Erase heading not required.)

Instructions regarding War Diaries and Intelligence Summaries are contained in F. S. Regs., Part II and the Staff Manual respectively. Title pages will be prepared in manuscript.

Hour, Date, Place	Summary of Events and Information	Remarks and references to Appendices
November 21st	A.R.C. arrived in narration of inspection with S.O. Murray. Quiet day. Lieut. O. R. Keefe, R.N. Sec. & Pt. Harvis reported for duty.	
November 22nd	S.O. was travelling Officer (Lt. Murray Canadian Cavalry Bde.) inspection of defences. Enemy T.M. activity on front opposite of our Artillery. Hostile gas fire enemy Baillescourt on town	
November 23rd	Major General Commanding 183 D. inspected sub calm OC of Left Group also Lieut. in charge T.M. Division also in afternoon. G.O.C. Division saw P.B. Lords temp. inst. Station. No enemy reconnaissance.	
November 24th	Very erratic enemy Artillery and T.M. activity on afternoon. Observed damage to front line & communication trenches.	
November 25th	P.B.C. indicates ordered in some T.M. and artillery activity in afternoon. Bombardment in left of front line B.P. 1360 under Capt. Frazer to shoot on enemy.	
November 26th	Lt. Murray Artillery Group Commander called to relieve the Lieut. Then as Major Gen. called informed G.O. (air) crew in take place T.M. & Artillery activity in afternoon.	

WAR DIARY or INTELLIGENCE SUMMARY.

Army Form C. 2118.

(Erase heading not required.)

Hour, Date, Place	Summary of Events and Information	Remarks and references to Appendices
November 24th	B.S.M. to inspect all entrenching tools, gas guards, box respirators and refitting. Damage to trenches.	
November 25th	Quiet day. Trench wards amount of work done	
November 29th	At about 2 am enemy commenced damages on our front line. Successive shots fired (10, 8 to 9"" + 6"") to explode obstacle. Communication was to dump about 30am. D.C. was & entire frontage on line O.T.O. Barney Cob. Guards of Monte C/C. 11th Battalion to report to duty with ? & ? Regt. ¶ L.O.Z. Box H.Q.R.F. in charge of Buff Sumner & persons by support by Canadian Sumners & forest by Y/7 & Buff. Unusual artillery activity during the occupation. Enemy Heavy enemy Trench mortar attack by in artillery in the 1 afternoon.	

L. Williams
Lieut. Adj.
for O.C. "24" London Regt.
The Queens

2/9/16

Army Form C. 2118.

1/24th B. London Regt

WAR DIARY
or
INTELLIGENCE SUMMARY.
(Erase heading not required.)

Instructions regarding War Diaries and Intelligence Summaries are contained in F.S. Regs., Part II and the Staff Manual respectively. Title pages will be prepared in manuscript.

Hour, Date, Place	Summary of Events and Information	Remarks and references to Appendices
Friday Dec 1st 1916	Quiet day. Midnight patrol from the front B.6.0.10.C.1/2 P.d. bay to C. reported all trenches to north or right or east of Bluff heads.	
Saturday Dec 2nd.	Quiet day. During evening night Lt. Mitchell & a patrol of 2 NCO's attempted to ambush patrol known to be out, but failed owing to enemy leaving patrol beaten. No activity afternoon. Enemy had TM & artillery embedded forward.	
Sunday Dec 3rd.	Quiet day. B.O.I. called (Col. Turner)	
Monday Dec 4th.	R.B.O. called. T.M. & Artillery activity in afternoon.	
Tuesday Dec 5th.	Quiet day. Canadian Tunneller blew a camouflet during the evening.	
Wednesday Dec 6th.	A.D.M.S. inspected B.L. OFF. Trench. Enemy carried T.M. activity in afternoon. Caused some damage to our trenches. 2/Lts Borrowman & Sanders proceeded on leave.	
Thursday Dec 7th.	B.O. & B.O.B. inspected Centr. Sub. sector. D.T.O. exposed artillery discombe Umi Batty. 20 days toil on trenches. Very heavy T.M. activity in afternoon. Our T.M. endeavoured to retaliate but our damage and trenches. Our artillery then retaliated.	
Friday Dec 8th.	Usual T.M. activity in afternoon. Relieved by 21st London Regt & moved to Dickebusch Huts, Bunt 9000 rs	

Army Form C. 2118.

WAR DIARY
or
INTELLIGENCE SUMMARY.
(Erase heading not required.)

Instructions regarding War Diaries and Intelligence Summaries are contained in F.S. Regs., Part II. and the Staff Manual respectively. Title pages will be prepared in manuscript.

Hour, Date, Place	Summary of Events and Information	Remarks and references to Appendices
Saturday Dec. 9th	Battalion in billets. Tak Barr in billets. Men have received General. Off. Hatherton Dismounted photography course received command. photography course	
Sunday Dec. 10th	Church Parade. B.M.B. called	
Monday Dec. 11th	Began training & drill	
Tuesday Dec. 12th	Men obtain remounts & repair of harness	
Wednesday Dec. 13th	Dining. Major Willmer takes Riding School at H.Q. Dec Coys	
Thursday Dec. 14th	R.M.B. checks rifles. Lectures & training	
Friday Dec. 15th	Major Willmer & Lt. Hetherton went to have Bt. Marked reins to Pickeltonne. Overtrained down	
Saturday Dec. 16th	Battalion finds Guard. H.Q. platoon as large. Capt. Pickersen retired from the Army. Lieut. Ash awarded commanded. 18 of Officer & Ribbon of Major Luard.	
Sunday Dec. 17th	Orders for Sunday Luncheon for the Band. Lt. Coyes in charge of peace to have reunion to H.Q. Church Parade distribution	
Monday Dec. 18th	Church Parade cancelled. 300 men listed. Interviewman	
Tuesday Dec. 19th	Major General inspection and change of Vancouver Camp R. Brigadier of Department H.Q. out to Bellomi at Railway dugouts. D reliefs Coming by B.C. Someday chant salage to Glasgow and Berry Posts. at Bottleset Farm. B.O. Guys at Belgian Chateau. Relief complete 600 pm.	

WAR DIARY
or
INTELLIGENCE SUMMARY.
(Erase heading not required.)

Army Form C. 2118.

Instructions regarding War Diaries and Intelligence Summaries are contained in F.S. Regs., Part II. and the Staff Manual respectively. Title pages will be prepared in manuscript.

Hour, Date, Place	Summary of Events and Information	Remarks and references to Appendices
Wednesday Dec 20	L.O. visits M.O. visits Battersea Farm and Forceway Capt Town returned to Antwerp on leave	
Thursday Dec 21st	C.O. visits Belgian Chateau. Capt Town returned from leave	
Friday Dec 22nd	C.O. visits Railway Dugouts Forceway & Battersea Farm with M.O. Erection cinema matinees	
Saturday Dec 23rd	C.O. visits Battersea Farm Reinforcement arrived in strength 3 officers 86 O.R. also visits Forceway, Tufts of Railway Dugouts & Bythe farm. Battersea farm. Journey of ris. prisoners	
Sunday Dec 24th	Orders became #8 #9 Bright moonlit night. No air raids. No siren. Read of ciel for to H.Q. placed back to respect Stoking Route Railway Dugouts Dudgesheur Reight Cup 515 S.A. Depot on ... Bright evening to life O. Lubeau Railway Dugouts H.Q. slightly wounded	
Monday Dec 25th	Emergency Ten guns to minutes for relieves M.O. 5 min, gas of Gas available ... 9 H.Q.	
Tuesday Dec 26th	Major Kerr a Staff member crossed front line discrimenting the shelling also barrage of Stay into Enemy TM in action Quiet casualties 3 officers any less any horses 2 armies under time attempts to run above R.S.O.R.G. at LE Touvet	
Wednesday Dec 27th	Q.B.S.O. Lord Bergens 900) arrived to H.Q. TM. Instrument ... afternoon front line to be cleared injury ... Major Kerr went to Bensham R.D. Main O.C. Battalion Ron H.Q. TM Instruments at 2.30 at 2.40 a firing less spill hand grenades exchanged of 3rd revolvers. One sergeant. Three Men Joyson. Sullivan + King 2 Others. B. ... on instrument. Corpl. Browning wounded ... Mac. ... left speaker ... returned back to ms flares	

WAR DIARY
or
INTELLIGENCE SUMMARY.
(Erase heading not required.)

Army Form C. 2118.

Instructions regarding War Diaries and Intelligence Summaries are contained in F.S. Regs., Part II. and the Staff Manual respectively. Title pages will be prepared in manuscript.

Hour, Date, Place	Summary of Events and Information	Remarks and references to Appendices
Thursday Dec 28cs	C.O. and 2nd in Command visited machine gun line Lt Col Kennedy 9/Lon. 6 R.C.E. Majr Cro visited P & MG	
Friday Dec 29cb	Lt Col Kennedy was round front line posts C.O. & Coy relieved in Chestnut line on left to Coy to Factory Dugouts.	
Saturday Dec 30cd	Lt Col Kennedy, R.M.O, went round billets & relieving C.O. unknown Maj Cro Major Hildon went to front line & Ferry Post. Capt Tadawa and Capt Odlum on leave.	
Sunday Dec 31cb	Majr Gen Smith M.G. [?] visited Brigade one Enemy airplane reached C.A. machine gun fire in morning and again during night Major Hilden arranged tournament to night inside officer's dug out. Tournament ABC-D [?] G.N.S.O.6. 29.30. visit made to see during the morning.	From Majr J. K. Nellor [?] Lieut Col lay 1/24 London Regt The Queen's

Army Form C. 2118.

1/24 London Regiment

WAR DIARY
INTELLIGENCE SUMMARY
(Erase heading not required.)

Instructions regarding War Diaries and Intelligence Summaries are contained in F.S. Regs., Part II. and the Staff Manual respectively. Title pages will be prepared in manuscript.

Hour, Date, Place	Summary of Events and Information	Remarks and references to Appendices
Monday 1. January 1917	Enemy Lovell's battery fired at new work in enemy's lines during the morning. Considerable T.M. activity in afternoon causing several casualties. Artillery activity at 5.40 p.m. mainly on left of battalion frontage, at first and subsequently also on our front. About 6.20 pm bombardment lifted off our front line and some of the enemy fired from nomansland. A raid, if intended, was stopped by our artillery barrage. Considerable damage to our trenches resulted. Quiet night followed. Casualties 9 killed and 8 wounded.	
Tuesday 2nd	Much sniping about dawn; enemy being observed moving along his trenches which were treated in a number of points. Some T.M. and artillery activity about midday. Acting B.G.C. (Col Kennedy. D.S.O.) called. C.O. attended Bde. H.Q. in afternoon.	
Wednesday 3rd	General Speeding R.A. called. Div.l Gas Officer called re: gas precautions. Quiet day. Relieved by 23rd London Regt. H.Q. and C. Coy less 2 platoons moved to Railway Dugouts. B. Coy to Battersea Farm (finding garrisons for Glasgow and Berry Posts by night.) Remainder to Chateau Belge.	

Army Form C. 2118.

WAR DIARY
or
INTELLIGENCE SUMMARY.
(Erase heading not required.)

Instructions regarding War Diaries and Intelligence Summaries are contained in F.S. Regs., Part II and the Staff Manual respectively. Title pages will be prepared in manuscript.

Hour, Date, Place	Summary of Events and Information	Remarks and references to Appendices
Thursday 4th January 1917	Quiet day. 2 Coys find working parties. C.O. 2 i/c and M.O. visited 13 and C Coys.	
Friday 5th.	Major Love R.E. called. G.O.C. Div. passed through area and saw 2nd in Cmd. Bombardment of enemy's trenches at 2.30 – 3.30 pm and again at 3.45–4.15 pm during which all ranks kept under cover in case of retaliation. G.S.O.1. (Col Dawson) went to visit Glasgow and Berry Pos/s. 2 Coys on night working parties in front line.	
Saturday 6th	Quiet day. 2 Coys on night working parties.	
Sunday 7th	Quiet day. 2 Coys on night working parties. C.O. on his daily round met A/BGC. Officers of relieving unit called.	
Monday 8th	Quiet day. C.O. and 2nd in Cmd took works officer of relieving unit round Dossway and Battersea Down. Relieved by 6/L London Reg.t Moved to Devonshire Lines, Busseboom.	

Army Form C. 2118.

WAR DIARY
or
INTELLIGENCE SUMMARY.
(Erase heading not required.)

Instructions regarding War Diaries and Intelligence Summaries are contained in F. S. Regs., Part II. and the Staff Manual respectively. Title pages will be prepared in manuscript.

Hour, Date, Place	Summary of Events and Information	Remarks and references to Appendices
Tuesday 9th January 1917	Battalion resting.	
Wednesday 10th	Battalion bathing and interior economy.	
Thursday 11th	Coy. training and Battalion route march.	
Friday 12th	C and A Coys Xmas dinner in "Sandbad" Y.M.C.A. Hut. and to Divisional Follies in the evening.	
Saturday 13th	D and B Coys: Xmas dinner in "Sandbad" Y.M.C.A. Hut. wet day.	
Sunday 14th	Brigade Church Parade. Officers Xmas Dinner.	
Monday 15th	Contact Patrol work ordered – Parade cancelled. Battalion Route March. Baths for 75 men. Major Milner to Sandbach to attend Board of Enquiry.	
Tuesday 16th	Physical Exercises – Drill – Musketry – Route March. C.O. visited Div. School. Div. Commander visited and inspected Camp.	

Army Form C. 2118.

WAR DIARY
or
INTELLIGENCE SUMMARY.
(Erase heading not required.)

Instructions regarding War Diaries and Intelligence Summaries are contained in F.S. Regs., Part II. and the Staff Manual respectively. Title pages will be prepared in manuscript.

Hour, Date, Place	Summary of Events and Information	Remarks and references to Appendices
Wednesday 17th January 17	Contact Patrol work ordered. Parade cancelled. Company Officers and Sergeant reconnoitred Buff. Sector. Baths for 50 men – Range, Rifle and Revolver.	
Thursday 18th	Bn relieved 19th in Canal Sector Right – Dispositions – A in Craters – C Centre – D Left – B in support in Tunnels. 1 Co 22nd attached. Relief completed 11 p.m.	
Friday 19th	C.O. visited Craters and front line. Lt Col Kennedy visited Bn HQ and discussed work on the Sector. Brig Gen Lord Hampden G.S.O.1. and A.D.M.S. visited HQ and obtained information as to accommodation in Tunnels. Major Gardener, A & S Highlanders attached for 6 days. Raid by 123rd Brigade on Right – our front and support lines bombarded – retaliation by our artillery.	
Saturday 20th	C.O. and Major Gardener visited front line. Lt Col Kennedy and B.M. visited Bn H.Q.	

Army Form C. 2118.

WAR DIARY
or
INTELLIGENCE SUMMARY.
(Erase heading not required.)

Instructions regarding War Diaries and Intelligence Summaries are contained in F.S. Regs., Part II and the Staff Manual respectively. Title pages will be prepared in manuscript.

Hour, Date, Place	Summary of Events and Information	Remarks and references to Appendices
Saturday, 20th January 1917. Contd.	Quiet day. S.O.S test for our Heavy Artillery between 10 and 11 p.m. 2nd Lt Hay reported for duty. 2nd Lt Busby returned from leave. Lt Ansell returned from course.	
Sunday, 21st.	C.O. visited front line. Conference C.O's at Brigade.	
Monday, 22nd	C.O. visited front line and craters. B Co relieved C. in Centre. Quiet day. Artillery S.O.S. test.	
Tuesday, 23rd.	C.O. visited front line. Bombardment by our Heavies 9 a.m. to 4.30 p.m.	
Wednesday, 24th.	C.O. visited front line. Lt Col Kennedy visited Bn. H.Q. Quiet day.	
Thursday, 25th.	C.O. visited front line. G.O.C. and Lt Col Kennedy visited front line. Officers 1/23 called and reconnoitred line — details given.	

Army Form C. 2118.

WAR DIARY
or
INTELLIGENCE SUMMARY.
(Erase heading not required.)

Instructions regarding War Diaries and Intelligence Summaries are contained in F.S. Regs., Part II. and the Staff Manual respectively. Title pages will be prepared in manuscript.

Hour, Date, Place	Summary of Events and Information	Remarks and references to Appendices
Friday 26 January 1917	Relief by 23 Honorons. postponed. Front line and Craters heavily shelled during morning. Retaliation by our Artillery. 2Lt. JASTRZEBSKI reported for duty. Lt. BASEDEN left for 2nd Army School. 2nd Lt. PERRY on leave. Major GARDENER. A & S Highlanders returned having completed tour. Our front line cleared for Artillery Shoot 11.30 a.m. Shoot was cancelled. Received warning from Brigade that there were indications that the enemy might attack on Div: front. Company Commanders warned to be on the alert - also Company Commander 22nd B⁹⁵ - Tunnelling Co - R.W.F. and R.E.	
Saturday 27/1/16	B.M. visited H.Q. Bombardment by Corps Heavy Artillery On relieve by 1/23. Relief completed 9.30 p.m. Bn. moved to Huts at Dickebusch.	

(73989) W.4141—463. 400,000. 9/14. H.&J.Ltd. Forms/C. 2118/10.

Army Form C. 2118.

WAR DIARY
or
INTELLIGENCE SUMMARY.
(Erase heading not required.)

Instructions regarding War Diaries and Intelligence Summaries are contained in F.S. Regs., Part II and the Staff Manual respectively. Title pages will be prepared in manuscript.

Hour, Date, Place	Summary of Events and Information	Remarks and references to Appendices
Sunday 28th January 1917.	C.O. visited SWAN CHATEAU, settled details of relief tonight. Bn. moved into support. Relief completed 10.10 p.m. A. S.P. 7 and 8. — B. SWAN CHATEAU — C. WOODCOTE FARM. — D. BLUFF TUNNELS.	
Monday 29th.	C.O. and M.O. visited WOODCOTE FARM and S.P. 8. Lt. Col. KENNEDY.	
Tuesday 30th.	C.O visited B.Co. and Borders. Orders received that Capt. FIGG. D.S.O. to report on 2nd Feb to y/17 London Regt. as 2nd in Command. Batts at SWAN CHATEAU.	
Wednesday 31st	C.O. and M.O. visited D.Co. in BLUFF TUNNELS.— A.Co in S.P. 7 and 8. Batts at SWAN CHATEAU	

Geo. Pemberton
Col.
C/O 1/24th London Regt

3 Feb 1917

Army Form C. 2118.

WAR DIARY
or
INTELLIGENCE SUMMARY.
(Erase heading not required.)

1/24th Batt. London Regt Vol 23

Instructions regarding War Diaries and Intelligence Summaries are contained in F.S. Regs., Part II and the Staff Manual respectively. Title pages will be prepared in manuscript.

Hour, Date, Place	Summary of Events and Information	Remarks and references to Appendices
Thursday 1st February	C.O. met G.O.C. at Brigade HQ with reference to commissions. C.O. visited Bluff Tunnel, SP7 and 8 and Woodcote Farm. Swan Chateau heavily shelled in the afternoon.	
Friday 2nd	C.O. and M.O. visited Bluff Tunnel, SP7 and 8, Woodcote Farm. Reconnoitring Party of 1/8 London Regt called.	
Saturday 3rd	C.O. and M.O. visited Woodcote Farm. Bboy lines and Chateau Segard. Relief by 1/8 London Regt completed 10pm. Battalion moved to Devonshire Camp.	
Sunday 4th	Interior Economy and cleaning up. C.O. on course to 2nd Army School at Wisques. Capt Nadaud in command. R.S.M. Norris and draft of 85 joined Battalion	
Monday 5th	Training – Route March.	
Tuesday 6th	Interior Economy. Corps Commander visited Camp in the morning. Brig. General visited Camp in the afternoon.	

Army Form C. 2118.

WAR DIARY
or
INTELLIGENCE SUMMARY.
(Erase heading not required.)

Instructions regarding War Diaries and Intelligence Summaries are contained in F.S. Regs., Part II and the Staff Manual respectively. Title pages will be prepared in manuscript.

Hour, Date, Place	Summary of Events and Information	Remarks and references to Appendices
Wednesday 7th February 17.	Training. Range for 2 Coys and Raiding Party. Bomb Throwing at Vancouver Camp. 80. OR's	
Thursday 8th.		
Friday 9th.	Baths - allotment 1/35. Practice signalling scheme with Aeroplanes. Complete HQ and Composite Coy. G.O.C. Div: visited Camp in the afternoon.	
Saturday 10th.	Coy Commanders and Adjutant reconnoitred LEFT SECTION — HILL 60 sub sector. Range for two Coys, Bombers and Raiding Party. C.O. returned from 2nd Army School.	
Sunday 11th.	Church Parade. Relieved 1/8 London in HILL 60. Left. Relief completed 11.30 pm.	
Monday 12th.	C.O. and M.O. visited Front Line. Brig: Gen: & B.M. visited Bn HQ. Defence Scheme Works Programme etc discussed. C.O. and Works Officer visited BATTERSEA FARM. Conference Company Commanders on points raised by Brigadiers.	

WAR DIARY
or
INTELLIGENCE SUMMARY.
(Erase heading not required.)

Army Form C. 2118.

Hour, Date, Place	Summary of Events and Information	Remarks and references to Appendices
Tuesday 13th February 17	C.O and M.O visited front line in morning and BATTERSEA FARM in the afternoon. Bombardment by our Heavy Artillery and 2" T.M, part of front line cleared 2.30 to 4.30 p.m. B.Coy relieved by Coy of 23rd London at BATTERSEA FARM. Patrol work GLASGOW and other posts by B.Coy. Capt J.B. Nadaud left for HAVRE as Instructor.	
Wednesday 14th.	Bombardment by 2" T.M 10-12 a.m. Brig: Gnl. visited Bn H.Q and settled Defence Scheme. He and C.O visited Tunnelling Coy and Infantry Tunnel. Major BOWRING 164 Reserve Training attached.	
Thursday 15th.	C.O visited front line. Wire cutting by 18 pdrs, part of front line trench cleared. Maj: Gnl & Brig: Gnl visited Bn H.Q	
Friday 16th.	C.O & M.O visited front line and Tunnels. Wire cutting by 18 pdrs and medium T.M. Bombardment by 6" fixed but did not take place. C.O attended conference at Brigade H.Q.	

WAR DIARY
or
INTELLIGENCE SUMMARY.
(Erase heading not required.)

Army Form C. 2118.

Instructions regarding War Diaries and Intelligence Summaries are contained in F.S. Regs., Part II and the Staff Manual respectively. Title pages will be prepared in manuscript.

Hour, Date, Place	Summary of Events and Information	Remarks and references to Appendices
Saturday 17th February 1917	C.O and M.O visited front line. C.O visited HQ Tunnellers and discussed Defence Scheme. Line cleared for wire cutting by 18 prs during morning and he wire cutting by T.M.B 2-5. Officers of 1/23 London Reg't reconnoitred line.	
Sunday 18th	Wire cutting continued by 18 prs in morning, line partly cleared. C.O and M.O visited front line. Wire cutting by 2" T.M 2-4. Brig'r B.M went round front line and visited HQ (Bn) and met left 1/23 London Reg't relieved 24th in Hill 60 left sub-sector. Relief completed 9.30 p.m. HQ and A Coy at RAILWAY DUGOUTS B Coy at BATTERSEA FARM. C + D Coys at BELGIUM CHATEAU. 1/23 found patrols for tonight. Carrying parties.	
Monday 19th	M.O visited BELGIAN CHATEAU. C.O and M.O visited A Coy. Carrying parties.	
Tuesday 20th	C.O visited BATTERSEA FARM. Raid by 140 Brigade. Carrying parties.	

Army Form C. 2118.

WAR DIARY
or
INTELLIGENCE SUMMARY.
(Erase heading not required.)

Instructions regarding War Diaries and Intelligence Summaries are contained in F.S. Regs., Part II. and the Staff Manual respectively. Title pages will be prepared in manuscript.

Hour, Date, Place	Summary of Events and Information	Remarks and references to Appendices
Wednesday 21st February 17	C.O. and Works Officer visited BELGIUM CHATEAU. Very quiet day.	
Thursday 22nd	C.O. M.O. and Works Officer visited BATTERSEA FARM. D.Coy. relieved B.Coy. at BATTERSEA FARM. Quiet day.	
Friday 23rd	C.O. and M.O. visited BATTERSEA FARM. Quiet day. C.Coy relieved A.Coy at RAILWAY DUG-OUTS.	
Saturday 24th	C.O. + M.O. visited BELGIUM CHATEAU. Adjutant and M.O. visited BATTERSEA FARM. Recd. by 41st Div. on Right.	
Sunday 25th	C.O. + M.O. visited BATTERSEA FARM.	
Saturday 26th	C.O. + M.O. visited BELGIUM CHATEAU.	
Monday 27th	C.O. + M.O. visited BATTERSEA FARM. Relief by 1/4" Lon. Regt. Relief completed 8.15.p.m. Bn. moved to DEVONSHIRE CAMP.	
Tuesday 28.	Bathing. Cleaning up, etc.	

Geo. And. Denchars
Lt. Col.
Comg. 1/24 Bn. London Regt.
The Queens

Army Form C. 2118.

WAR DIARY
or
INTELLIGENCE SUMMARY.
(Erase heading not required.)

1/24th Batt London Regt

Vol 2

Hour, Date, Place	Summary of Events and Information	Remarks and references to Appendices
Thursday 1st March 1917.	Training – Route March.	
Friday 2nd "	Shell Gas Testing – "A" & "B" Companies. Training – Interior Economy.	
Saturday 3rd "	Shell Gas Testing "C" & "D" Companies. Training – L.G. and Raiding Party on Range. B.M. C. visited Camp.	
Sunday 4th "	Camp Inspection by C.O. Church Parade under Bishop of Khartoum. Corps Commander visited Camp.	
Monday 5th "	Training – Route March cancelled owing to snow. Medical Inspection.	
Tuesday 6th "	Training – Camp visited by Div. Commander. Route March – Adjutant arranged details of relief with O.C. 1/19th Bn London Regt.	
Wednesday 7th "	Foot inspection and preparation for move to Kendles. Relieved 1/19th London Regt in CANAL SECTION. Relief completed 10.35 pm	

WAR DIARY
or
INTELLIGENCE SUMMARY.
(Erase heading not required.)

Army Form C. 2118.

Instructions regarding War Diaries and Intelligence Summaries are contained in F.S. Regs., Part II and the Staff Manual respectively. Title pages will be prepared in manuscript.

Hour, Date, Place	Summary of Events and Information	Remarks and references to Appendices
Thursday 8th March 1917	C.O. visited Craters and Front line. and again with BGC and B.M. Div. General visited Bn.H.Q.	
Friday 9th "	C.O. visited Front line and Tunnels. Called on R.W.F. and Tunnelling Coy - discussing scheme for clearance of Tunnels in the event of emergency	
Saturday 10th "	C.O. visited Front line at 8. AM and again at 11 a.m with D.U.C - King St. Craters. Tunnels etc.	
Sunday 11th "	C.O. visited Front Line and Tunnels. Capt. BROMHEAD 2/1st London Regt. visited Bn H.Q. on tour.	
Monday 12th "	C.O. and Works Officer visited Tunnels and Front line. G.O.C. Div. & B.G.C. visited Front line. Capt. BROMHEAD left.	
Tuesday 13th "	C.O. and Works Officer visited Front line. B.U.C. visited Bn. H.Q. Conference with C.O. and Works Officer as to work. Visited King St and Hedge Row	

Army Form C. 2118.

WAR DIARY
or
INTELLIGENCE SUMMARY.
(Erase heading not required.)

Hour, Date, Place	Summary of Events and Information	Remarks and references to Appendices
Wednesday 14th March 1917	C.O. visited front line. 1/23rd Bn relieved 1/24th Bn. Relief completed	
	11.40 p.m. Battalion moved to DICKEBUSCH CAMP.	
Thursday 15th "	Rev Cohen, C.F. joined Battalion.	
Friday 16th "	Baths – Cleaning up – Interior Economy.	
Saturday 17th "	Baths – Interior Economy – Training.	
Sunday 18th "	— " — " — " —	
Monday 19th "	— " — " — " —	
Tuesday 20th "	— " — " — " —	
Wednesday 21st "	1/8th Bn relieved 1/24th Bn at DICKEBUSCH. Relief completed	
	4 p.m. 1/24 Bn moved to DEVONSHIRE CAMP.	
Thursday 22nd "	Interior Economy. Foot Inspection. Battalion Concert.	
Friday 23rd "	Brigade moved to STEENVOORDE area.	
	1/24 Bn billeted at GODEWAERSVELDE.	
Saturday 24th "	Brigade moved to NOORDPEENE area.	
	1/24 Bn billeted at ZERMEZEELE and WAEMERS CAPEL.	
Sunday 25th "	Brigade moved to 2nd ARMY TRAINING area.	
	1/24 Bn to EPERLECQUES. C.O. visited Training Ground with B.G.C.	

Army Form C. 2118.

WAR DIARY
or
INTELLIGENCE SUMMARY.
(Erase heading not required.)

Instructions regarding War Diaries and Intelligence Summaries are contained in F.S. Regs., Part II. and the Staff Manual respectively. Title pages will be prepared in manuscript.

Hour, Date, Place	Summary of Events and Information	Remarks and references to Appendices
Monday 26th March 1917	Training on Area.	
Tuesday 27th "	" " "	
Wednesday 28th "	" " "	
Thursday 29th "	Training in Billets. Major MILLNER joined Battalion. Conference with Brig: General.	
Friday 30th "	Route March. Training in Billets.	
Saturday 31st "	Training on Area. Capt: BATTS Capt: YATES and Lt WILLIAMS joined Battalion.	

Geo A. Paston Jones
Lt. Col.
Cdg. 1/24 Bn London Regt.
The Queens.

H.6

142 Inf Bde.

The attached War Diary
for April is forwarded, please

P. Matthews
  Lt. & Adjt
for O.C. 1/24 LONDON REG.
        The Queens.

Army Form C. 2118.

WAR DIARY
or
INTELLIGENCE SUMMARY.
(Erase heading not required.)

1/4 London R [handwritten]

Instructions regarding War Diaries and Intelligence Summaries are contained in F.S. Regs., Part II and the Staff Manual respectively. Title pages will be prepared in manuscript.

Hour, Date, Place	Summary of Events and Information	Remarks and references to Appendices
1st.April 1917.	Musketry on open range by Companies from 8.30 a.m. to 5.30 p.m. Inspection of transport horses and distribution of prizes by A.D.V.S assisted by Capt.CRAIG,A.V.C. from 2.30 p.m. to 4.30 p.m.	
2nd.April.	Company training during morning. Lecture by 2nd.in Command on "Situation reports during active operations" to all officers.	
3rd.April.	Training programme cancelled owing to snow. Route march substituted. C.O. calls at Brigade H.Q. Major MILLNER President of F.G.C.M.	
4th.April.	Battalion battle practice. C.O. attends conference at Brigade H.Q. Major MILLNER President of F.G.C.M.	
5th.April.	Brigade battle practice. Divnl.Commander present.	
6th.April.	Battalion battle practice.	
7th.April.	Brigade Battle practice. Corps Commander present.	
8th.April.	C.O. proceeds to England on special leave. Major G.E.MILLNER assumes command. Brigade on the move. Battalion leaves EPERLECQUES and billets for the night at WAEMARS-CAPPEL and ZERMEZEELE.	
9th.April.	March resumed. Billet for night at GODEWAERSVELDE.	
10th.April.	Battalion resting. C.O.visits billets. 2/Lt.MATTHEWS appointed Acting Adjutant vice Lt.WILLIAMS who becomes Signalling Officer. 2/Lt.HERIVEL becomes Assistant Adjutant.	
11th.April.	March to Devonshire Lines, BUSSEBOOM. Major T.O.BURY,R.W.F.reports for duty as 2fond in Command.	
12th.April.	Relieved 6th.Battn.in BLUFF Sector.Relief complete 1.50 a.m.	

Army Form C. 2118.

WAR DIARY
or
INTELLIGENCE SUMMARY.
(Erase heading not required.)

Instructions regarding War Diaries and Intelligence Summaries are contained in F.S. Regs., Part II. and the Staff Manual respectively. Title pages will be prepared in manuscript.

Hour, Date, Place	Summary of Events and Information	Remarks and references to Appendices
13th.April.	Quiet day. C.O. visited line in morning.	
14th.April.	About 9 p.m. small hostile party attempted raid at Craters E. of BLUFF. They approached close to our posts and threw bombs which failed to explode, and were shortly driven by Lewis Gun Fire. 2 O.Rs wounded.	
15th.April.	C.O. visited trenches in evening. Lt.-Col.TURNER, G.S.O.1. and Staff Captain 142nd.Inf.Bde. called. Quiet day. Lieut.DALZIEL reported for duty. 2/Lt.WETTONE to hospital sick.	
16th.April.	A.D.M.S. called and inspected Tunnels, dugouts etc.,. Major NICKALLS, commanding X Battery called to apologise for firing "shorts" on afternoon of 15th.inst. attributed to faulty ammunition. Cpl.M.E.GREEN recommended for immediate award of Military Medal for work on 14th.inst. during hostile raid.	
17th.April.	Brigade Commander called and C.O. accompanied him round the line. Staff Captain called. Enemy obtained hit with 77 m.m.Gun on Lewis Gun position in B Crater putting the gun out of action.	
18th.April.	Brigade Commander and Major SPENCER,M.G.C. called during the day. also reconnoitring party 23rd.Battn. 1 Officer and 20 O.Rs. Artists Rifles (candidates for direct commission) reported, to be attached for instruction.	
19th.April.	Brigade Commander and Brigade Major called. Relieved by 23rd.Batn and moved to SWAN CHATEAU. A.B. and D. Coys at CHATEAU SEGARD and C Coy at S.P. 7 & 8. 1 Platoon of A and B Coys remained at BLUFF Tunnels at disposal of O.C. 23rd.Battn. 1 O.R. Artists Rifles wounded.	
20th.April.	C.O. visited Coys. at CHATEAU SEGARD.	

Army Form C. 2118.

WAR DIARY
or
INTELLIGENCE SUMMARY.
(Erase heading not required.)

Instructions regarding War Diaries and Intelligence Summaries are contained in F.S. Regs., Part II and the Staff Manual respectively. Title pages will be prepared in manuscript.

Hour, Date, Place	Summary of Events and Information	Remarks and references to Appendices
21st. April.	C.O. visited C Coy at S.P.7 & 8. Major BURY at F.G.C.M. at HALIFAX CAMP.	
22nd. April.	Voluntary Divine Service at SWAN CHATEAU.	
23rd. April.	Major BOWRING left to take over duties of Major on H.Q. 2/8th. King's Liverpool Regiment. Major BURY at F.G.C.M. at HALIFAX CAMP.	
24th. April.	Relieved by 7th. Bn. Lon. Regt., and moved to OTTAWA CAMP near OUDERDOM. Lieut. BUSBY and 1 O.R. wounded.	
25th. April.	Interior economy. Rifle inspection etc. C.O. and 2nd. in command visited Transport Lines. 2/Lt. ALLISON rejoined from Brigade School.	
26th. April.	Squad Drill. Physical Training and Specialist Training carried out. Conference with Company Commanders and Specialist Officers at Bn. H.Q. 20 O.Rs H.Q. Platoon visited Divisional Follies. Farewell dinner to Lt. Col. CARR, D.S.O. at H.Q. Mess.	
27th. April.	Interior economy. Major BICKFORD C.F. called. 50 O.Rs per Company visited Divisional Follies.	
28th. April.	All Drummers, C Coy and all Company Cooks segregated as Diphtheria Contacts and moved to H.Q. 5th. London Field Ambulance. Relieved 23rd. Battn. (less 1 Company) in Right Canal Sub-Sector. THE BLUFF. Relief completed 11.45 p.m. "A" Coy. Craters. D Coy. trenches N of Craters to HEDGE ROW C.T. "B" Coy. Support. 1 Coy. 23rd. Battn. Reserve. Capt. RICHARDSON left to attend Corps Tactical Course. Hon. Lieut. & Q.M. Barrett left to take over duties as Q.M. of Corps Rest Camp near AUDRESSELLES. Lieut. H.S. MITCHELL left to attend Corps Sniping Course at MONT DES CATS.	

Army Form C. 2118.

WAR DIARY
or
INTELLIGENCE SUMMARY.
(Erase heading not required.)

Instructions regarding War Diaries and Intelligence Summaries are contained in F.S. Regs., Part II. and the Staff Manual respectively. Title pages will be prepared in manuscript.

Hour, Date, Place	Summary of Events and Information	Remarks and references to Appendices
29th. April.	C.O. visited line at "Stand to" at 4.30 a.m. 2 Platoons (one "A" and one "B") rejoined from work at PACIFIC SIDING. On instructions of Brigade Commander "B" Coy. 23rd. London Regt., less their Lewis Guns and Gun Teams withdraw to OTTAWA CAMP. Conference of Company Commanders and Specialist Officers at Battn. H.Q. at 3 p.m.	
30th. April.	A.D.M.S. called. About 1.45 p.m. a fire broke out in Signallers' Dugout in A Tunnel and spread rapidly. Prompt assistance was given by 2nd. Australian and 1st. Canadian Tunnelling Coys. and by blocking tunnels with wet sand bags, fire confined to small area. Battn. H.Q. moved to dugout near. Smoke of fire was observed by enemy who shelled Canal S. of BLUFF. Casualties 3 O.Rs wounded and 1 O.R. burnt.	

M. Mullens

Major Cdg., "THE QUEENS"
1/24th. Bn. Lon. Regt.,

1/24th. LONDON REGIMENT.
SECRET.   O.O. 149   COPY.

1. The 24th. Bn. will relieve the 6th. London Regiment in the
CANAL SUB-SECTOR on the 12th. April 1917.

2. TABLE OF RELIEF.
                Left Coy.   Right Coy.   Support Coy.   Reserve Coy.
   6th. Bn.
   24th. Bn.   C.   A.   D.   B.

3. ADVANCE PARTIES.

   A Coy. will send up garrisons for CRATERS including
Lewis Guns.
   Guides for these parties at WOODCOTE HOUSE 4.p.m.

        2 Guides for Platoons
        3 Guides for Lewis Guns.

   Lewis Gun teams for the guns in the CRATERS will
proceed to the TRANSPORT LINES reporting there at 1.p.m. to
load limber and magazines.

   One Officer and 1 N.C.O. per Coy. and the R.S.M.
will report at the 6th. Bn. H.Qs. at 2.p.m. to take over
stores etc. Separate receipts will be given for Gumboots,
Water, Iron Ration Dumps, and biscuit portion of Iron Rations.
Trench Stores must be checked with the greatest care.

   Copies of Receipts MUST be at Bn.H.Qs. as early as
possible to-morrow evening.

4. PARADE.

   The Bn. less Lewis Guns and A Coy's advance party
will move off at 5 minutes interval in the following order:-

        H.Q., C., A, D, B.

   H.Qs. will move off at 7.5.p.m.

   Bn. will entrain at G.S.c.9.2. and detrain at
ASYLUM, YPRES. Train leaves at 8.45.p.m.. Coys. etc. will
be at place of entrainment at 8.15.p.m.

   2/Lt. S.H.Walker will act as entraining Officer.
He will report to R.T.O. at G.S.c.9.2. at 8.15.p.m. O.C. Coys.
will arrange to send their entraining strength to the Bn.O.R.
by 4.p.m.

5. GUIDES. at LANGHOFF FARM at 9.45.p.m.

        H.Qs. 1: Right Coy. 2: Left Coy. 4: Reserve Coy. 4:
                Support Coy. 4:

Lewis Guns. Three Lewis Gun limbers leave TRANSPORT LINES
at 6.p.m.
        13 Guides for Lewis Guns at LANGHOFF FARM at
9.p.m. Sgts. BOUSHER & LANCASTER will be in charge of guns.

6. ROUTINE.

   T.O. will collect Cookers, Water Cart, Blankets etc., as
follows:-

        Cookers ready for teams by   5.30.p.m.
        Blankets at Guard Tent by   9.a.m.
        Officers' Valises   12.noon.
        Officers' Mess Gear   5.30.p.m.
        Cookers' dixies, etc. for line   5.30.p.m.
        C.O's., 2nd. i/c., M.O's., Adjt's chargers 7.30.p.m.

(2).

7.   2/Lt. Burroughs will report to H.Qs. of the 6th. Bn. at 11.a.m. and take over details of work.

8.   Code word for relief:- BURY.

P. Matthews

2/Lt. & Adjt.

11/4/1917.

Army Form C. 2118.

1/24th Batt London Regt

WAR DIARY
or
INTELLIGENCE SUMMARY.
(Erase heading not required.)

Instructions regarding War Diaries and Intelligence Summaries are contained in F.S. Regs., Part II and the Staff Manual respectively. Title pages will be prepared in manuscript.

Hour, Date, Place	Summary of Events and Information	Remarks and references to Appendices
Tuesday, May 1st.	Draft of 18 o.rs reported at Transport Lines. Practice Creeping Barrage carried out on 41st Div: Front.S. of YPRES - COMMINES CANAL which was observed from our lines by Major Bury and reported on by the Battalion on instructions of Brigade. 2 Sections Lewis Gunners Army Cyclist Corps reported for duty as re-inforcements for Garrison. 1 o.r. wounded.	
Wednesday, May 2nd.	Capt Richardson rejoined from Corps Tactical Course. Major Bury attended at Div.H.Q. re F.G.C.M. on L/Cpl Tutenberg 21st. Battalion. Transport Lines slightly shelled with shrapnel about 10.a.m. 1 o.r. wounded. Bde Commander 140 Bde called. At 10.10.p.m. Strombos Horns were heard. Battalion stood with Box Respirators. Bde H.Q. telephoned that enemy had discharged Gas N. No Gas on Battalion front.	
Thursday, May 3rd.	Brig.Genl Bailey called also Major Spencer M.G.C. and Major Commanding Australians Tunnellers. Quiet day. Conference of Company Commanders and Specialist Officers at 3 p.m Left Company Sector held from 11.p.m. to 4.a.m. (4th) by 6 Lewis Gun Sections under Lieut Dalziel, remainder of Company Garrison being used for working parties.	
Friday, 4th.	Quiet day. Major Genl went round line. Bde Major also Major Spencer called. Usual conference 3.p.m. 2/Lt S.H.Walker Transport Officer vice Lieut J.Robinson for duty as Bde T.O.	
Saturday, 5th.	Brig.Genl. Bailey called. Usual conference 5.p.m. Question of proposed new rank of Temp. W.O. Class 1 discussed and not approved. At midnight severe bombardment of back areas by hostile artillery.	

(73989) W.14141—463. 400,000. 9/14. H.&J.Ltd. Forms/C. 2118/10.

Army Form C. 2118.

WAR DIARY
or
INTELLIGENCE SUMMARY.
(Erase heading not required.)

Hour, Date, Place	Summary of Events and Information	Remarks and references to Appendices
Sunday, May 6th.	Capt H.C.Watts to Lewis Gun School at LeTouquet. Lieut Strachan and 2/Lt Adams rejoined from Div.School. 2/Lt Keeble, Lieut Sanders and 2/Lt Perry to Div.School. Lieut Shields, M.C. rejoined. Relieved by 23rd Battn. Relief interfered with by hostile shelling. Casualties 2 o.rs. wounded. Moved to OTTAWA CAMP. Attached details Artists Rifles left to rejoin their unit.	
Monday 7th.	Battalion resting. At 8.45.p.m. and 11.p.m. Artillery along Army front bombarded hostile Communications as retaliation for shelling of back areas. Major Hargreaves D.S.O. 23rd London Regt. reported for duty training young Officers.	
Tuesday 8th.	Company Training. Farewell dinner to Lt.Col.Parker. D.S.O.	
Wednesday, 9th.	Coffee bar established under Sgt cook. Battalion bathing at HOPOUTRE. Lewis Gunners at Bde Range. 2/Lt Cazeaux posted to this Battn. 2/Lt Wettone rejoined from hospital.	
Thursday, 10th.	Battn. Drill and Company Training. 2 Platoon Commanders from each Company under 2nd i/c for Tactical Scheme. 2/Lts Burroughs and Herivel to Gas School.	
Friday 11th.	Battn.Drill and Company Training. Lewis Gunners on Range. Tactical Scheme under 2nd i/c for Platoon Commanders. Football match - Officers v Sergeants.	
Saturday, 12th.	2/Lt Cattell to 2nd Army School. Battn Drill and Company Training. Lewis Gunners on Range. Tactical Scheme under 2nd i/c for Platoon Commanders.	
Sunday, 13th.	2/Lt Cazeaux to hospital sick. Battn inspection by C.O. followed by Church Parade under Capt. Cohen. Bde Staff dined at Bn.H.Q. I.O. goes up line to arrange relief.	

Army Form C. 2118.

WAR DIARY
or
INTELLIGENCE SUMMARY.
(*Erase heading not required.*)

Instructions regarding War Diaries and Intelligence Summaries are contained in F.S. Regs., Part II and the Staff Manual respectively. Title pages will be prepared in manuscript.

Hour, Date, Place	Summary of Events and Information	Remarks and references to Appendices
Monday 14.	2/Lt Longley rejoined and posted to "A" Coy. Conference of Company Commanders and Specialist Officers. C.O. attended Conference at Bde.H.Q. at WINNIPEG CAMP morning and afternoon. Relieved 23rd London Regt in Right Canal Sub-sector THE BLUFF. "A" Coy Craters, "C" Coy trenches N of Craters, "D" and "B" Support and Reserve respectively in Tunnels.	
Tuesday 15	2/Lt Longley to Gas School. Usual conference at 5.p.m. C.O. visited line at 9.p.m. Lt.Col.Parry D.S.O. Cdg 18th London Regt. called. 1.o.r. wounded and 1.o.r. accidentally wounded. G.S.O.3. 41st Div and a Bde. Intell. Officer of same Div. wounded in BEEF St.	
Wednesday 16.	Brig.Genl.McDowell called also 2nd i/c 18th Bn, C.R.E, Major Cammell, Siege Arty Major Cooper (A 236) Major Maxse R.E.m Capt Plumtree.C.F. Corps G.S.O. and another. Capt Gamer C.F. Capt Watts rejoined from Lewis Gun Course LeTOUQUET. Quiet day. Usual conference at 5.p.m.	
Thursday 17.	1.o.r. killed by sniper in "B" Crater. Usual conference. 6" Battery wire cutting S.of Canal fired a few shorts one of which, a direct hit on front line cut off temporarily, communication with O.P. of Liaison Officer attached to this Bn. Officers 3rd Bn Rifle Brigade called reconnoitring approaches to line.	
Friday 18.	Major Genl. also Brig.Gen.Bailey called, also Major Maxse R.E and Lieut.Tompson & Major Cooper R.E.A. (A.236)½ C.O. and 2 i/c called at H.Q. 1/18th.Bn. Officers 1st.Bn. Royal Fusiliers called reconnoitring approaches to line. Usual conference. 2nd.Lt.Carr joined.	
Saturday 19.	1 O.R. wounded. C.O. and Coy.Commanders 7th.Bn.Northamptonshire Regt. called reconnoitring approaches to line. Wire cutting	

WAR DIARY
or
INTELLIGENCE SUMMARY.
(Erase heading not required.)

Army Form C. 2118.

Instructions regarding War Diaries and Intelligence Summaries are contained in F.S. Regs., Part II and the Staff Manual respectively. Title pages will be prepared in manuscript.

Hour, Date, Place	Summary of Events and Information	Remarks and references to Appendices
Saturday 19th.	on wire round hostile sap opposite "A" Crater by C.104 Batty. unsuccessful. Capt.C.White acting D.T.M.O. called. Usual conference.	
Sunday 20th.	Quiet day. Usual conference. Brigade Commander called but did not see C.O.	
Monday 21st.	C.O. and Adjt.20th.Bn. called reconnoitring preparatory to relief. Major Walford D.S.O. called with reference to wire cutting of sap also Major Wood R.F.A. Capt.White Acting D.T.M.O called. Platoon of "A" Coy. under Lieut.I.W.Jones R.W.F. and Sergeant Fox raided hostile sap. See copy of operation order and report attached.	
Tuesday 22nd.	Lieut.I.W.Jones R.W.F. (attached) proceeded to England on 10 day's leave. Quiet day. Relieved by 23rd.Bn.(Lt.Col Matthews D.S.O.) and move to ONTARIO camp near RENNINGHELST. Arrive 6 a.m. 23rd.Battn having breakfasted on line of march.	
Wednesday 23rd.	Resting. C.O. and 2 I/c visited HOPOUTRE to make arrangements for baths &c. to-morrow.	
Thursday 24th.	Baths at HOPOUTRE Dinnees at H.Q. Div.Train,later entrained for GODEWAERSVELDE and thence by march route to billets N.W of STEENVOORDE. H.Q. at Farm at K.19.c.5.8. (Belgium & France sheet 27.) Company Commanders conference at 9 p.m	
Friday 25th.	Brig.Genl.Bailey and Bde.Major called in morning. Practice Trench to Trench attack carried out from 3 to 7 p.m on training ground at K.27.c. Central. Bde.Major attended also artillery Liason Officer (Lieut Lucas M.C.)	
Saturday	Practice Trench to Trench attack carried out from 9.30 to 1.30 p.m Bde.Commander attended and addressed officers and	

WAR DIARY
or
INTELLIGENCE SUMMARY.
(Erase heading not required.)

Army Form C. 2118.

Hour, Date, Place	Summary of Events and Information	Remarks and references to Appendices
Saturday 26.	Warrant Officers and Sergeants. Lieut Lucas R.F.A. also attended Conference Coy Commanders and Specialist Officers at 2.30.p.m. Officers dine at Hotel Faucou Steenvoorde. Lieut Sanders and 2/Lts Perry and Keeble rejoin from Div.School.	
Sunday 27.	Practice Trench to Trench Attack carried out 8.30.a.m. to 12.30.p.m. Bde Commander and Lt.Col.Kemble 1/23 London Regt attended also Lieut Lucas and Bde Signalling Officer. The following Officers and N.C.O. mentioned in despatches (Gazette of Tuesday 15-5-17 Times 26-5-17.) Temp.Capt C.J.Saunders., Act.Capt H.C.Watts., Lieut J.Robinson 2/Lt R.V.Todd., 2/Lt S.H Walker and 720220 Act L/Sgt Garwood.J.R.	
Monday 28.	Practice Trench to Trench Attack carried out as yesterday. 2/Lt Martin to hospital sick.	
Tuesday 29.	Practice Trench to Trench Attack as yesterday, one practice being carried out after all Coy & Platoon Commanders and Coy Sgt Mjrs withdrawn. Half an hours ceremonial drill. C.O. dined at H.Q. 142nd Inf Bde., ABEELE frontier cross reads.	
Wednesday 30.	Practice Trench to Trench Attack as yesterday. Bde Commander attended. Capt Saunders Staff Capt, 142nd Inf Bde called.	
Thursday 31.	Moved by march route via ABEELE-HOPOUTRE to Camp at M.3.c.2.5. (Belgium & France sheet 28). Dinners at HOPOUTRE. C.O. stepped at Bde H.Q. ABEELE frontier cross reads for short conference with Bde Commander. 2/Lt L.P.Arnold 1/24 London Regt and 2/Lts G.L.Scott and E.C.Mave 1/17th London Regt joined the Battalion, on posting.	

O.O. 185.   1/24 BATT. LONDON REGT. (THE QUEENS)   SECRET.
                                                     COPY No. 3

MINOR ENTERPRISE ON O 4 a 8/.85 and O 4 a 8/.80.
REFERENCE:- BLUE PRINT MAP No 3.

1. INTENTION:- To raid enemy sap O 4 a 8/.85 and Crater O 4 a 8/.80.
To secure prisoners and reconnoitre the sap and crater.

2. STRENGTH:- 1 PLATOON viz:- LIEUT. I.W. JONES.
                                   Sgt. Y.H. FOX.
                                   1 SECTION BOMBERS
                                   1 SECTION RIFLE BOMBERS
                                   1 SECTION RIFLEMEN
                                   SUPPORTED BY 1 SECTION LEWIS GUN.

3. ARTILLERY:-
(a) Bombardment to open at ZERO. Infantry approach as close as possible by ZERO and at ZERO + 2' reach objective.
(b) There will be no fire on actual objective. 18 Pounders will barrage trenches NORTH and SOUTH of CANAL from which fire could be brought to bear on Infantry and will form a box barrage round objective. 4.5" Howitzers will fire on trench junctions, known trench mortar and machine gun positions.
(c) Rates of fire:- ZERO to ZERO + 4 minutes - intense.
                    ZERO + 4 minutes till withdrawal complete — moderate.
                    Slow down and stop as soon after withdrawal as possible.

4. ARMS &c. Each man will carry rifle and bayonet, two bandoliers and two bombs. Half the bombers will carry 10 bombs each.
No equipment identification marks, badges, pay-books, maps or letters &c will be carried. Box respirators will be worn at the alert position.

5. TIME TABLE. At ZERO minus 5' infantry will proceed from "B" Crater via "C" & "D" CRATERS to "E" CRATER.
At ZERO party will reach the sap at a point about O 4 a 8/.90. The riflemen will hold captured sap, while a section of bombers will advance to each flank i.e. towards the head of the sap and towards the CRATER. O 4 a 8/.80.
At ZERO + 20' parties will withdraw from enemy Crater, at ZERO + 25' parties will withdraw from sap via "E" "D" + "C" CRATERS and return.

6. ACTION ON RETURN. On returning all ranks will report forthwith to the CANTEEN to MAJOR. T.O. BORY who will call the roll and take over all captured booty and prisoners.

7. ADVANCED AID POST and COMPANY HQs will be at S.O.S. phone in NORTH ST TUNNEL.

8. TIME. ZERO will be 10.45 pm on 21st inst. Watches of all concerned including ARTILLERY will be synchronised at ZERO minus 60' and ZERO minus 30' by 2nd LT J. HERIVEL, who will obtain correct time from Brigade Headquarters at 10 o'clock pm.

9. CODE WORDS:-

ISSUED AT 12 NOON 18th MAY 1917.

COPY No. 1	Bde	No 10	143rd Bde
2	Lt Jones	11	141st Bde
3	A. Coy	12	Artillery
4	B "	13	Right Batt.
5	C "	14	Left Batt
6	D "	15	Australian Tunnellers
7	L.S.B.	16	R.E.
8	T.O. + QM	17	R.W.F.
9	H.Q. Officers	18	141st M.G. Coy
		19	142nd M.G. Coy
		20	T.M.

P.J. Mathew
Lt + adjt.

REPORT ON WORK DONE IN .... COMPANY'S SECTION.

During tour of Company from 12 midnight .... to 12 midnight ....

DETAILS	CONDITION WHEN TAKEN OVER	WORK DONE	NUMBER OF MEN / HOURS EMPLOYED	CONDITION AT END OF WORK
TRENCHES				
DO.				
WIRE				
FRENCH				
DUGOUTS				
SHELTERS				
COMMUNICATION TRENCHES				

War Diary

SECRET.

REF. OO/55.

AFTER ORDERS.

1. STOKES MORTARS.

The TMs will fire on known machine gun emplacement at I 34 d.10.35 at ZERO and onwards in connection with ARTILLERY.

2. STRETCHER BEARERS.

2 Stretcher Bearers will accompany party (para 2) The Reserve SB's will be at ADVANCED AID POST at S.O.5 phone in NORTH ST TUNNEL.

3. CODE WORDS. (PARA 9)

Raiding party has started — BULL.
Raiding party has completely withdrawn — DUN.
The operation is postponed — POP
Password — SAPPY.

P.D. Mathews
Lt. & Adjt.

Headquarters,

    142nd. Infantry Brigade.

    Report on my O.O. 155and artillery activity during night of the 21/22nd. May.

Preliminary.   (a)   About 9.25.p.m. last night enemy commenced a bombardment by T.Ms. on our Craters and south of the Canal.

    About 10.p.m. there was intense enemy artillery fire on this same front, L.H.V. shells enfilading the Craters from both flanks. The fire continued until 10.45.p.m. Our retaliation appeared effective.

  (b)   About 10.p.m. the fire was increased in depth and covered the Canal, the Wynde, King Street and the vicinity of Battn. H.Qs, and the Aid Post, where it ceased about 10.42.p.m.

  (c)   In regard to the intensity of the L.H.V. fire, it appeared to the O.C. Crater Coy. that this was more due to the rate at which the guns were firing than to the number of guns employed.

  (d)   The light T.M. detachment in the Wynde retaliated during this and the subsequent enemy's bombardment.

Our Artillery Barrage.   2.

  (a)   The bombardment commencing at Zero appears to have been carried out as ordered. It was accurate and effective in neutralising the enemy machine guns. In this connection it may be stated that the M.G. fire which invariably sweeps this subsector after dusk was entirely stopped, no shot being heard before 1.10.a.m. and to this must, in a great measure, be attributed the partial success of the enterprise.

  (b)   It appears probable that our bombardment was regarded by the enemy as retaliation for his activity until our party was seen in the vicinity of his Crater.

  (c)   With regard to the rate of fire, the word "intense" applied to the 18 pr. fire between Zero and Zero plus 7 minutes was not a correct description from the point of view of the raiding party. It was regarded by them as slow as compared to the previous activity. The subsequent "moderate" fire also suffered in comparison.

  (d)   All artillery fire was ordered to slacken at 11.15.p.m. to cease about 11.25.p.m., when the raiding party was reported back. Throughout the preparations for the raid, as during the raid, and the subsequent bombardment my liaison officer, 2/Lt. MATEER, R.F.A. rendered valuable assistance.

Raiders. 3. The raid was carried out as ordered in Para.5 of the O.Os., but the section of bombers intended to move towards the Crater O.4.d.87.80, lost direction slightly to the left owing to the state of the ground with the result that they struck the enemy trench about the junction of the Crater and the front line where the wire was several yards thick and without gaps. The Crater was held by enemy bombers and a bombing fight ensued but our party could gain no ground on account of the wire and retired when their stock of bombs became exhausted. The sap was carefully examined from the point where it was raided (near the centre) to the head. It is only a ditch with a little sandbagging and nothing of interest was observed. The enemy who fires very lights at intervals of from 15 to 60 minutes every night from near the head of the sap and whose presence there the previous night had again been verified by our patrols, must have been withdrawn in view of the enemy bombardment which preceded our raid.

Lt. I. W. Jones, who was the first to enter the sap, and Sgt. V. H. Fox, who showed both courage and coolness in assisting Lt. Jones in directing and leading the raid, led the right and centre parties respectively, got into touch with the detachment which had lost direction, but owing to the necessity of adhering to the time table which had been laid down by higher authority, there was not sufficient time left to organise an advance on the side of the Crater adjacent to the Canal where it is believed the wire was damaged and where access to the Crater might have been gained. As it was, the party were late in returning. One man was wounded by an enemy bomb and one man lost his way back but turned up about an hour later.

Subsequent Bombardment. 4. At 3.a.m. an intense barrage was simultaneously opened on our front. The front line companies stood to. The Crater Company called for retaliation on the S.O.S. phone line and the reply was immediate from the 18 pr. batteries, but some time elapsed before the heavy artillery responded. The left Company phone lines were cut and rifle & lewis gun fire was opened. During the the night about 8,000 rounds were expended. It appeared to the Officer on duty that as the enemy's fire did not slacken that the enemy might attempt a raid, two bombardments by him in one night being unusual, and he fired an S.O.S. rocket. In the opinion of the O.C. left company, retaliation did not follow for about 15 minutes. Firing ceased about 4.a.m.

Damage.
(a) Damage was done to posts in both "A" & "B" Craters.
(b) Front Line trenches are not damaged, but one trench dump has been destroyed.
(c) The M.G. in Beef Street was destroyed and this trench and King Street is blown in in 9 places including about 30 yards near junction with the Wynde and the Wynde including the T.M. emplacement.
(d) Hedge Row is blown in in 9 places and is impassable.

(e) Peartree Walk now impassable.
(f) About 30 yards of railway track blown up near "A" tunnel.
(g) Entrance to R.E's quarters partly blown in.
(h) Dump in King's way blown in and tank pierced.
(I) Duckboards blown up in several places.

Total Casualties.   6.   2 killed & 10 wounded - several slightly wounded and remained at duty.

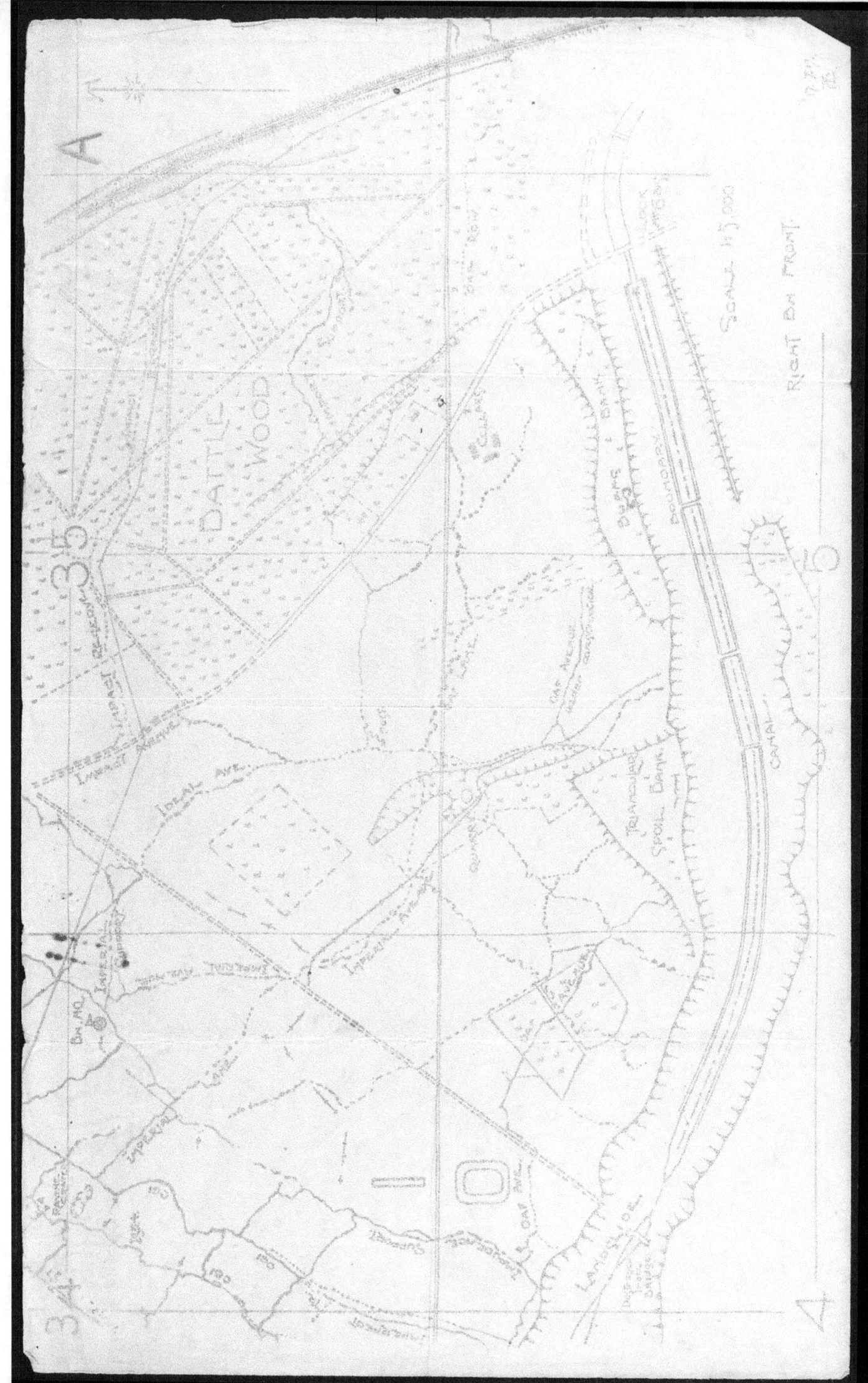

WAR DIARY
or
INTELLIGENCE SUMMARY.
(Erase heading not required.)

Army Form C. 2118.

/24th Battn London Regt.

Hour, Date, Place	Summary of Events and Information	Remarks and references to Appendices
1-6-17.	Battalion resting.	
2-6-17.	At 3.30.p.m. Battalion is inspected by Major Genl.Gorringe who afterwards presents medal ribbons to the undermentioned N.C.O's and men. The Battalion having been addressed by the Major General marched past in column of route. 720660 C.Q.M.S.Summerfield D. 720858 L/C Hills.F.H. 721956 Pte Perrons C.A. 720466 L/C Thompson A.B. 722051 Pte Neve C.M. 721629 Pte Baker A. 722939 Pte Andrews A.E. Lt.Col Hobbs D.S.O. 7th Northants dined at H.Q. Battalion Smoking Concert. 2/Lieut H.W.Fuller, 17th London Regt joined the Battalion on posting.	
3-6-17.	Voluntary Service at 6.p.m. by Capt Cohen C.F. Battalion resting. Privates S.Thresher and J.Prime awarded M.M. (Vide Corps R.O 2/Lieut Beck 17th London Regt joined the Battalion on posting	
4-6-17.	Battalion moved by march route to road junction 400x S.E. of MILLE KAPELLEKEN Fm N.E. of OUDERDOM and bivouacked until 9.p.m. later relieving 20th Bn LONDON Regt in Right Sector Canal Sub-sector THE BLUFF. Company Commanders conference at 6.p.m. Major T.O.Bury, 8 other Officers and 59 o.rs proceed to Brigade Reinforcement Camp (Mick Mack) S.E. of OUDERDOM.	
5-6-17.	2/Lieut P.W.Burroughs and 15 o.r. rejoined from leave to BOULOGNE, and reported to Brigade Reinforcement Camp. 2/Lieut H.Adams wounded. 2/Lieut J.J.Herivel proceeds to BEDFORD HOUSE as O.C. Div. Ammunition Dump. 2/Lieut H.Gover proceeds to H.13 central as O.C. Detonating Party Div.Dump. Lieut G.Dalziel takes over duties of Liaison Officer with 69th Inf.Bde.	

Army Form C. 2118.

WAR DIARY
or
INTELLIGENCE SUMMARY.
(*Erase heading not required.*)

Instructions regarding War Diaries and Intelligence Summaries are contained in F.S.Regs., Part II and the Staff Manual respectively. Title pages will be prepared in manuscript.

Hour, Date, Place	Summary of Events and Information	Remarks and references to Appendices
6-6-17.	Major T.O.Bury took over command of 142nd Brigade Reinforcement Camp. 2/Lieut P.W.Burroughs proceeds to BLUFF to replace 2/Lieut H.Adams.	
7-6-17.	At 3.10.a.m. Battalion attacks according to plan capturing and holding the four objectives allotted to it (see attached narrative).	
8-6-17.	2/Lieuts Sanders and Shields rejoin Battalion from Reinforcement Camp. R.Q.M.S. A.J.Beer awarded Meritorious Service Medal.	
9-6-17.	2/Lieut McAdam joins from an Entrenching Battalion. Major T.O.Bury rejoins Battalion from Reinforcement Camp. Battalion withdrawn from O.G. lines 1,2,3, and 4 to Support Trenches KING St, BEEF St, FIR LANE and RENNIE St in O.B. line, and was during the night and following day subjected to severe shell fire. Capt Cohen.C.F. conducted short service at graves of Capt F.Richardson and 2/Lieut S.H.Coates at CHESTER FARM CEMETERY	
10-6-17.	At 9.30.p.m. Battalion is withdrawn to SWAN CHATEAU and neighbouring trenches.	
11-6-17.	At SWAN CHATEAU.	
12-6-17.	At 10.p.m. Battalion moves by march route to rest camp near HEKSDEN.	
13-6-17.	At rest camp. Capt & Adjt L.C.Gamage M.C. rejoins from England. C.O., 2nd i/c., and several other Officers visit grave of Lieut I.W.Jones at 10th C.C.S. near HOPOUTRE. Lieut B.H.Strachan to hospital sick.	

Army Form C. 2118.

WAR DIARY
or
INTELLIGENCE SUMMARY.
(Erase heading not required.)

Instructions regarding War Diaries and Intelligence Summaries are contained in F.S. Regs., Part II. and the Staff Manual respectively. Title pages will be prepared in manuscript.

Hour, Date, Place	Summary of Events and Information	Remarks and references to Appendices
14-6-17.	At 10.15.a.m. Battalion is inspected by Brig.Genl Bailey, D.S.O. who also addressed the Battalion expressing appreciation and thanks of higher Commands for services of Battalion during recent operations. In the evening Battalion moves by march route to CAESTRE with remainder of 142nd Inf Bde en route to SERCUS. Packs of all ranks carried in motor lorries and sent direct to SERCUS. Battalion billeted in and near CAESTRE. 2/Lieut J.J.Hesivel to 10th Corps School General Course.	
15-6-17.	Battalion moves to billets in neighbourhood of SERCUS. Very hot weather.	
16-6-17.	Battalion resting. "C" Coy. "21680 L/C T.Ruel, accidentally drowned whilst bathing in a pond near his platoon billets. R.Q.M.S. A.J.Beer appointed Quartermaster with the honorary rank of Lieutenant.	
17-6-17.	Divisional Commander attends combined Drum-head Service of 21st and 24th Battalions under Capt Plumtree M.C. C.F. Body of L/C T.Ruel recovered after pond systematically dragged, and buried in Parish Church Yard SERCUS. At 7.30.p.m. Battalion moves by march route to billets in and near ST MARTIN AU LAERT for musketry.	
18-6-17.	Musketry Practices intended to be carried out by "C" and "D" Coys in afternoon cancelled owing to severe cyclone.	

WAR DIARY
or
INTELLIGENCE SUMMARY.
(Erase heading not required.)

Army Form C. 2118.

Hour, Date, Place	Summary of Events and Information	Remarks and references to Appendices
19-6-17.	On instructions of 142nd Inf Bde, Court of Enquiry assembles to inquire into circumstances attending death of L/C Ruel. President:- Major T.O.Bury. Members:- Capt L.Baseden and 2/Lieut H.Gover. "C" and "D" Coys carry out musketry practice from 12 to 3 at CORMETTE Range. "B" Coy on minature Range in quarry near ST MARTIN AU LAERT. 2/Lieuts Mitchell and Turner to England on leave.	
20-6-17.	"A" and "B" Coys at musketry at CORMETTE Range. "C" Coy on minature Range. At 3.p.m. C.O. and 2nd i/c inspect "A" and "D" Coys respectively.	
21-6-17.	"C" and "D" Coys musketry practices at CORMETTE. "A" Coy on minature Range. "B" Coy finding duties. 2/Lieut Longley rejoins from Lewis Gun Course LE TOUQUET.	
22-6-17.	Very wet weather. Musketry practices cancelled. Div.Commander and Lt.Col Greenwood (Acting Bde Commander) inspect Coys at work in billets. Lieut B.H.Strachan rejoins from hospital. Div.Follies give entertainment at 9.p.m.	
23-6-17.	C.O. writes with Military Medal ribbons to Ptes E.F.C. Watkins and W.Davey wounded in recent operations when attached to Bde H.Qrs as signallers and awarded decorations on recommendation of Brigade Commander. At 6.15.p.m. Battalion moves by march route to billets at and near SERCUS. 2/Lieut F.Morgan joins Battalion on posting. 2/Lieut C.Shields to Second Army School. (Coy Commanders-).	

WAR DIARY
or
INTELLIGENCE SUMMARY.
(Erase heading not required.)

Army Form C. 2118.

Instructions regarding War Diaries and Intelligence Summaries are contained in F.S. Regs., Part II and the Staff Manual respectively. Title pages will be prepared in manuscript.

Hour, Date, Place	Summary of Events and Information	Remarks and references to Appendices

23-6-17. ST.MARTIN AU LAERT.	The following are the Practices fired by the Battalion whilst at ST.MARTIN AU LAERT.
	   5 rounds at 200 yards. Grouping.
	  10 rounds at 200 yards. Application.
	   5 rounds at 200 yards. Snapshooting.
	   5 rounds at 300 yards. Application.
	  10 rounds at 300 yards. Rapid.
	H.P.Score.145.
	Prizes provided out of Canteen Funds as under:-
	50 Francs Best Platoon. Winners No.15 Platoon Average Score 63.68.
	20 Francs Best Individual. " 721423 L/C Lidbetter. 8 Platoon and 720807 Pte Wilson 8. 15 Platoon each with score of 110.
	Prizes of 50 Francs also given for best Platoon in each Company and 5 Francs for best individual shot in each Platoon.	

24-6-17.	Divisional Commander and Lt.Col Greenwood attend combined Drum Head Service of 21st and 24th Battalions and presents Military Cross ribbons to the undermentioned Officers. Capt W.J.Williams. Lieut G.A.Coombe and 2/Lieut H.W.Allison. The ribbons for Crosses awarded to 2/Lieut C.V.Keeble (wounded) and Capt C.Bannigan R.A.M.C. late attached to this unit handed to Lt.Col.G.E.Milner. G.O.C. also presents 18 Military Medal ribbons. Ribbons of absent N.C.O's and men handed to Lt.Col G.E.Milner. Capt C.Bannigan calls in afternoon and receives ribbon from Lt.Col.G.E.Milner.	
25-6-17.	Battalion, Company and Section Drill. Lt.Col Greenwood A/Bde Commander visits Bn when at work. 2/Lieuts G.L.Scott E.C.Nave and H.W.Fuller leave to join 1/17th Bn on re-posting. 2/Lieut H.J.Grose joins the Battalion on posting.	

WAR DIARY
or
INTELLIGENCE SUMMARY.
(Erase heading not required.)

Army Form C. 2118.

Instructions regarding War Diaries and Intelligence Summaries are contained in F.S. Regs., Part II. and the Staff Manual respectively. Title pages will be prepared in manuscript.

Hour, Date, Place	Summary of Events and Information	Remarks and references to Appendices
26-6-17.	Coys at disposal of Coy Commanders and Specialists under Specialists Officers in morning. At 2.30.p.m. Divisional Aquatic Sports and Fete near Canal at BLARINGHAM.	
27-6-17.	At 6.30.a.m. Battalion moves by march route to billets at METEREN.	
28-6-17.	At 5.15.a.m. Battalion moves by march route, destination RIDGE WOOD area E of DICKEBUSCH. Destination later altered to Trenches adjacent to VOORMEZEELE. At 3.p.m. C.O. and Coy Commanders reconnoitre trenches in vicinity of RAVINE WOOD to be taken over on relief of 26th Bn Royal Fusiliers tomorrow. Following awards notified in Brigade Orders. Military Cross. C.S.M. A.J. Baxter "B" Coy. D.C.M. Sergeant V. Avramachis. Bar to M.M. Private S. Thresher. Depot formed at ROZENHILL CAMP near La CLYTE M.6.b.6.4. (Sheet 28)	
28-6-17.	Battalion relieves 26th Bn in trenches near RAVINE WOOD. Front line. "A" Coy. Support. "C" & "D" Coys. Reserve "B" Coy.	
30-6-17.	Very wet. Major T.O. Bury attends F.G.C.M. at ROZENHILL CAMP as President.	

Lt.Col.-Cdg.
1/24th Bn. LONDON REGIMENT.
"THE QUEENS."

NARRATIVE OF ATTACK.
by 1/24th. LONDON REGIMENT, "THE QUEENS", on 7/6/1917.

Before going into the details of the actual attack, the following points are thought worthy of mention as having an important bearing in the ultimate success of the operation.

For the period of some months the battalion when holding the line always occupied the trenches from which the attack was to be made with the result that all company and platoon commanders, became thoroughly acquainted with the ground in front of them, and by areful observation of hostile barrages the most advantageous positions for the assembly of the battalion prior to the attack could be decided upon.

At EPERLECQUES & STEENVOORDE the battalion carried out training over a course laid out with flags representing as nearly as possible the position of trenches to be captured and the value of this training cannot be overestimated. One practice attack was carried out without Officers, Warrant Officers or N.C.Os. Platoon Commanders. During the period of training great care was taken not to overwork the men with the result that when they moved up the line they were in excellent heart.

Although up to this time no definite orders or instructions had been received, the objectives to be captured had been allotted and frontages and work of each company definitely fixed as shown on the attached map.

The Attack. The Battalion moved up to the trenches on the night 4/5th June and on the night of the 5/6th, June at 2.30.a.m. a fighting Patrol was sent out into the enemy front line trenches, but no signs of the enemy could be found.

The ZERO hour for the attack was fixed at 3.10.a.m. on the 7th. June and at midnight on the 6/7th. the Battalion moved forward to their position of assembly in the front line trench and CRATERS immediately north of the YPRES-COMMINES CANAL. This was a difficult and delicate operation owing the the close proximity of the enemy trenches, but largely owing to much attention hwing been paid to thispart of the work during practices it was successfully carried out without loss.

The strength of the attacking platoons averaged from twenty five to thirty and the attack was carried out on a two Comapny front distributed in four waves of two lines each as follows.-

    A Coy. two leading right waves.
    B Coy. (less 1 platoon) two leading left waves.
    C Coy. two following right waves.
    D Coy. two following left waves.

Intervals between lines intended to be 10 yards and Intervals between waves intended to be 30 yards but were in practice very much less. The Moppers Up were included in the second lines of the waves.

Definite times were laid down at which the various advances & assaults were to be made, but these were in the actual attack regulated by the artillery barrage. It was also laid down that all troops for the four abjectives should be over the parapet within four minutes after Zero. This was strictly adhered to and the companies detailed to take the third and fourth objectives reformed on the road parallel to and between the second and third objectives. The barrages being timed to allow of this being done and to cover the rally.

All troops were out of the trench immediately after the mine at Hill 60 was fired: The broken nature of the ground prevented good lines being kept, but these were always in touch with troops on the flanks and there was little or no confusion:

Our artillery barrage was so accurate that the attacking troops were able to approach within 30 or 40 yards of it and there is no doubt that this prevented hostile machine guns being brought into action: "B" Company lost their Commander, Capt: H.C.WATTS at ZERO: He was the only casualty in the Company and was undoubtedly wounded by a fragment of one of our own shells: The command of the Company then devolved on Lieut G.A.COOMBE who from that moment led the company with considerable ability: The company on reaching the second objective discovered a machine gun section about to bring their gun into action, killed the crew and captured the gun: This Company was two minutes late in capturing the first objective but then went forward with a rush and reached the second objective a minute or so before scheduled time:

A platoon of "B" Company left "A" Crater at 3.25 a.m. and proceeded up the North Bank of the Canal in order to deal with a small trench and suspected machine gun emplacement South of the Canal at O.4.b.9.1. They made their way to a point about 200 yards from their objective but were there held up by a hostile machine gun and the garrison of the tunnels in the Spoil Bank in O.4.b.6.4. They established a post there until they got touched with a platoon of "C" Company advancing on the opposite side of the canal: After this platoon had cleared the tunnels the detached platoon moved on to their objective which they consolidated being in touch with 7th Bn:Lon:Regt: on the South of the Canal who came up into line soon after: This platoon was under the command of Sgt.AVRAMACHIS and lost 16 men out of 24 in this gallant effort: 2/Lt:H:ADAMS, the officer commanding this platoon had been wounded the previous day but the success of this minor enterprise was in no way lessened through his absence: No 2 Platoon of "A" Company started from the craters under the command of Lieut:I:W:JONES R:W:F: attached, although this gallant officer knew the ground well, having continually patrolled it for months and having raided the line opposite, he could not get his platoon over the lips of the craters without 50 per cent loss and he was himself mortally wounded: It is more than probable that all these casualties were due to our barrage fire owing to the height of the lips of the craters and the Canal Bank:

"A" and "B" Companies met with little opposition:

"C" and "D" Companies moved forward passing through "A" and "B" Companies and although the waves were disorganized owing to the difficulty in maintaining direction due to darkness and smoke and the craters formed by our shelling they were successfully reorganized on the road already referred to: At 3:47 a.m. under cover of the barrage they assaulted the third and fourth objectives, the fourth objective being captured at 3:58 a.m. or one minute later than the time laid down in the instructions laid down for the attack:

No:9 Platoon commanded by 2/Lt:H:F: WETTONE sustained even heavier casualties than number two platoon of "A" Company in starting from the craters: The Officer and all section commanders becoming casualties the command of this platoon devolved on Sgt:PASHLEY after 2/Lt:WETTONE was sent back from the fourth objective which, although wounded, he had reached:

2/Lt:H:W:ALLISON there met 2/Lt:R:W:TURNER commanding respectively the leading lines of "D" and "C" Companies and after a short consultation concluded that they had reached their final objective but the conditions and confusion caused by the shelling were of such a nature that there was some doubt about it on the right: Reconnoitring patrols were pushed out as far as the Spoil Bank under 2/Lt:COATES "D" Company and Sgt: PHELPS "C" Company and fire was directed on the retreating enemy but were withdrawn later owing to our barrage fire:

Capt: W.J.WILLIAMS commanding "C" Company thoroughly grasping the situation arranged for fire to be directed on the enemy on a line with him South of The Canal where it would appear the attack had not progressed soo quickly:

Capt: RICHARDSON O.C: "D" Company on moving forward with his H.Q lost direction slightly to the left owing to the difficulty of seeing at that time and the obstacles formed by shell holes but 2/Lt:ALLISON in the fourth objective, whose iniative was conspicuous throughout the operation, immediately got into touch with the 22nd:Bn:Lon:Regt: in their fourth objective on his left:

The two Stokes guns which followed the Companies assaulting the third and fourth objectives were not brought into action, the one on the right being trained later on an enemy M:G: emplacement covering the front of the 1/23rd Lon:Regt: which passed through the 1/24th:Bn in the second phase of the attack: The left gun was similarly employed but owing to the loss of all their ammunition it could not have been used at once had it been required: The two M:Gs of the 142nd:M:G:Coy: followed close in rear of "C" and "D" Companies under the able direction of Lieut:TREGURTHA who did extraordinary good work making a personal reconnaisance of the Spoil Bank in advance of our final objective: The right gun was got into position 15 yards from the Canal in the Fourth objective: The left gun was brought into position just beyond our left flank from a spot where our front could best be covered: The N:C:O: commanding this gun shewed iniative and a good grasp of the situation:

At 3:55 a.m. Battalion H:Q: moved forward from the Bluff Tunnels and was established in a German dugout, the Adjutant being slightly wounded on the way but remaining at duty

The following incidents are Worthy of record: In addition to the M:G: previously referred to as captured by "B" Company another gun was found, the crew of which had been unable to remove the lock: They also captured a Granatenwerfer with considerable supplies of ammunition: Nos:6 and 8: platoons commanded by 2/Lts:BATCHELOR & SIEVERS captured over 40 of the enemy and number 5 Platoon commanded by Sergeant KENT killed at least 10:

On the right of the first objective a Feldwebel was captured by Sgt SPEAR "A" Company No:4 Platoon and another was taken prisoner by 2/Lt KEEBLE who was wounded at the time: This officer also shot 5 of the enemy:

Lieut:STRACHAN'S platoon captured 6 of the enemy but there seemed to be some doubt as to the number killed in this part of the line: There were probably few of the enemy:

Sgt:BAXTER "B" Company No:8 Platoon took a reconnoitring patrol to get into touch with the 22nd Lon:Regt: in their first second and third objectives and made a number of prisoners The Number is believed to be about 25:

Private A:BROOKS "B" Company No:8 Platoon went out singlehanded on his own iniative in search of a sniper who was giving much trouble and having located him stalked him from behind and shot him with a revolver: He also personally accounted for 6 prisoners:

Before "C" Company reached their third objective they opened fire on a number of the enemy who were running away, and five of the enemy including a Schwereminenwerfer Feldwebel were captured in the third objective after putting up some resistance, and the Schwereminenwerfer was captured intact close by:

-4-

Between the third and fourth objectives a machine Gun intact was captured: The gun was at once overhauled by Sgt: WEST who filled the water jacket with cocoa and got the weapon into action in the third objective at a time when a counter attack appeared imminent:

The mopping up of the tunnels was undertaken by a small party under the gallant direction of Sgt:Shadgett some 15 prisoners being captured: In this connection it may be stated that moppers up should invariably be provided with electric torces without which it is not possible to ascertain extent of dugouts:

"D" Company on the left did not encounter any enemy until passing through the third objective: 2/Lt:ALLISON personally killing four: Between the third and fourth objectives this Company in all encountered about 30 enemy retiring: They were suitably dealt with:

A Machine Gun was captured in the fourth objective but the trench had been evacuated by all the enemy capable of getting away: About 30 of the enemy were noticed on the triangular Spoil Bank which was then swept by Lewis Gun fire:

At 6 a.m. 2/Lt:COATES whilst in an exposed position was shot through the head by an enemy sniper using an ~~explosive~~ [armour piercing] bullet of which a number were subsequently found:

This officer had throughout behaved with exceeding gallantry exposing himself freely whenever he felt that his duty required him and by his cheerfulness and remarkable example inspired all ranks under his command:

Some two hours later Capt:RICHARDSON whose conduct throughout the attack and in organising the consolidation had been beyond praise was also killed by a sniper:

It was about this time that an escort of two men of the 23rdLon:Regt: were bringing back some 25 of the enemy when this sniper picked off one of the escort: The Lewis gun was immediately turned on the spot where the sniper was believed to be, namely about 80 to 100 yards away in the entrance to the tunnels on the left front in the area of the 22nd Bn:

This Company which also many of its leaders also suffered through the death of Acting Company Sergeant Major TIMON who had recently been awarded the Italian Bronze Medal for valer: This very gallant N:C:O: ~~who~~ has been out with the Battalion throughout their active operations and not missed a single engagement and his loss as one of the most capable leaders will be keenly felt:

The following day the enemy's guns commenced registering and during the frequent bombardments the garrison of the ~~kxft~~ left portion of the fourth objective suffered acute losses:

2/Lt:ALLISON then in command of "D" Company sent for 2/Lt:PERRY to come up ~~kxxkkx~~ from the third objective and was ably assisted by this officer who worked unceasingly until about 6 P.M. on the 10th June:

In view of the loss of so many of the leaders the fact that the work of consolidation and forwarding of information reflects the highest credit on those remaining and it is impossible adequately to describe the gallantry displayed by 2/Lt:ALLISON and the able and willing assistance afforded by Sgt:WREN and all other ranks of the company: As an example of the punishment which they suffered it may be recorded that one shell killed 6 men wounded 6, one man only escaping: On another occasion one or two shells in close proximity killed

/continued

— 5 —

four and wounded about 12: These were not isolated cases and it is not astonishing to know that among one or two others a senior N.C.O: of proved worth and a brave man in every sense of the word lost his reason:

On June 8th: owing to the heavy losses additional officers were brought into the line : 2/Lt:C:R:C:SHIELDS M:C: who took over the command of "D" Company was able to relieve the leaders of that company of some of the strain: From the moment he arrived this officer worked incessantly until his company was relieved: On the night of the line conditions were not so acute but the services rendered here by 2/Lt:TURNER who worked without rest throughout the whole period should be noted: This officer on the right and 2/Lt ALLISON on the left rallied a considerable number of men of other units who had become demoralized owing to the heavy shelling:

Lt. Saunders M.C. came up and re-inforced C. Coy and performed very useful work

The Battalion was relieved by three companies of the 18th London Regiment on the night of the 9th/10th June and moved back to the old British trenches where for 24 hours until move to SWAN CHATEAU they were subjected to an almost continuous bombardment by hostile artillery:

CONSOLIDATION: The work of consolidation of the third and fourth objectives was confined in the first place to making posts at intervals along the captured trench, each post having its own small dump of ammunition and bombs: These posts were firestepped and when completed, the work of linking up was commenced:

The Companies occupying the first two objectives consolidated to the extent of providing cover for the garrison by excavating the trench where blown in and the men were mainly utilised for providing, carrying and working parties to the further objectives:

GENERAL: The Battalion laid a line for communication between Battalion H.Q in the tunnels and the attacking companies: This line was one of the few which held but the value of it to the Battalion was negative through other units teeing into it: It was also used to considerable extent by F:O:Os: At one time it was disconnected at Brigade H.Q on the grounds that it was not part of the scheme of inter-communication but was eventually connected up again: The line was used to such an extent by other units that it ceased to be of much value to the Battalion

The communication between company and Battalion H.Q. was carried on by means of runners and telephone: Visual signalling although practised beforehand proved to be of little or no value owing to smoke and dust:

Some use was made of the message maps which have been issued to companies but were not of much practical value owing to the smallness of the scale:

AEROPLANES Contact aeroplanes were good but planes dropped signals with which the infantry were not acquainted namely a red and white light together and red and green lights together The Artillery officers could afford no explanation: Flares were lighted when called for by contact aeroplanes:

CARRYING PARTIES: Battalion made use of the drummers to provide carrying parties and did all its own carrying: This proved to be an excellent arrangement and the attacking companies were provided with hot tea within a few minutes of the objectives being captured: *R.S.M. H.W. NORRIS did admirable work in organizing and supervising these carrying parties.*

CASUALTIES: Total casualties sustained by the Battalion were 10 Officers and 175 other ranks and a large number of these was sustained during the period spent in the line after the attack: About 12 men were knocked out in the assembly trenches whilst waiting for their turn to advance: A few casualties were caused by shell fire between jumping off place and the second objective mainly owing to the men following very close to the barrage but after the second objective there were practically no casualties from shell fire:

ARTILLERY BARRAGE: This was excellent but one company commander reports that a number of Germans were able to run back and escape and suggests that it might be possible to take steps to prevent this occuring in future:

EQUIPMENT: The troops were equipped in a manner laid down in instructions for "Training Divisions in Offensive Action" and proved suitable:- The chain visers were universally deprecated and were not used as it is impossible to see to the chain mail in bad light and the weight of the chain if not properly fixed causes loss of balance in the helmet while if properly fixed does not allow of the rapid removal of the helmet should the respirator require to be used:

The men experienced difficulty in carrying two Mills Poms and a "P" Bomb in their pockets and in getting at the same readily: This difficulty would be overcome if tunics were used of the same pattern as those supplied to the Australian Troops:

MEDICAL ARRANGEMENTS: These were satisfactory except for the congestion in the Aid Post due to the lack of bearers to carry from there: They should have been available much earlier than they were:

Throughout, the operation was completely successful as far as this Battalion is concerned and this is largely due to the fact that every N.C.O. and man had a definite task: Maps had been carefully studied and discussed and aeroplane maps had been passed round and all had an excellent idea of the ground and places where opposition was likely to be met: N.C.O's and men were invited to raise points *there were* gone into and *this* gave the N C O's and men an increased interest:

OFFICERS. The following Officers took part in the attack:

H.Q. Lt. Col. G.E. MILLNER. M.C.
　　LIEUT. P.T. MATTHEWS. (Adjutant) Wounded at duty.
　　2/LIEUT. H.S. MITCHELL. Intelligence Officer.

'A' Coy. CAPT. L. BASEDEN. M.C.
　　2/LIEUT. C.V. KEEBLE (Wounded)
　　LIEUT. I.W. JONES. R.W.F. (attached) Died of Wounds.
　　LIEUT. B.H. STRACHAN.

'B' Coy. CAPT. H.C. WATTS. (Wounded).
　　LIEUT. G.A. COOMBE. (Wounded at duty)
　　2/LIEUT. R.F. SIEVERS.
　　2/LIEUT. E. BATCHELOR.

'C' Coy. CAPT. W.J. WILLIAMS. Royal Fus. (attached).
　　2/LIEUT. R.W. TURNER.
　　2/LIEUT. H.F. WETTONE (Wounded).

'D' Coy. CAPT. F. RICHARDSON. (Killed).
　　2/LIEUT. S.H. COATES. (Killed)
　　2/LIEUT. P.R.W. PERRY (Wounded)
　　2/LIEUT. H.W. ALLISON.

RATION OFFICER. 2/LIEUT. P.W. BURROUGHS. (Wounded)

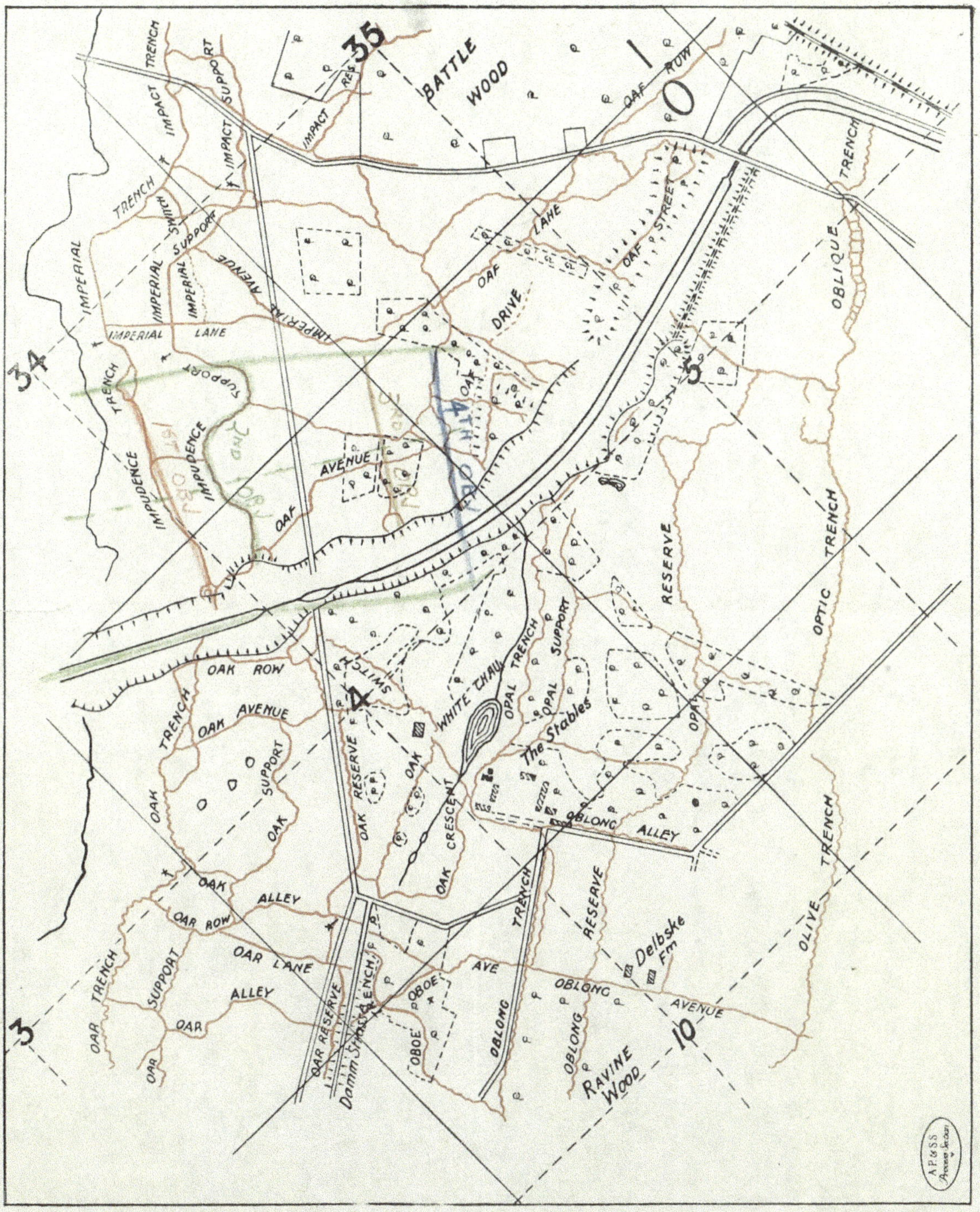

PRINTED BY No 2 ADVANCED SECTION A P & S S

.... DIVISION
.... Map reference or
          Mark on MAP on
                    Back.

1. I am at ....
2. I am at .... and am consolidating
3. I am at .... and have consolidated
4. Am held up by M.G. at ....
5. I need :- Ammunition
            Bombs
            Rifle Grenades
            Water
            Very Lights
            Stokes shells
6. Counter attack forming up at ....
7. I am in touch with .... RIGHT at ....
                                 on LEFT ....
8. I am not in touch on RIGHT ....
9. Am being shelled from ....
10. I estimate my present strength at .... rifles
11. Hostile { BATTERY
             MACHINE GUN } active at ....
             TRENCH MORTAR

Time .... m   Name ....
Date ....   Platoon ....
                     Company ....
                     Battalion ....

Army Form C. 2118.

1/24 London
Vol 2 8

WAR DIARY
or
INTELLIGENCE SUMMARY.
(Erase heading not required.)

Instructions regarding War Diaries and Intelligence Summaries are contained in F.S. Regs., Part II and the Staff Manual respectively. Title pages will be prepared in manuscript.

Hour, Date, Place	Summary of Events and Information	Remarks and references to Appendices
July 1st. SUNDAY.	During night of 30th/1st. ration party of "B" and "D" Companies caught by hostile shell fire. Casualties 3 killed and 9 wounded. "B" Company relieves "A" Company in front line. Company Commanders Conference 2.30 p.m. 2/Lieut.BECK joins 1/17th.Battn. Capt.BASEDEN and Lieut.MATTHEWS to England on leave. Strength of Battalion:- 33 officers and 832 O.Rs.	
July 2nd. MONDAY.	Staff Captain calls. Company Commanders Conference 2.30 p.m. 3 O.Rs. "B" company wounded. Considerable hostile aircraft activity at one time 16 planes over our line.	
July 3rd. TUESDAY.	Battalion relieved as under and withdrawn to OLD FRENCH TRENCH running from BOIS CONFLUENT to BUS HOUSE. H.Q. in BOIS CONFLUENT (Sheet 28 S.W. WYCHAETE):- "B" Company. Front Line by 1 company 10th.Royal Warwicks. "A" Company. Support by 1 company 8th.North Staffs. "C" Company. Reserve by 1 company 8th.North Staffs. "D" Company. withdrawn - no relief. Major BURY at F.G.O.M. ROZENHILL CAMP, LA CLYTTE.	
July 4th. WEDNESDAY.	Quiet day. H.M. THE KING and H.R.H. THE PRINCE OF WALES pass ROZENHILL CAMP in motor cars. Troops line banks on roadside and cheer. 4 O.R. wounded on working party. Company Commanders Conference 2.30 p.m.	
July 5th. THURSDAY.	No.721480 Private W.Ryan awarded Military Medal. 2/Lieuts.CARR and ARNOLD - 100 O.RS. attached to 1st.Canadian Tunnelling Company and proceed to LA CLYTTE. Company Commanders Conference 2.30 p.m.	
July 6th. FRIDAY.	BrigadeCommander calls. Company Commanders Conference 2.30 p.m. Adjutant and M.O. visit Depot in afternoon. 1 O.R. (Q.M's Groom) wounded.	

WAR DIARY
or
INTELLIGENCE SUMMARY.
(Erase heading not required.)

Army Form C. 2118.

Instructions regarding War Diaries and Intelligence Summaries are contained in F.S.Regs., Part II and the Staff Manual respectively. Title pages will be prepared in manuscript.

Hour, Date, Place	Summary of Events and Information	Remarks and references to Appendices
July 7th. SATURDAY.	O.O. and Company Commanders 15th.Battalion reconnoitre position preparatory to relief. Company Commanders Conference 2.30 p.m. O.O. and 2nd. in command visit Depot.	
July 8th. SUNDAY.	Lt. & Q.M. BEER to England on leave. Battalion relieved by 15th. Battalion and proceeds to MURRUMBIDGEE CAMP LA CLYTTE. Relief complete at 10.15 p.m. During period 3rd. to 8th. Battalion supplied daily working parties of 100 O.Rs. to R.Es for work on forward lines. A good deal of work was also carried out cleaning up ground in neighbourhood of OLD FRENCH TRENCH draining, limewashing dugouts &c.,. Party attached to 1st. Canadian Tunnelling Company relieved and proceed to MURRUMBIDGEE CAMP.	
July 9th. MONDAY.	Battalion resting. O.O. and 2nd. in command ride to WESTOUTRE in connection with arrangements for baths and afterwards to Brigade H.Q. at RENINGHELST. Capt.J.R.TRUELOVE calls and dines at H.Q.	
July 10th. TUESDAY.	Companies at disposal of Company Commanders for interior economy and 1 hour's bayonet training and physical exercises. Company Commanders Conference 12 noon. Battalion bathing. Brig.Genl.BAILEY calls.	
July 11th. WEDNESDAY.	Battalion drill and Company training. Company Commanders Conference 3.30 p.m. Riding School for officers 4 p.m. Capt.SPENCER,M.C. and Lieut.MURRAY,M.C. 1st. Canadian Tunnelling Company dine at H.Q. Lieut.ROBINSON to hospital sick. 2/Lieut.ANSELL and 2/Lieut.Millward-Oliver (17th.Battn.) report for duty.	
July 12th. THURSDAY.	Battalion drill. Company drill and rifle grenade training &c.,. Company Commanders Conference 2.30 p.m. Riding School and jumping for officers. Officers dinner.	

WAR DIARY
or
INTELLIGENCE SUMMARY.
(Erase heading not required.)

Army Form C. 2118.

Instructions regarding War Diaries and Intelligence Summaries are contained in F.S. Regs., Part II and the Staff Manual respectively. Title pages will be prepared in manuscript.

Hour, Date, Place	Summary of Events and Information	Remarks and references to Appendices
July 13th. FRIDAY.	Company Commanders Conference. Brigade Commander inspects cookhouses &c... C.O. and Adjutant dine with Capt.TRUELOVE at RENINGHELST.	
July 14th. SATURDAY.	C.O. and 4 Company Commanders reconnoitre trenches Right Canal Sector (THE BLUFF). G.O.C.,accompanied by Brigade Commander and A.A.& Q.M.G. inspect Battalion in close column of Companies and presents Military Medal ribbon to L/Cpl.PRIME. Battalion marches past in column of route. Regimental Sports in afternoon and evening, concluding with concert at which Orchestra of 1st.Entrenching Battalion performs. Capt.BASEDEN and Lieut.MATTHEWS rejoin off leave. 2/Lt.HERIVEL rejoins from Xth. Corps School.	
July 15th. SUNDAY.	DRUMHEAD service under Capt.COHEN,C.F. Battalion relieves 18th.Battalion in Right Section CANAL SUB-SECTOR THE BLUFF holding following line. (see attached map). Right Boundary YPRES COMINES CANAL near S.W.corner of TRIANGULAR SPOIL BANK, thence BUFFS BANK to BATTLE WOOD inclusive. H.Q. in concrete dugout in old German support line. Relief Complete 1.30 a.m. 2/Lieut.ALLISON,M.O. and 11 O.Rs.to Rest Camp at BOULOGNE. 2/Lieut.CARR, Lieut.STRACHAN and 2/Lieut.MORGAN to Xth.Corps School.	
July 16th. MONDAY.	Divisional Commander and Brigade Commander visit line. Quiet day. Hostile artillery active during night obtaining direct hit on Battn.H.Q. with 4.2 shell. Killing Lance corporal WELLS (Runner) and wounding Lieut.ROSS, R.F.A. (Liason officer) and 2 signallers and 1 other runner. TOTAL casualties 3 killed and 2 O.R.wounded. 2 O.RS wounded at duty.	

WAR DIARY
or
INTELLIGENCE SUMMARY.
(Erase heading not required.)

Army Form C. 2118.

Instructions regarding War Diaries and Intelligence Summaries are contained in F.S. Regs., Part II and the Staff Manual respectively. Title pages will be prepared in manuscript.

Hour, Date, Place	Summary of Events and Information	Remarks and references to Appendices
July 17th. TUESDAY.	2 platoons "C" Company BATTLE WOOD relieved by 1 platoon "D" Company and withdrawn to RAT ALLEY and adjacent trenches in old British line and old German line. At 9.50 p.m. minor operation carried out by 19th.Division and 140th.Inf.Bde. S of CANAL. Casualties 1 O.R. killed 3 O.R. wounded and 1 wounded at duty. 2 O.R. (N.Y.D.) shell shock.	
July 18th. WEDNESDAY.	O.O. and Adjutant visit forward Coys. at 11.a.m. Major Nadaud (from Base) and 2/Lieut.A.C.Shaw (from England) report at Depot. Fairly quiet day. Enemy artillery again very active during night on front, support and reserve lines. 2 platoons "B" Company in BUFFS BANK relieved by 2 platoons "A" Company. Battalion now disposed as follows:- "A" Company. 3 platoons in TRIANGULAR SPOIL BANK and 1 platoon in STRONG POINT in IDEAL AVENUE C.T. "B" Company. Right Support Company in IMPERIAL SUPPORT and BLUFF TUNNELS. "C" Company. Left Support Company. 1 platoon IMPERIAL SUPPORT near Battn.H.Q., and 3 platoons in RAT ALLEY. "D" Company. BATTLE WOOD.	
July 19th. THURSDAY.	Fairly quiet day. 2nd.Lieut.Milward-Oliver, 17th.Bn, (attached) to hospital N.Y.D.(Not yet diagnosed). O.O.visits Bde.H.Q. and H.Q. 23rd. Battn. (in support). Intermittent hostile shell fire during night more particularly on trenches held by "D" Company in BATTLE WOOD. 2nd.Lieut.POLL reports at Depot on joining Battn.	
July 20th. FRIDAY.	Adjutant and Company Commanders 23rd.Battn. reconnoitre position preparatory to relief. Fairly quiet day. During night hostile bombardment of positions in rear of Battn front including shells emitting new sneezing gas which affected H.Q. and	

WAR DIARY or INTELLIGENCE SUMMARY.

(Erase heading not required.)

Army Form C. 2118.

Hour, Date, Place	Summary of Events and Information	Remarks and references to Appendices
July 20th. FRIDAY. (continued)	support and reserve companies. 3 O.R. "D" Company wounded. Lt. & Q.M. BEER rejoins off leave.	
July 21st. SATURDAY.	Lieut. BATCHELOR to England on leave. Major of R.E. calls. Battn. relieved by 23rd Battn. and withdraws to support disposed as follows:- "B" Company BLUFF TUNNELS - remainder of Battn. in trenches in OLD British Line extending from BLUFF Craters to RAVINE. H.Q. in RAVINE WOOD about 400 yds. S.W. of VERBRANDENMOLEN. During night gas shells again used by enemy. Casualties:- 2 O.R. N.Y.D.N.	
July 22nd. SUNDAY.	Brigade Commander and Brigade Major call.	
July 23rd. MONDAY.	O.Os and other officers of 10th.Bn.Royal West Kents and Durham Light Infantry reconnoitre previous to relief. 2nd.Lieuts.MITCHELL and MATTHEWS accompany O.Os of 21st.K.R.R.C. and D.L.I. reconnoitring forward lines previous to relief. Gas shells again used by enemy during night. 2nd.Lieut.CAZEAUX rejoins from hospital.	
July 26th. WEDNESDAY.	Wet day. Battalion relieved by three Companies of three different Battalions 41st.Division, and on relief moves to ASCOT CAMP N.W. of WESTOUTRE. The tour in the trenches was notable in that the precise position of the enemy on our front was never definitely located although patrols were sent out nightly. There was very little machine gun or rifle fire directed at our positions. Hostile shell fire was at times very severe especially on our positions in BATTLE WOOD held by "D" Company (Capt.DALZIEL). By judicious thinning of his line by this officer his casualties were lessened. The new gas shells used by the enemy chiefly during the hours of darkness, although not causing any fatal casualties, were at times serious and caused considerable	

WAR DIARY
or
INTELLIGENCE SUMMARY.
(Erase heading not required.)

Army Form C. 2118.

Hour, Date, Place	Summary of Events and Information	Remarks and references to Appendices
July 25th. WEDNESDAY. (Continued)	annoyance producing violent fits of sneezing and also sickness. During the period spent in support working parties of not less than 200 O.R. were supplied nightly to R.Es and 175th. TUNNELLING COMPANY.	
July 26th. THURSDAY.	Battalion resting. Brigade Commander and Staff Captain visit Camp in afternoon. 2nd.Lieut.SHIELDS,M.O. rejoins off Second Army School.	
July 27th. FRIDAY.	Major Genl. GORRINGE accompanied by Brigade Commander visit the Camp. Battalion Parade. Promulgation of sentence of F.G.C.M. on Private WEBSTER, C.O. 2nd. in command and other officers attend Divisional Train Sports near RENINGHELST., C.O. and 2nd. in command taking part in jumping competition. Major NADAUD posted to command of "B" Company. The following officers proceed to England on leave:- Capt. COOMBE,M.C. - 2/Lieut.CATTELL - 2/Lieut.SANDERS, M.C. - 2/Lieut.GOVER - 2/Lieut.McADAM - 2/Lieut.WALKER.	
July 28th. SATURDAY.	Battalion bathing at WESTOUTRE. Companies carry out physical Training and bayonet fighting practice. Riding School for officers. R.S.M.NORRIS returns off leave.	
July 29th. SUNDAY.	Drumhead service of 23rd, and 24th.Battns. interfered with by heavy rainstorm. Lt.Col.MILLNER proceeds to England on leave.	
July 30th. MONDAY.	Very wet. 2nd.Lieut. ALLISON,M.C. and 14 O.R. rejoin from Rest Camp near BOULOGNE. Battalion parade and Company training.	
July 31st. TUESDAY.	Brigade Commander presents Bar to Military Medal to L/Cpl.THRESHER "D" Company and afterwards inspects First Line Transport and Cookhouses in connection with Divisional Competition. Lecture on Bombs by 2nd.Lieut.REEVES, Brigade Bombing officer	

Army Form C. 2118.

WAR DIARY
or
INTELLIGENCE SUMMARY.
(Erase heading not required.)

Instructions regarding War Diaries and Intelligence Summaries are contained in F.S. Regs., Part II. and the Staff Manual respectively. Title pages will be prepared in manuscript.

Hour, Date, Place	Summary of Events and Information	Remarks and references to Appendices
July 31st. TUESDAY.	at 2.30 p.m. Company and Specialist training. Boxing Competition in evening. Capt. BANNIGAN, M.O. R.A.M.C. rejoins vice Capt. T.A. TOWNSEND, M.O. to 4th.London Field Ambulance. Strength of Battalion:- 34 Officers and 791 O.RS.	

T. Sweetbury
Major O.C.,
1/24th.Battalion Lon.Regt.,
"THE QUEENS"

Army Form C. 2118.

WAR DIARY
or
INTELLIGENCE SUMMARY.
(Erase heading not required.)

1/24th B. London Reg.

Instructions regarding War Diaries and Intelligence Summaries are contained in F.S. Regs., Part II. and the Staff Manual respectively. Title pages will be prepared in manuscript.

Hour, Date, Place	Summary of Events and Information	Remarks and references to Appendices
August 1st, 1917.	Very wet. Parades cancelled. Greatcoats fumigated at Laundry. WESTOUTRE. C.O. receives Extract from Routine Orders of Lewis Gun School, BOULOGNE containing congratulatory order by Inspector General, L.O.G., with reference to courageous act of 2nd. Lieut. R.C. LONGLEY, and other officers in rescuing two ladies from drowning on the 17th, June 1917. Lieut. B.H. Straachan rejoins from Xth. Corps School.	
August 2nd.	Weather cold and wet. Corps Commander and Brigade Commander make informal Inspection of Camp. 2nd. Lieut. R.C. Longley proceeds to Veterinary Course at BOULOGNE. 2nd. Lieut. A.E. Ansell to Xth. Corps School. 2nd. Lieut. E. Batchelor rejoins from leave.	
August 3rd.	Demonstration of Daylight Sapping at CONQUEROR CAMP to Officers and N.C.Os.	
August 4th.	2nd. Lieut. R.F. Stevens rejoins from leave. Major Bury, Major Nedand and Capt. Baseden attend lecture on T.G.M. by D.A.G., 2nd. Army at RENINGHELST. Bombing practice by Bombing Sections carried out at Brigade School.	
August 5th.	Combined Divarhead Service, 23rd. & 24th. Batts. - Capt. Cohen, C.F. 2nd. Lieut. R.W. Turner returns from Course.	
August 6th.	Companies carry out miniature range practice at Brigade School. Officers' riding class.	
August 7th.	Bn. parade and Company training. Major T.C. Bury and 2nd. Lieut. H.S. Mitchell attend Conference of C.Os. and Intelligence Officers at RENINGHELST. Staff Captain calls. Concert in evening. Massed Drums of 23rd. and 24th. Battns. play at Tattoo.	

Army Form C. 2118.

WAR DIARY
or
INTELLIGENCE SUMMARY.
(Erase heading not required.)

Instructions regarding War Diaries and Intelligence Summaries are contained in F.S. Regs., Part II and the Staff Manual respectively. Title pages will be prepared in manuscript.

Hour, Date, Place	Summary of Events and Information	Remarks and references to Appendices
August 8th.	Battalion Parade and Company Training. First Line Transport leaves for WALLON CAPEL en route to ACQUIN. 2nd. Lieuts. Sanders, Gover, Cattoll and McAdam rejoin off leave.	
August 9th.	At 11 a.m. Battalion leaves ASCOT CAMP and moves by march route to ACQUIN. Battalion marching past General H.Q. Plumer, Army Commander en route. At ARNEKE, Battalion entrains for ST. OMER, arriving 5 p.m. and marching thence to billets at ACQUIN arriving 9 p.m. Capt. G. A. Coombe rejoins off leave. 2nd. Lieuts. Allison & Shields to England on leave.	
August 10th.	Platoon Training from 2 to 5 p.m. Brigadier General Bailey and Staff Captain call. Lt. Col. G. E. Milner, M.C. rejoins off leave.	
August 11th.	Platoon Training 8.30 a.m. – 12.30 p.m. O.C. and 2nd. in Command visit Brigade H.Q. at BOISINGHEM.	
August 12th.	Wet weather. Church Parade cancelled. Officers' riding school in evening. 2nd. Lieut. Longley rejoins from A.V. Course. Capt. L. Basedon, M.C. and 9 O.Rs. proceed to Rest Camp near BOULOGNE. Capt. W. J. Williams, M.C., proceeds to 2nd. Army Company Comm anders' Course.	
August 13th.	Companies march to Rifle Range, MOULLE and fire following practices:— 200 yards 5 rounds application & 5 rounds rapid. 300 yards 5 rounds application, 5 rounds rapid & 5 rounds snapshooting. 2/Lieut. S. H. Walker, rejoins off leave.	

Army Form C. 2118.

WAR DIARY
or
INTELLIGENCE SUMMARY.
(Erase heading not required.)

Instructions regarding War Diaries and Intelligence Summaries are contained in F.S. Regs., Part II and the Staff Manual respectively. Title pages will be prepared in manuscript.

Hour, Date, Place	Summary of Events and Information	Remarks and references to Appendices
August 14th.	Platoon Training in morning. At 5.30.p.m. Battalion is inspected in MASS by General Plumer afterwards marching past in column of route.	
August 15th.	Wet weather. Indoor Training and Interior economy. Brigadier General Bailey, Brigade Major & Staff Captain dine at Battalion H.Q.	
August 16th.	2/Lieut. A.C.S.Bean and 8 O.Rs. join Battalion.	
August 17th.	At 1.p.m. Battalion moves by march route to WIZERNES and entrains for OUDERDOM arriving 1.a.m. marching thence to Dominion Camp.	
August 18th.	Battalion resting.	
August 19th.	At 8.p.m. Battalion marches to Billets in Ramparts of YPRES, taking over from 2nd. Scottish Rifles and 2nd. East Lancashire Regiment. H.Q. at LILLE GATE. 2nd. Lieut. M.Cover proceeds to Xth. Corps School.	
August 20th.	Brigadier General calls. Forward Tracks reconnoitred by Officers.	
August 21st.	Major General Gorringe and Brigade Commander call and Inspect Billets. During night 21/22nd. carrying party under 2/Lt. R.F.Sievers, B Coy. who had been ordered to carry S.A.A. at all costs to neighbourhood of BELLEWARDE RIDGE succeeded inspite of very severe hostile barrage of H.E. and Gas Shells. CASUALTIES:- 1 Officer (2nd. Lieut. R.F.Sievers) and 33 O.Rs. "B" Coy., wounded gas and 2 O.Rs. wounded	
August 22nd.	QUIET day. 2nd. Lieut. C.P.O.Shields,M.C. rejoins off leave. 2nd.Lieut. A.C.S.Bean to hospital sick.	

Army Form C. 2118.

WAR DIARY
or
INTELLIGENCE SUMMARY.
(Erase heading not required.)

Instructions regarding War Diaries and Intelligence Summaries are contained in F.S. Regs., Part II and the Staff Manual respectively. Title pages will be prepared in manuscript.

Hour, Date, Place	Summary of Events and Information	Remarks and references to Appendices
August 23rd.	At 5.30.a.m., C.O., I.O., and Company Commanders reconnoitre forward Trenches preliminary to relief.	
August 24th.	2/Lieut. H.W. Allison, M.O., rejoins off leave. During night 24/25th. Battalion relieves 20th. Battalion holding front line trenches N. & N. of WESTHOEK. DISPOSITIONS:- Right front:- C Coy. plus 2 L.Gs. D.Coy. Left front:- B Coy. plus 3 L.Gs. A.Coy. Right Support:- D Coy. less 2 L.Gs. Left Support:- A Coy. less 3 L.Gs. H.Q. near cross roads 500 yards N.W. by N. of WESTHOEK. Prior to relief on instructions of Brigade Commander, Platoons in each Company reduced to 3 in number. The following Platoons are temporarily broken up and Platoon Sergeants and Section Commanders returned to Depot:- Nos. 3, 5, 9, 13. Battalion stands to in afternoon, enemy reported massing in NONNEN BOSCHEN WOOD.	
August 25th.	C.S.O., I, and Brigade Commander calls H.Q. dug-out hit by shell - 2 O.Rs. wounded. Major Love, R.E's. calls. Artillery fire at 11.p.m. lasts about 90 minutes to cover advance some 1500 yards to the North. Casualties 5 killed 14 wounded.	
August 26th.	Hostile Artillery active 3.45.a.m. and 5.a.m. Quiet later. One of the enemy surrenders in afternoon to B.Coy. (A Belgian who had been compelled to join) and another in evening (a Prussian who had lost his way from enemy's front line posts when fetching coffee). Brigade Major and Staff Captain call.	

Army Form C. 2118.

WAR DIARY
or
INTELLIGENCE SUMMARY.
(Erase heading not required.)

Instructions regarding War Diaries and Intelligence Summaries are contained in F.S. Regs., Part II and the Staff Manual respectively. Title pages will be prepared in manuscript.

Hour, Date, Place	Summary of Events and Information	Remarks and references to Appendices
August 27th.	Commanding Officers 2nd. Wilts. and another Battalion and their Brigade Commander call and discuss situation in view of future operations. Our artillery active at 12.55.p.m. Very wet day. Great difficulty getting up rations. S.O.S. put up by 8th. London Regt. on our right. 2nd. Lieut. L.P. Arnold and 1 O.R. wounded and 2 N.Y.D.N.	
August 28th.	At 1.a.m. Staff Captain calls regarding rations which he personally saw delivered and which reached Bn. H.Q. just before dawn, carrying party out 12 hours. After dawn reconnoitring party 23rd. Battalion call. G.S.O. 2. and G.S.O. for Intelligence 47th. Division call. Quiet day. Relieved by 23rd. Battalion and move to Tunnels in Railway Wood. While awaiting relief C Coy. H.Q. in front line raided by a platoon of 8th. London Regiment. Reason obviously due to absolute impossibility of moving in or out after bad weather on ground out up by shell fire. Fortunately no casualties owing to most of attacking party being stuck in mud and the Officer having slipped and his revolver useless through mud. Relief complete 1.a.m. Casualties:- 1 killed, 14 O.Rs. wounded and 1 died of wounds.	
August 29th.	Resting and cleaning up. Staff Captain calls.	
August 30th.	Major General and Brigade Commander call also Brigade Major and Lieut. R.C. Longley to hospital sick.	
August 31st.	Quiet day. Brigade Commander calls in evening.	

Lieut. Col. O.G.
1/24th. Bn. Lon. Regt. "THE QUEENS".

Army Form C. 2118.

WAR DIARY
or
INTELLIGENCE SUMMARY.
(Erase heading not required.)

Instructions regarding War Diaries and Intelligence Summaries are contained in F.S. Regs., Part II and the Staff Manual respectively. Title pages will be prepared in manuscript.

Hour, Date, Place	Summary of Events and Information	Remarks and references to Appendices
Saturday, Sept.1.1917.	Relieved by 1/4th Bn.East Lancs and move to SWAN CHATEAU.	
" 2. "	At 2.p.m. Battalion moves to DEVONSHIRE LINES near RENINGHELST. Bombed at night. Major H.L.T.B.Nadaud rejoins off leave. Bombed at night.	
" 3. "	Cleaning up and work on clearing camp.	
" 4. "	Divisional and Brigade Commanders visit Camp.	
" 5. "	Major T.O.Bury to England on leave. Battalion moves to STEENVOORDE area. Good billets for men, poor for Officers.	
" 6. "	Company training 2½ hours. Brigade Commander calls during afternoon.	
" 7. "	Conference at Brigade H.Q. in morning. Company training 2½ hours. 720989 Cpl J.C.Cantle and 722400 Private P.Hopkins awarded Military Medal.	
" 8. "	Company training 2½ hours. 2/Lieut R.F.Sievers awarded Military Cross. D Company Supper and Concert., 2/Lieut G.C. Heathcote reports for duty.	
" 9. "	Church Parade 9.a.m. following which Brigade Commander presents ribbons for recently awarded Military Cross and Military Medals. 120 other ranks proceed by Motor Bus to DEN GRONEN JAGER CABARET for work on Trench Tramways.	
" 10. "	Battalion proceeds by Motor Busses to VLAMERTINGHE and relieves 11th Cheshires (25th Div) near DICKEBUSCH. Brigade Commander calls also Lt.Col.Turner G.S.O.1.	

Army Form C. 2118.

WAR DIARY
or
INTELLIGENCE SUMMARY.
(Erase heading not required.)

Instructions regarding War Diaries and Intelligence Summaries are contained in F.S. Regs., Part II. and the Staff Manual respectively. Title pages will be prepared in manuscript.

Hour, Date, Place	Summary of Events and Information	Remarks and references to Appendices
Tuesday, Sept. 11.1917.	Men work on improving Camp. Capt F.Gordon Gill joins Battalion and takes over duties of Lewis Gun Officer.	
Wednesday, " 12.1917.	Brigade Commander calls. Inspection of horses by Divisional Commander during afternoon. 2/Lt. LONGLEY rejoins from hospital. Work on improving Camp and Physical Training and Bayonet Fighting.	
Thursday, " 13.1917.	Brigade Commander and Staff Captain call and inspect Leave and other Battalion Rosters. Brigadier congratulates Adjutant on his card index system. Working Party on French Tramways reported to be working exceedingly well. Battalion wins first round Transport Competition.	
Friday, " 14.1917.	C.O. at Brigade H.Q. and discusses proposed Scheme for transferring suitable officers to units requiring competent Seconds in Command and Company Commanders. Adjutants of 21st. and 23rd. Battalions London Regt., call to see Battalion system of keeping records. Furnished working party of 100 O.R. to bury cable. Casualties 35 wounded Gas 3 O.R.Killed.	
Saturday, " 15.1917.	2nd/Lieuts. SIEVERS AND CAZEAUX to hospital as gas casualties. Furnished further working party of 100 O.R. 2 wounded.	
Sunday " 16.1917.	Battalion is relieved and moves to CONNAUGHT CAMP near REMY SIDING, taking over from 11th. Canadians. 11 additional casualties to hospital as result of gas on 14th. instant.	
Monday. " 17.1917.	Company Training. Brigade Commanders calls. Divisional "Follies" perform. Major BURY returns off leave.	
Tuesday. " 18.1917.	Battalion moves by march route to billets in neighbourhood of TERDEGHEM. Billetted in farms and tents over wide area.	

Army Form C. 2118.

WAR DIARY
or
INTELLIGENCE SUMMARY.
(Erase heading not required.)

Instructions regarding War Diaries and Intelligence Summaries are contained in F.S. Regs., Part II. and the Staff Manual respectively. Title pages will be prepared in manuscript.

Hour, Date, Place	Summary of Events and Information	Remarks and references to Appendices
Wednesday. Sept.19.1917.	Brigade Commander and Staff Captain call. 2nd.Lieuts.LONGLEY and CARR to England on leave. Major BURY and Capt.COOMBE attend first meeting of Brigade Sports Committee.	
" 20.1917. Thursday.	Major BURY President F.G.C.M. at H.Q. 23rd.Battalion London Regt near STEENVOORDE.	
" 21.1917. Friday.	Major BURY President F.G.C.M. at H.Q.22nd.Battalion London Regt.	
" 22.1917. Saturday.	At 4.30 a.m. Battalion leaves Camp and moves by march route to BAVINCHOVE and at 9.21 entrains for MAROEUIL arriving 2.35 p.m. and proceeding thence by tramway to Camp between ROCLINCOURT and ECURIE.	
" 23.1917. Sunday.	Combined Drumhead service with 23rd.Battalion. C.O., Intelligence Officer and Company Commanders reconnoitre front line trenches S.of OPPY WOOD preparatory to relief.	
" 24.1917. Monday.	Relieved, by day, 7th.Royal Fusiliers,63rd.Division in front line trenches on a front of approximately 1200 yards S.of OPPY WOOD. Dispositions:- Right Front and Immediate Support "C" Coy. Centre "B" Coy. Left Front and Immediate Support "D" Coy. Support "A" Coy. Brigade Commander and Staff Captain also Major WATSON R.F.A. C/317 Battery call. Very quiet night.	
" 25.1917. Tuesday.	Quiet day. Brigade Commander calls. Company Commanders' Conference 10.30 a.m. Brigade Commander calls during afternoon also Capt. THORNTON R.F.A. B/317 Battery and Capt.SMITH R.F.A. D/317. Capt. COOMBE M.C. leaves for duty as an Instructor at XIIIth.Corps School. Casualties 1 O.R. wounded. Capt.DALZIEL rejoins from leave.	

(73989) W4141—463. 400,000. 9/14. H.&J.Ltd. Forms/C. 2118/10.

Army Form C. 2118.

WAR DIARY
or
INTELLIGENCE SUMMARY.
(Erase heading not required.)

Instructions regarding War Diaries and Intelligence Summaries are contained in F.S.Regs., Part II and the Staff Manual respectively. Title pages will be prepared in manuscript.

Hour, Date, Place	Summary of Events and Information	Remarks and references to Appendices
Wednesday. Sept.26.1917.	O.O. attends Conference at Brigade H.Q. and inspects trenches E. of GAVRELLE from O.P. 2nd.Lieut.BATCHELOR and 1 O.R. killed by Trench Mortar Bomb falling in trench. 2 officers and 4 O.R. 21st.London Regt on working party, wounded at the same time. 2/1Lieut.MORGAN proceeds to England on leave.	
Thursday " 27.1917.	Quiet day. Hostile aircraft active in evening.	
Friday " 28.1917.	Capt.TOLLERTON, Commanding 21st London Regt calls. Divisional Commander and Brigade Commander call. Company Commanders' Conference. "A" Company relieves "D" Company.	
Saturday " 29.1917.	Capt.DALZIEL leaves for 1st.Army Company Commanders' School, BOULOGNE. Company Commanders' Conference. Quiet day. Staff Captain calls.	
Sunday " 30.1917.	Quiet day except for some trench mortar activity on "B" Coy.front. Major HARGREAVES and Capt.BRETT, 23rd.London Regt reconnoitre line preparatory to relief. Major HYSLOP Commanding 21st.London Regt.calls.	

Lieut.Col.Cdg.,
1/24th. Battalion London Regiment,
"THE QUEENS".

Army Form C. 2118.

WAR DIARY
or
INTELLIGENCE SUMMARY.
(Erase heading not required.)

Instructions regarding War Diaries and Intelligence Summaries are contained in F. S. Regs., Part II. and the Staff Manual respectively. Title pages will be prepared in manuscript.

2/4th London Regt.

Vol 31

Place	Date	Hour	Summary of Events and Information	Remarks and references to Appendices
OCTOBER.				
	Monday 1st.		2/Lt.GROSE proceeded to England on leave. Trenches in neighbourhood of Bn.H.Q. shelled with 5.9's and 4.2's from 10.30 a.m. to 12 noon. No casualties. Cpl.LeGrove "C" Coy.hit by sniper and dies of wounds. This very excellent N.C.O. had seen 28 months active service and been wounded three times. His death was a great loss.	
	Tuesday 2nd.		Capt.GAMAGE,M.O. to England on leave. Relieved by 23rd.Bn.London Regiment and move to shelters and dugouts 600 yards S.W. of village of BAILLEUL. Relief carried out by daylight.	
	Wednesday 3rd.		Col.MILLNER,M.C. and I.O. reconnoitre trenches E.& S.E. of GAVRELLE in connection with proposed future/operations. Brig.Genl.BAILEY calls in afternoon.2/Lt.CARR returns from leave. Lt.HEATHCOTE wounded at duty on working party.	
	Thursday 4th.		2nd. i/c and Company Commanders reconnoitre trenches E. & S.E. of GAVRELLE. Lt.STRACHAN rejoins from Lewis Gun Course.	
	Friday 5th.		2/Lt.MILLER to XIIIth.Corps School. Capt.LONGLEY rejoins from leave. Brig.Genl.BAILEY calls in afternoon. C.O. and 2nd. i/c attend short Memorial Service at dark at graveside of the late Lieut.BATCHELOR conducted by Capt.MARSHALL,C.F. Major BICKFORD C.F. calls.	
	Saturday 6th.		Quiet day.	

Army Form C. 2118.

WAR DIARY
or
INTELLIGENCE SUMMARY.
(Erase heading not required.)

Instructions regarding War Diaries and Intelligence Summaries are contained in F. S. Regs., Part II. and the Staff Manual respectively. Title pages will be prepared in manuscript.

Place	Date	Hour	Summary of Events and Information	Remarks and references to Appendices
	OCTOBER. (continued)			
	Sunday 7th.		Capt. LONGLEY proceeded to ~~Veterinary~~ Transport Course at Divisional Train H.Q. Voluntary R.C. & C.E. Services near Bn.H.Q. 40 O.Rs. proceed to Corps Reinforcement Camp for Musketry Instruction.	
	Monday 8th.		Capt. BASEDEN,M.C., Lieut.SANDERS,M.C. and Lieut. CATTELL ordered to England for 6 months home service in connection with scheme for resting war worn officers. Capt.W.J.WILLIAMS,M.C. proceeds to England on leave. Capt.GILL assumes Command of 'A' Company.	
	Tuesday 9th.		Lt.Col.Mildren and Adjutant call reconnoitring preparatory to relief. Lt. MITCHELL proceeds to England on leave. Capt.BASEDEN,M.C. and Lieut.SANDERS,M.C. proceed to England. 2/Lt. MORGAN rejoins from leave.	
	Wednesday 10th.		Battn. relieved by 6th.Bn.Lon.Regt. and move to WAKEFIELD CAMP near ROCLINCOURT. During period spent in Reserve, Battn. provided daily 2 working parties of 1 Officer and 40 O.Rs., 2 Officers and 30 O.Rs. on construction of forward posts, laying pipe lines in forward area. Also pushing parties for rations & R.E. material and a few men on salvage. All other available men employed on cleaning out and making accommodation in old German tunnels in RAILWAY CUTTING.	

Army Form C. 2118.

WAR DIARY
or
INTELLIGENCE SUMMARY.
(Erase heading not required.)

Instructions regarding War Diaries and Intelligence Summaries are contained in F. S. Regs., Part II. and the Staff Manual respectively. Title pages will be prepared in manuscript.

Place	Date	Hour	Summary of Events and Information	Remarks and references to Appendices
OCTOBER. (continued)	Thursday 11th.		Resting and cleaning up. C Company supply Platoon for Guard Duties at Divisional H.Q. under 2/Lt.POLL. Lt.Col.MILLNER,M.C., President of Court of Enquiry at Chinese Labour Company Camp at MAROEUIL. Official notification received from Director of P.S.W.O. that Capt. LONGLEY awarded Bronze Medal, Royal Humane Society for assisting to save two French Nursing Sisters from drowning at PARIS PLAGE on 17th.June 1917.	
	FRIDAY 12th.		Lt.Col.MILLNER,M.C., at Court of Enquiry, MAROEUIL. Major WILKINSON, M.C., C.F., Senior Chaplain calls.	
	Saturday 13th.		Major General GORRINGE inspects new horse standings. Lt.Col.MILLNER,M.C., at Court of Enquiry, MAROEUIL. Capt. SAUMAREZ acting Brigade Major calls. Battn. provides working party of 200 for work burying cable, W. of GAVRELLE. Capt. GAMAGE,M.C. returns off leave.	
	Sunday 14th.		Divine Service at Divisional Cinema, ROCLINCOURT under Capt. MUNRO. Brigadier General BATLEY presents bar to Military Medal to Corporal SHOWELL and Lance Corporal JARMAN. Lt.Col.MILLNER,M.C. at Court of Enquiry at MAROEUIL.	
	Monday 15th.		Lt.Col.MILLNER,M.C. at Court of Enquiry at MAROEUIL. Lt.MATTHEWS to England on leave. Lt.McADAM rejoins from Course.	

Army Form C. 2118.

WAR DIARY
or
INTELLIGENCE SUMMARY.
(Erase heading not required.)

Place	Date	Hour	Summary of Events and Information	Remarks and references to Appendices
	OCTOBER.(continued)			
	Tuesday 16th.		Practice combined attack with 23rd.Bn. over flagged course representing trenches E of GAVRELLE attended by G.O.C.,Corps,Division and two General Officers U.S.A.Army. Lt.Col.MILLNER,M.C. engaged on work of Court of Enquiry. 2/Lt.POLL to England on leave.	
	Wednesday.17th.		Practice combined attack with 23rd.Bn. Major BURY & reconnoitring party reconnoitre trenches E of GAVRELLE preparatory to relief. Brig.Gen. calls in afternoon.Capt.SAVILE joins for duty and is posted to A Coy.	
	Thursday 18th.		Relieve 20th.Bn.Lon.Regt. in trenches E.& S.E. of GAVRELLE. Dispositions:- Right Front A Coy. Left Front, B Coy., Support, C.Coy., Reserve, D Coy. Relief complete at 1.40.p.m. C.O. & 2nd. i/c visit line in afternoon. Col. TURNER G.S.O.1., calls.	
	Friday 19th.		Quiet day. Lt.Col.FASSETT,G.S. 31st.Div.and Capt.MCCUNNIFFE, A de C. to G.O.C. 31st. Division U.S.A. Army spend the night at H.Q. making a tour of the line at midnight with Major BURY. Brig.Gen.BAILEY calls also Capt. SAUMAREZ, acting/ Brigade Major calls. Also Major HARGREAVES 23rd. Bn. 1 Company 21st. Bn. billeted in NAVAL TRENCH for work in forward posts.	
	Saturday 20th.		Brig.Gen.BAILEY calls. Lt. JONES, R.G.E. calls with reference to wire cutting to-morrow.	

Army Form C. 2118.

WAR DIARY
or
INTELLIGENCE SUMMARY.
(Erase heading not required.)

Instructions regarding War Diaries and Intelligence Summaries are contained in F.S. Regs., Part II. and the Staff Manual respectively. Title pages will be prepared in manuscript.

Place	Date	Hour	Summary of Events and Information	Remarks and references to Appendices
OCTOBER. (continued)				
	Sunday 21st.		Lt. BAILEY joins for duty, posted to C Coy. Wire cutting by 6 inch Howitzers commenced. Capt.W.J.WILLIAMS, M.O. & Lt.H.S.MITCHELL rejoin off leave. Lt.BAILEY reports for duty.	
	Monday 22nd.		Brigadier General BAILEY calls.	
	Tuesday 23rd.		Major HARGREAVES calls.	
	Wednesday 24th.		MAJOR HATFIELD, R.F.A. calls. Artillery strafe by the Division on our right. Enemy retaliate with 7.7.m.m. and T.M. on our front and support lines. During night 140th. Inf. Bde. on our left carry out minor operation. Also Bde. on right. Casualties 2 O.Rs.wounded. Lt. TURNER to England on leave.	
	Thursday 25th.		Major LOVE, R.E. calls. Practice assembly carried out by A & B Companies for forthcoming minor operation.	
	Friday 26th.		Relieved by 23rd. Bn. and move into Support Trenches W. and S.W. of GAVRELLE. Lt. ANSELL proceeds to join R.F.C.	
	Saturday 27th.		Brigadier General and Staff Captain call.	
	Sunday 28th.		Brigadier General ERSKINE Cdg. 47th. Division, Brigadier General BAILEY and Col.TURNER,G.S.O.1. call also Lt. Hope, T.M. Battery. 2/Lt. KING, American Army reports for attachment to H.Q. for instruction for 3 days.	

Army Form C. 2118.

WAR DIARY
or
INTELLIGENCE SUMMARY.
(Erase heading not required.)

Instructions regarding War Diaries and Intelligence Summaries are contained in F.S. Regs., Part II. and the Staff Manual respectively. Title pages will be prepared in manuscript.

Place	Date	Hour	Summary of Events and Information	Remarks and references to Appendices
	OCTOBER. (continued)			
	Monday 29th.		Lt. LINDSAY, R.A.M.C. relieves Capt. BANNIGAN, M.C. proceeding on leave. Lt.Col.ALLEN, R.F.A., Commanding Artillery Group calls.	
	Tuesday 30th.		Relieved by 22nd. Bn. A & B Companies move to billets at ECURIE; also Lt.Col.MILLNER,M.C. and Adjutant. C Coy. moves into Support Line, right front and D Coy. to NAVAL TRENCH, Reserve Company. Front line being held by 2 Coys. 23rd. Bn. Major Murr relieves Command of sector with Captain WILLIAMS as Adjutant.	
	Wednesday 31st.		2/Lt. TAGGART, Corps Signals also Lt.Col.MCMILLAN, R.A.M.C. call. Wire cutting by 6 inch howitzers and 4.5 howitzers and T.Ms. Major HATFIELD, D.S.O., R.F.A. calls; also Capt. C.G.DAVIES, M.C. 142nd. M.G.Company.	

M.R. Millner

Lieut.Col.Cdg.,

1/24th.Battalion London Regiment,

"THE QUEENS".

CONFIDENTIAL.

Headquarters,
    142nd. Inf. Bde.

Herewith War Diary for month of
November 1917.

[signature]
        Major for O.C.
    1/24th. Battalion London Regiment,
        "THE QUEE S".

2.12.17.

Army Form C. 2118.

WAR DIARY
or
INTELLIGENCE SUMMARY.
(Erase heading not required.)

Instructions regarding War Diaries and Intelligence Summaries are contained in F. S. Regs., Part II. and the Staff Manual respectively. Title pages will be prepared in manuscript.

1/24 Batt London Regt

Vol 32

Place	Date	Hour	Summary of Events and Information	Remarks and references to Appendices
NOVEMBER.1917.				
	Thursday 1st.		Major LOVEDAY commanding 230th.Siege Battery R.G.A. calls with reference to cutting hostile wire on our front. Lt.Col.MATTHEWS R.W.F. and Lt.Col.DAWSON and Capt.ROBINSON,R.A.M.C. call.	
	Friday 2nd.		Brigade Intelligence Officer calls also O.C.87th.Siege Battery,R.G.A. Wire cutting continued. Practice Barrage on OPPY front. Enemy retaliation on GAVRELLE village. At 9.30 p.m. enemy opens slow bombardment on our support trenches and O.T. also GAVRELLE village and continues for one hour. Casualties 1 Opl.22nd.Bn.(working party) killed and 1 sergeant wounded.	
	Saturday 3rd.		Major MARSHALL, Commanding 15th.Bn. and his Adjutant and Company Commanders reconnoitre preparatory to relief. Capt.ROBINSON, R.A.M.C. - Capt.SMITH, R.E. - Lieut.HOPE, T.M.B., Brigade Major, Div.Sig.Officer and Lt.Col.GREENWOOD call.	
	SUNday 4th.		Major BRAY, R.E., calls. At 4.30 p.m. "A" and "B" Coys.with 2 sections "C" and "D" Coys. carry out a raid with 2 Coys. 23rd.Bn. on enemy front and support lines on a front of 800 yards FXXX E. & S.E. of GAVRELLE VILLAGE. All objectives reached and Raid successful in all respects. (See attached copy of Operation Orders and Narrative). Congratulatory messages received from Army, Corps, Divisional and Brigade Commanders.	
	Monday 5th.		Relieved by 15th.Bn. and move to billets at MAROEUIL. Relief complete 12.15 p.m. Genl. BAILEY addresses Bn. in evening.	
	Tuesday 6th.		Resting and cleaning up. Company Commanders' Conference 2 p.m.	
	Wednesday 7th.		Divisional and A/Brigade Commanders pay informal visit and inspect billets.	
	Thursday 8th.		Genl.HORNE, Commanding 1st.Army inspects Battalion and is accompanied by Corps, Divisional and Brigade Commander. After inspection he addresses Bn. and congratulates them on successful raid. Col.STIMPSON,C.M.G., 1st.Army School calls. O.O. and 2nd. i/c attend conference of C.Os at Brigade H.Q. in evening. Officers Dinner at the CHATEAU, MAROEUIL.	

Army Form C. 2118.

WAR DIARY
or
INTELLIGENCE SUMMARY.
(Erase heading not required.)

Instructions regarding War Diaries and Intelligence Summaries are contained in F.S. Regs., Part II. and the Staff Manual respectively. Title pages will be prepared in manuscript.

Place	Date	Hour	Summary of Events and Information	Remarks and references to Appendices
	Friday 9th.		Company training and fatigues. 2nd/Lt. GIBBONS, 17th.Bn. reports for duty on attachment and is attached to "A" Company.	
	Saturday 10th.		Wet weather. Company training. Smoking concert.	
	Sunday 11th.		Lt.Col.MILLNER proceeds to England on leave. C. of E. service at Y.M.C.A. Tent by the Rev. MARSHALL, C.F. Major FAIR, 19th. Bn. calls.	
	Monday 12th.		Major BURY and Company Commanders reconnoitre Right Bn.Sub-Sector GAVRELLE. During period spent at MAROEUIL daily working parties supplied to Town Major for cleaning roads and other fatigues.	
	Tuesday 13th.		Relieved 7th.Bn. in Right Sub-Sector,GAVRELLE taking over line on new Winter Post dispositions. Relief complete 3 p.m.	
	Wednesday 14th.		Quiet day. Company Commanders Conference 11.15 a.m. The following call:- Lt.Col.MILDREN, A/Bde. Commander; O.C. 142nd.M.G.Company, Tunnelling Officer and Captain BLOFIELD, T.M.B.	
	Thursday 15th.		G.S.O.1., 31st.Div. calls and goes round line, Capt.SMITH R.E. and Capt.CHRISTOPHERSON A/235 Battery R.F.A. call. The following awarded M.M. for conspicuous behaviour and gallantry during raid on 4.11.17. 720982 L/Sgt.M.E.GREEN - 720819 Sgt.G.E.BANTING - 720127 L/Cpl.E.A.PORTER.- 720677 L/Cpl.S.CUTLER 722340 Pte.T.RUSSELL - 721615 L/Cpl.R.F.GRIMSEY - 723406 L/Cpl.W.ALLSWORTH. (XIIIth.Corps R.Os.) At 7.30 p.m. Raid by Division on our right attracts retaliation on our front and support lines.	
	Friday 16th.		The following call:- Lt.Col.MILDREN - Lieut.OWEN and Lieut.de SOUSA,R.W.F. Company Commanders Conference 11.15 a.m.	
	Saturday 17th.		Adjutant 10th.E.Yorks reconnoitres previous to relief. Divisional and A/Brigade Commanders call.	

Army Form C. 2118.

WAR DIARY
or
INTELLIGENCE SUMMARY.
(Erase heading not required.)

Instructions regarding War Diaries and Intelligence Summaries are contained in F. S. Regs., Part II. and the Staff Manual respectively. Title pages will be prepared in manuscript.

Place	Date	Hour	Summary of Events and Information	Remarks and references to Appendices
	Sunday 18th.		G.O.C. 92nd.Inf.Bde.calls also 4 Company Commanders and Signalling Officer 10th.E.Yorks reconnoitre. Message received from Brigade stating Divisional Commander wished particularly to commend Capt.SAVILL and 2nd/Lieut.GROSE in charge of patrols on night of 16th/17th. Practice Barrage on our right provokes retaliation. Casualty 1 O.R. killed.	
	Monday 19th.		Relieved by 10th.E.Yorks and move to ROUNDHAY CAMP and railway cutting S.E. of ROCLINCOURT. Relief complete 1.15 p.m. Casualties 1 O.R. killed and 1 O.R. wounded.	
	Tuesday 20th.		Relieved by 11th.E.Lancs and move to SPRINGVALE CAMP near ECURIE. Relief complete 11 a.m.	
	Wednesday 21st.		At 9.30 a.m. Bn. moves by march route to FRASER CAMP, /ST.ELOY. Very wet. All ranks in huts. Accommodation for officers not good. Draft of 40 O.R.join. Lieut.COOMBE, M.O. rejoins from Corps Reinforcement Camp.	
	Thursday 22nd.		At 9 a.m. Bn. moves by march route to billets at BERNEVILLE. Billets bad, especially for officers. Lieut.A/Capt.R.C.LONGLEY and Lieut.CARR awarded M.C. and the undermentioned the D.C.M. in connection with the Raid on 4.11.17:- Sgt.BAXTER, Pte.RUDHALL and Cpl.THEIS. (Corps R.Os 21.11.17.) Company Commanders Conference.	
	Friday 23rd.		Refitting and re-equipping. A/Bde. Commander calls. Lt.& Q.M. Beer rejoins from leave.	
	Saturday 24th.		Bn. moves by march route to GOMMIECOURT and billets in tents. Very uncomfortable owing to wet weather.	
	Sunday 25th.		At 1 p.m. Bn. moves by march route to hutments hear BARASTRE. March considerably delayed owing to long and repeated checks. Draft of 10 O.Rs arrived.	
	Monday 26th.		Battalion resting.	
	Tuesday 27th.		At 1 p.m. Bn. moves by march route to tents near BEAUMETZ LES CAMBRAI. Lt.Col.MILLNER rejoins from leave. Major MADAUD, Capt.GILL, Lieut.MATTHEWS, Lieut.STRACHAN and Lieut.SHIELDS with 66 O.R. proceed to Reinforcement Camp MAILLY-MAILLET area.	

Army Form C. 2118.

WAR DIARY
or
INTELLIGENCE SUMMARY.

(Erase heading not required.)

Place	Date	Hour	Summary of Events and Information	Remarks and references to Appendices
	Wednesday 28th.		Bn. relieves 20th. Bn. in Hindenburg Line S.W. of BOURLON WOOD. Transport lines remain at BEAUMETZ.	
	Thursday 29th.		No change.	
	Friday 30th.		No change.	

T. Sweetburg

Major for Lt.Col.Cdg.,
1/24th. Battalion London Regiment,
"THE QUEEN'S".

1/24th. BATTALION LONDON REGIMENT,

"THE QUEENS"

R E P O R T

ON

RAID carried out on NOVEMBER 4th, 1917.

ATTACHED.

(1)   24th. Battn. OPERATION ORDER No. 196.
(2)   24th. Battn. OPERATION ORDER No. 197.
(3)   PATROL MAP.

1/24th. LONDON REGIMENT.

REPORT
on the RAID
carried out on November 4th, 1917.

1. PREPARATION

   (a) ARTILLERY and T.M. Action before the RAID:-
   The enemy's front line wire was strong along the front
   of the attack – his support line was not wired at all.
   For the fortnight preceding the raid, wirecutting was
   carried out along the front of 47th. and neighbouring
   Divisions by Field Guns, 6" howitzers, and 2" trench
   mortars. Gaps so formed were kept under continual
   Lewis Gun fire by the trench garrison during the hours
   of darkness and in misty weather.

   (b) Our Wire.
   12 Zig-Zag gaps were cut in our wire by the raiding
   Companies during the time they were holding our front
   line. The last few strands were left uncut until the
   night preceding the raid, when they were cut by the
   troops garrisoning the front line.
   The gaps were all numbered and boards indicating them
   were fixed in the parapet front line firebays.
   Owing to the distance of our wire from the trenches
   (some 25 yds. to 60 yds. in places), lengths of telephone
   wire were run from these boards to the exit of the
   gaps to guide the assaulting troops.
   To guide troops returning from the raid, white discs
   were provided – these were dropped at the exits of the
   gaps by last man to leave the gaps in the advance.

   (c) Our Trenches.
   Firebays serving as points of exit were built up with
   sandbags so as to form steps.
   These were most successful.

   (d) Reconnaissance.
   Advantage was taken of the period spent in the line
   to make every officer, N.C.O. and man familiar with
   his Assembly Position, and a practice Assembly was
   held on the actual ground.
   Patrols were sent out every night composed of officers
   and men of the raiding party, and thus a thorough
   knowledge of No Man's Land and the enemy front line
   and wire was obtained by all concerned. These Patrols
   also served the purpose of driving the enemy from
   No Man's Land and preventing him from obtaining any
   knowledge of our wire.
       (See Patrol Map attached).

   (e) Practice.
   The two Raiding Companies had two practices over a
   flagged course while the Brigade was in Reserve.
   Subsequently on October 30th, the two Companies were
   withdrawn from the line, and had three day's practice
   over a course consisting partly of trenches and partly
   of flags – the last practice taking place at the time
   fixed for Zero. The Communication Trenches leading
   to the Assembly Position were marked with flags, and
   on each day, the assembly was practised.
   Watches were synchronised daily. During the training
   period every man was shown maps and aeroplane photographs
   and invited to make suggestions.

2. MOVEMENT INTO POSITION.

The Raiding Companies moved into the line on the morning of November 4th. Every move was carefully timed. (See O.O.197 attached), and worked without a hitch, except at the Entraining Point, where the presence of a Staff Officer or one of the Railway Company's Officers would have been of great assistance as the train conductor did not know which units he was to move and had been given a different map reference as point of entrainment to that indicated in the wire from Brigade notifying the train arrangements. The Companies reached their primary assembly position (NAVAL TRENCH) at 12.10.p.m. and their final assembly position at 3.55.p.m. The Assembly Practices enabled this latter move to be effected very rapidly and easily. Bn.H.Q. was established in the Advanced H.Q. at 3.p.m.

3. DIVERSIONS.

To confuse the enemy, practice barrages were put down on the days preceding Z day, on the enemy's line opposite neighbouring Divisions, and wirecutting operations which were done very thoroughly on the frontage attacked were similarly dispersed.
At ZERO rockets of every description were sent up on the whole Divisional Front, and that of neighbouring Divisions.
A smoke discharge which should have been coincided with this did not take place, owing to the direction of the wind.
Sufficient, however, had been done to puzzle the enemy and in consequence his barrage was dispersed, spasmodic and ineffective.

4. ARTILLERY, TM. and M.G. ACTION DURING OPERATIONS.

For detail of areas and lifts, see Maps B.C.& D.
One battery opened fire 30 seconds before ZERO.
The barrage itself was excellent, except on the right flank where it was inclined to be ragged and the lift wasn not simultaneous. It is considered that the rate of the 'creep' might have been slightly accelerated with advantage as the going in No Man's Land was so uniformly good that the men had to wait for the barrage to lift while the enemy were fleeing from the trenches in front of them. Rifle and Lewis Gun fire, together with our barrage undoubtedly caused them severe casualties, but a quicker lift in our barrage would have resulted in greater numbers being killed or captured. During the actual operation, the assistance afforded by Major STAPLEY, R.F.A. was of the greatest value throughout.

5. SMOKE BARRAGES.

In addition to those mentioned in para. 3, it was planned to discharge at ZERO harmless, but evil-smelling smoke from projectors, on the front of attack, with the object of making the enemy put on his gas masks. Owing to the easterly direction of the wind, the projection had to be cancelled.

6. COMMUNICATIONS.

Previous to Z day, wires had been run by alternative routes to Stations in the Assembly Position from Advanced H.Q., and the line thence to Advanced Brigade H.Q. triplicated.

NARRATIVE. (continued)

permitted. The enemy in his flight took with him all the M.Gs. and T.Ms. that were in the line — these were apparently all of a light pattern. Of the two light M.Gs. that were captured, one was found between the 1st. and 2nd. objectives, with its squad dead beside it, and the other was taken in the 2nd. objective while being carried away by the enemy. Only on the left were any enemy found in the trenches — one man getting into CHAFF TRENCH, accounted for 9 singlehanded, and one officer for four or five.

The Withdrawal was timed entirely by watch, and was carried out on the lines of a rearguard action. It was effected in excellent order and without a single casualty. On arriving 25 yards from our wire, the white discs marking the gaps were seen very plainly and the men were able rapidly to regain our front line.

During the night and early morning a search party voluntarily went out under 2nd. Lieut. J.W.CARR to find the body of one of the killed — this was eventually recovered from the enemy wire. The other man killed was so blown to pieces that recovery of his body was impossible. There were no men missing. Before dawn, 4 out of the 12 gaps in our wire had been repaired.

8. RESULTS.

(a) CAPTURES.
4 Other Ranks, (1 of whom was wounded) 459th. I.R., 236 Division.
2 Light Machine Guns.
Large quantities of documents, papers, etc. — rifles bombs, kit etc.

(b) KILLED.
In trenches — 25 — in the open 40 (estimated)
In dugouts — these cannot be accurately estimated.

(c) DESTRUCTION.
9 dugouts.
Large quantities of T.M. Bombs, Grenades, Rifles, Packs, Tools, etc.
Trenches and T.M. Emplacements wrecked generally.

(d) INFORMATION regarding Enemy Trenches.
(1) Front Line (SOUTH GAVRELLE TRENCH) — about 4' deep, without any kind of revetment — no duckboards — practically no firesteps in the firebays — dugouts about 15' deep — the majority being only staircases of dugouts in course of construction. No examination of these dugouts was made, as they were destroyed immediately.
(2) Support Line (COD and CRAWL) — Similar in character to the front line, except that the dugouts in Crawl were further advanced, being 25' deep. On each step of the staircase, a niche was cut out from the side, to form a sleeping place.
COD was very shallow, about 3' deep, and full of mud. The enemy were apparently at work on it at the time.
(3) CHINK A communication trench about 4' deep without traverses.
The T.M. position marked at C.25.D.43.52. was found to be a very foul latrine. A plate for a light T.M. was found 30 yds. S of junction of CHINK and CRAWL — this was destroyed.
(4) MISCELLANEOUS.
(a) No gas cylinders or emplacements for same were found.
(b)

COMMUNICATIONS. (continued).

Each of the Raiding Companies established Signal Stations in 1st. objective, which were linked up laterally and another Station was pushed forward to the 2nd. objective. Communication by telephone was continuous throughout the whole operation, both from the attacking Companies and to Brigade H.Q. This was due entirely to the work of the Battalion Signallers and the buried cable.

7. NARRATIVE.

4.30.p.m.	Barrage started, and raiding Companies advanced towards their objective. On reaching the barrage fire was opened on the fleeing enemy and several were seen to fall.
4.32.p.m.	Enemy barrage opened in desultory fashion on our front line.
4.35.p.m.	Raiding Companies assaulted and carried 1st. objective. (Report received at 4.42.p.m.) Enemy barrage opened fairly heavily on WILLIE SUPPORT and TOWY ALLEY.
4.40.p.m.	2nd. objective carried — casualties slight. (Report received 4.50.p.m.) — resistance NIL. Fleeing enemy pursued with Lewis Gun and Rifle fire.
4.55.p.m.	Our barrage reported too short on the right: this was immediately rectified by the Artillery Liaison Officer attached to Bn.H.Q.
5.5.p.m.	Withdrawal from 2nd objective commenced — covered by Lewis Gun sections.
5.10.p.m.	Withdrawal from 1st. objective commenced — covered by Lewis Gun sections.
5.35.p.m.	Companies reported "all correct".
5.40.p.m.	Artillery informed "All clear".
6.20.p.m.	Enemy fire still heavy — counter-battery work called for.
6.37.p.m.	All batteries firing on enemy front and support line for 5 minutes.
6.55.p.m.	All counter batteries firing for 5 minutes.
9.30.p.m.	Situation normal.
3.a.m.	Patrol reports enemy had not yet returned to his front line.

The whole Attack went like clockwork. The enemy's wire was found to be absolutely flattened and offered no obstacles. The garrison, including a large working party estimated at 150 men, caught in their flight by Lewis Guns and Rifle Fire and by the barrage, suffered considerable casualties, of which 40 is a moderate estimate. One of the Raiding Platoons alone fired an average of 100 rounds per man. In addition 9 dugouts were destroyed, 2 or 3 being demolished by the R.E.
(The special training they had received from Major LOVE,R.E. enabled them to carry out their duties quickly and efficiently. Their conduct throughout the operation was of the highest order,) and the remainder set on fire by 'P' Bombs — 2 of these dugouts are known to have been inhabited at the time.
Into the blazing dugouts all enemy stores which could not be removed, were thrown, including a large stores of 'pineapple' bombs, tools, tunnelling sets, etc.
The trenches themselves were demolished so far as time

MISCELLANEOUS. (continued)
(b) Enemy appear to be using our MILLS bombs: a number were found in their front line, neatly placed beside some of the ordinary German hand grenades.

9. CASUALTIES.

OFFICERS   —   2 wounded.

OTHER RANKS   —   2 killed.
                       8 wounded.

10. DETAIL of TROOPS engaged.

    8 Officers: 225 Other Ranks.

    6 Other Ranks (R.E.) attached.

11. CONCLUSIONS.

The moral of the troops engaged was excellent owing to their having spent several days in comfortable quarters and the arrangements made for their amusement. The Divisional Follies gave a free entertainment which was much appreciated. During this period no more work was done than actually necessary to ensure that each man knew his job.

(Signed)   G.E.MILLER.

Lieut. Col., Cdg.,
1/24th. Bn. London Regiment,
'The Queens'.

7.11.1917.

SECRET.   24th.Battalion London Regiment.

O.O. No.195.   Copy No. 9.

In Connection with Minor Operation.

NOTE.   All previous instructions are cancelled.

Refce. MAPS.   COPY 2 and Special Maps.

1. INTENTION.   A raid will be carried out by 142nd.Inf.Bde.in the
                   GAVRELLE Sector, at a date and ZERO time to be
                   notified later, with a view to:-
                   (1) Capturing and killing as many of the enemy
                        as possible.
                   (2) Capturing and destroying war material.
                   (3) Destroying dugouts.

2. DETAIL OF TROOPS.   "A" and "B" Companies (plus 2 Sections of
                   "C" and 2 Sections of "D" Companies) 24th.Bn.LON.REGT.
                   will attack on the RIGHT.
                   2 Companies 23rd.Bn.LON.REGT. will attack on the LEFT.
                   6 O.R. (R.E.) will be attached to each Battalion.

3. OBJECTIVES ETC.   Objectives, inter-Battalion and inter-Company
                   boundaries are shown on MAP A attached.

4. ASSEMBLY. (1) Assaulting Companies will assemble in WULUE
                   TRENCH, which will be evacuated by the garrisoning
                   troops prior to time of assembly.
               (2) Assembly will be complete by ZERO minus 20.
               (3) Each Section will be detailed to leave assembly
                   position for the assault, by a definite 'gap'
                   in our wire, and will assemble opposite that gap.
               (4) 2 Sections of "C" Company will assemble with "A"
                   Company.
                   2 Sections of "D" Company and 6 O.R. (R.E.) will
                   assemble with "B" Company.
               (5) 4 Signallers will assemble with each Company H.Q.

5. ASSAULT and WITHDRAWAL.

               (1) TIME TABLE as shown in Appendix 1.
               (2) ASSAULT will be carried out in two waves as
                   follows:-
                   (a) First Wave - 1 Platoon of "A" (plus 2 Sections
                                    of "C") and 1 Platoon of "B"
                                    plus 1 Section of "D" and
                                    6 O.R. (R.E.)
                       Second Wave - 2 Platoons of "A" and 2 Platoons
                                    of "B" (plus 1 section of "D").
                       The first wave will occupy the first objective.
                       The second wave will occupy the second objective.
                   (b) Distance between waves ------ 10 yards.
                       Distance between lines ------   5 yards.
                   (c) The leading sections of the first wave will
                       extend immediately on emerging from our wire.
                   (d) 1 Section of "C" Coy.will seize junction of
                       CHINK and first objective and clear T.M.
                       emplacement (C.25.D.45.52.) and dugout
                       adjoining.
                       1 Section of "C" Coy. will be responsible for
                       clearing CHINK.
                       1 Section of "D" Coy.will 'mop up' 4 enemy
                       dugouts reported in first objective from
                       C.25.D.45.85. to C.25.D.35.90.
                       1 Section of "D" Coy.will constitute 'moppers
                       up' party for No.6 Platoon in 2nd.objective.
                   (e) LEWIS GUNS. The 3 Platoon Guns will advance
                       with their Platoons. Platoons detailed for
                       the 2nd.objective will establish their Lewis
                       Guns on the flanks and in advance of the

(2)

2nd.objective, cooperating with the bombers
and rifle grenadiers forming the bombing
stops.
The Reserve Company Gun will advance with
the 2nd.wave of each Company, and will take
up position in the 1st.objective in the
vicinity of Company H.Q., and be at the
disposal of the O.C.Company.

(f) MOPPERS-UP. During "mopping-up" operations
a man will be posted at the entrances of
all dugouts in which "mopping-up" operations
are proceeding, to prevent bombs etc., being
thrown into same.

(g) COVERING PARTIES. Covering parties will be
thrown out on the flanks and in advance of
the 2nd.objective. Bombing Posts, double
blocked, will be established in all
communication trenches and on the flanks.

(h) SAPPERS. The 6 Sappers attached to "B"
Company will assist mopping-up parties in
destroying dugouts and emplacements, and
releasing fixed machine-guns etc... They
will advance with First Wave to 1st.objective
and will then act under the orders of O.C.
Company.

(j) WITHDRAWAL. The troops occupying the 1st.
objective will always be prepared to cover
the withdrawal of the troops in front of
them. While in occupation of the 1st.
objective they will cut further gaps in the
enemy wire, to facilitate withdrawal.

(k) LINGUISTS. One man, if available, with a
knowledge of German will be attached to
each O.C.Company.

(l) TREACHERY. All ranks are to be warned
against treachery and the misuse of the
White Flag by the enemy.

(m) CASUALTIES. All wounded, and as far as
possible all dead, are to be carried back
to our line.

6. REASSEMBLY. Companies will reassemble in their assembly
positions. Rolls will be called and casualties checked.

7. ARTILLERY etc.SUPPORT. The raid will be covered by

(1) A creeping and standing barrage as shown on MAP B
attached.
(2) Heavy Artillery and all available Artillery on
GAVRELLE SUPPORT and counter-battery work.
(3) M.Gs. of 47th. and 61st.DIVISIONS.
(4) T.Ms. co-operating on each flank of the attack.

8. COMMUNICATIONS.

(1) Each Company will establish a Signal Station in 1st.
objective near junction of CHINK and enemy front line -
these will be amalgamated, if possible.
"A" Company will also establish a forward station in
2nd.objective, near junction of CHINK and CRAMP.
(2) Battalion runners will establish a Relay Runner Post
at junction of TOWN ALLEY and WILLIE TRENCH.
(3) Code for telephone messages as shown in Appendix III.

9. SMOKE. (1) A smoke screen by 4" Stokes Mortars will be placed
on both flanks of the raiding party.
(2) A projection of harmless smoke on the front of attack
will be made at ZERO minus 30 seconds.

(2).

        (3) A Smoke discharge of candles will be made on 61st. Divisional Front.

10. ROCKETS. Rockets of every nature will be sent up along the front of 47th. and neighbouring Divisions, copying, if possible, those normally used by the enemy.

11. SYNCHRONISATION. Watches will be synchronised daily during practice.
On Z day, a synchronised watch will be sent to both Companies at ZERO minus 5 hours and ZERO minus 1 hour.

12. ADMINISTRATIVE INSTRUCTIONS. See Appendix II.

13. AID POST will be adjoining Bn.H.Q. in conjunction with 23rd. LONDON REGIMENT.

14. BN.H.Q. will be established, together with H.Q. 23rd.LON.REGT. at former RIGHT COMPANY H.Q., WILLIE SUPPORT (C.25.C.40.32.)

        Issued at
          8 P.M.
            1.11.17.

DISTRIBUTION.

Copy No.1. File.
     2. "A" Coy.
     3. "B" Coy.
     4. "C" Coy.
     5. "D" Coy.
     6. H.Q.
     7. 23rd.LON.REGT. (for information)
     8. 142nd.Inf.Bde. (for information).

                                L. C. James.
                           Captain and Adjutant.

APPENDIX 1.

TIME TABLE.

TIME.	INFANTRY.	ARTILLERY. (see Map 'B' attached)
ZERO.	Begins to assemble outside our wire close to barrage.	Commences firing on all objectives. Creeping barrage across enemy re-entrant with special battery on base of RED TRIANGLE from 0.25.d.25.45. to 0.25.b.13.12.
PLUS 3.		Standing barrage lifts from 2nd. objective to line of GAVRELLE SUPPORT. Creeping barrage. Special RED Battery lifts to line of enemy re-entrant.
PLUS 5.	Assaults 1st. Objective (except in re-entrant) as soon as possible after barrage lifts.	Standing barrage lifts from flanks of 2nd. Objective. Creeping barrage lifts from BLUE Line to BROWN Line and also to the BLACK line between 0.25.d.30.65. and 0.25.b.55.14.
PLUS 6.	Assault re-entrant as soon as possible after barrage lifts.	Special RED Battery ceases fire.
PLUS 10.	Assaulting troops for 2nd.Objective assemble behind creeping barrage.	Creeping barrage lifts from BROWN LINE to BLACK LINE.
PLUS 13.	Assaults 2nd. Objective as soon as possible after barrage lifts.	Creeping barrage lifts from BLACK LINE to YELLOW LINE.
PLUS 45.	Troops in 2nd. Objective commence to withdraw.	

APPENDIX 1. (continued).

TIME TABLE.

TIME.	INFANTRY.	ARTILLERY. (see Map 'B' attached.)
PLUS. 50.	Troops in 1st. Objective commence to withdraw.	
PLUS 80.	Infantry withdrawal to be complete.	Start gradually to slacken and to cease fire when Infantry report 'All Clear'.
N O T E.	A withdrawal Signal will be fired at ZERO plus 45 when troops in 2nd. Objective commence to withdraw.	

APPENDIX II.

Administrative Instructions in connection with 24th.Battalion Instructions No.1.

1. **MEDICAL ARRANGEMENTS.**

    (1) 5th.LON.FLD.AMBULANCE will take over AID POSTS of RIGHT and SUPPORT Battalions as advanced Dressing Stations and clear all wounded from the Regimental Aid Post to them.
    (2) To avoid congestion, walking wounded will be sent as far as possible down INVICTA TRENCH, and thence via WILLIE SUPPORT to TOWY ALLEY.
    (3) All ranks will be warned that walking cases should carry back their rifle and equipment, if possible.
    (4) M.O. will arrange for S.Bs of "C" and "D" Companies to take over stretcher cases in WILLIE TRENCH.

2. **CASUALTIES.** Company Commanders will send an estimate of their total casualties to Bn.H.Q. as soon as possible after reassembly.

3. **PRISONERS** (1) will be sent back under escort to shelter previously used by Right Bn. as a drying room and Canteen. This is in TOWY ALLEY, adjoining RIGHT Bn.H.Q.
    (2) 2/Lt.D.E.POLL and 6 O.R. of "C" Coy. will there marshal all prisoners, and finally conduct them to POINT DU JOUR (H.3.D.0.0.) where they will be handed over to A.P.M. and a receipt taken.
    2/Lt.D.E.POLL will be responsible for searching all prisoners, and will personally see that all prisoners are handed over to A.P.M.
    All ranks will be searched immediately after capture for arms, ammunition etc.,. Only officers and N.C.Os will have papers, maps etc., taken from them. Such papers will be handed over to A.P.M. by the escort.
    Under NO circumstances will the Identity Disc or pay book be taken from a prisoner of war. Numbers of Prisoners will be reported to Bn.H.Q. by 2/Lt.D.E.POLL, by runner, immediately before he marches them off.

4. **CAPTURED WAR MATERIAL ETC.**

    Company Commanders will notify as soon as possible after reassembly the capture of any Machine Guns, Mortars, arms and stores of any description.
    All captures that cannot be carried back will be left at convenient places in reassembly position, position being notified to Bn. H.Q. They will be subsequently moved under Bn. arrangements.
    Attention is directed to G.R.O.1879 as amended by G.R.O.s 1901 and 2207.

5. **EQUIPMENT.**

    (a) **OFFICERS.**   Tunics as worn by O.R.
    Web equipment.
    Box Respirator at alert position.
    Revolver and Ammunition.
    2 Bombs (Mills No.5.) in pockets of tunic.

    (b) **MEN.**   Skeleton Drill Order.
    Rifle and Bayonet fixed.
    Entrenching tool.
    Water-Bottle.
    Box Respirator at alert position.
    S.A.A. 110 rounds in pouches 10 in magazine

5.   EQUIPMENT. – MEN (continued)

                              3 Bombs (Mills No. 5) in pockets of
                              tunic.
                              2 Sandbags (for carrying back spoil).

   (c) BOMBERS.   As in (b) except that

                              (1) They will NOT carry sandbags.
                              (2) They will only carry 40 rounds
                                  S.A.A. in pouches and 10 in
                                  magazine, and 16 Mills No.5. in
                                  a bomb bucket.

   (d) RIFLE GRENADIERS. As in (b) except that

                              (1) They will NOT carry the sandbags
                                  & S.A.A.
                              (2) They will carry 50 rounds S.A.A. in
                                  bandolier – Blank S.A.A. in pouches
                                  – 10 bombs (Mills No. 23) in a
                                  bomb bucket.
   The one man attached to each Rifle Grenadier will
   carry 16 bombs (Mills No.23) in a bomb bucket.

   (e) LEWIS GUNNERS.   as in (b) except that

                              (1) They will not carry the sandbags.
                              (2) No. 1 & 2 on each gun will carry
                                  revolver & webley ammunition instead
                                  of Rifle & Bayonet & S.A.A.

   (f) TECHNICAL GEAR. Wire cutters 'Turnover' – 50 per Coy.
                       Wire cutters 'Large Hand' – 9 per Coy.
                       Wire cutters 'Small Hand' – 9 per Coy.
                       Rope:– six 15' lengths per Coy.
                       Electric Torches – 9 per Coy.
                       'P' Bombs (for Moppers Up) – 25 per Coy.
                       ~~Bombs No. 27. – 25 per Coy.~~

   (g) All identity discs, paybooks, letters, papers etc., &
       all means of identification will be left behind in the
       packs, in the position occupied before Companies move
       into assembly position.
       Special Maps only to be used.

6.   HOT FOOD & RUM.

            Hot Food will be issued immediately before
   marching up to assembly position and immediately after
   reassembly.
            A small RUM issue will be made to all ranks
   immediately before assault, and a full issue on reassembly.
            O.C. 'D' Coy. will detail 20 O.Rs. to carry food
   from cookhouse to Companies.

7.   TRENCH CONTROL.

   (1) Control Posts will be established at junctions of INVICTA
       TRENCH, TOWN ALLEY, and COLOUR TRENCH with WILLIE TRENCH –
       also at GAP BOARDS No. 5, No. 6 & No.10 to direct runners,
       wounded, etc. These will be furnished by 'C' Company, and
       will be established immediately after the assault is
       launched.
       They will see that walking wounded are directed down INVICTA
       TRENCH – stretcher cases and prisoners down TOWN ALLEY –
       runners down COLOUR TRENCH.

TRENCH CONTROL (continued)

(2) Further Control Posts will be established by ZERO at junction of INVICTA TRENCH, TOWN ALLEY, and COLOUR TRENCH & WILLIE SUPPORT to direct wounded to AID POST, and runners to Bn.H.Q.

APPENDIX III

SECRET

N.1.2.3.4.5.6.7.8.9.0.	1.2.3.4.5.6.7.8.9.0.
Bread	First line captured.
Butter	Second line captured.
Apple	Prisoner.
Plum	Machine Gun.
Peach	Trench Gun.
Potato	All comrades have returned.
Turnip	Slight casualties.
Bean	Fairly heavy casualties.
Cabbage	Heavy casualties.
Beef	Barrage not short enough.
Mutton	Barrage too short.
Pudding	Heavy enemy fire.
Savoury	Enemy fire not heavy.
Dessert	All quiet.
Sheep	No resistance from enemy.
Cow	Fair resistance from enemy.
Mule	Heavy resistance from enemy.
Horse	Enemy counterattacked.
Viper	Enemy counterattacking.
Cat	We are returning.
Cigar	"A" Coy. 24th Battalion.
Cigarette	"B" Coy. 24th Battalion.
Pipe	"C" Coy. 22nd Battalion.
Tobacco	"A" Coy. 22nd Battalion.

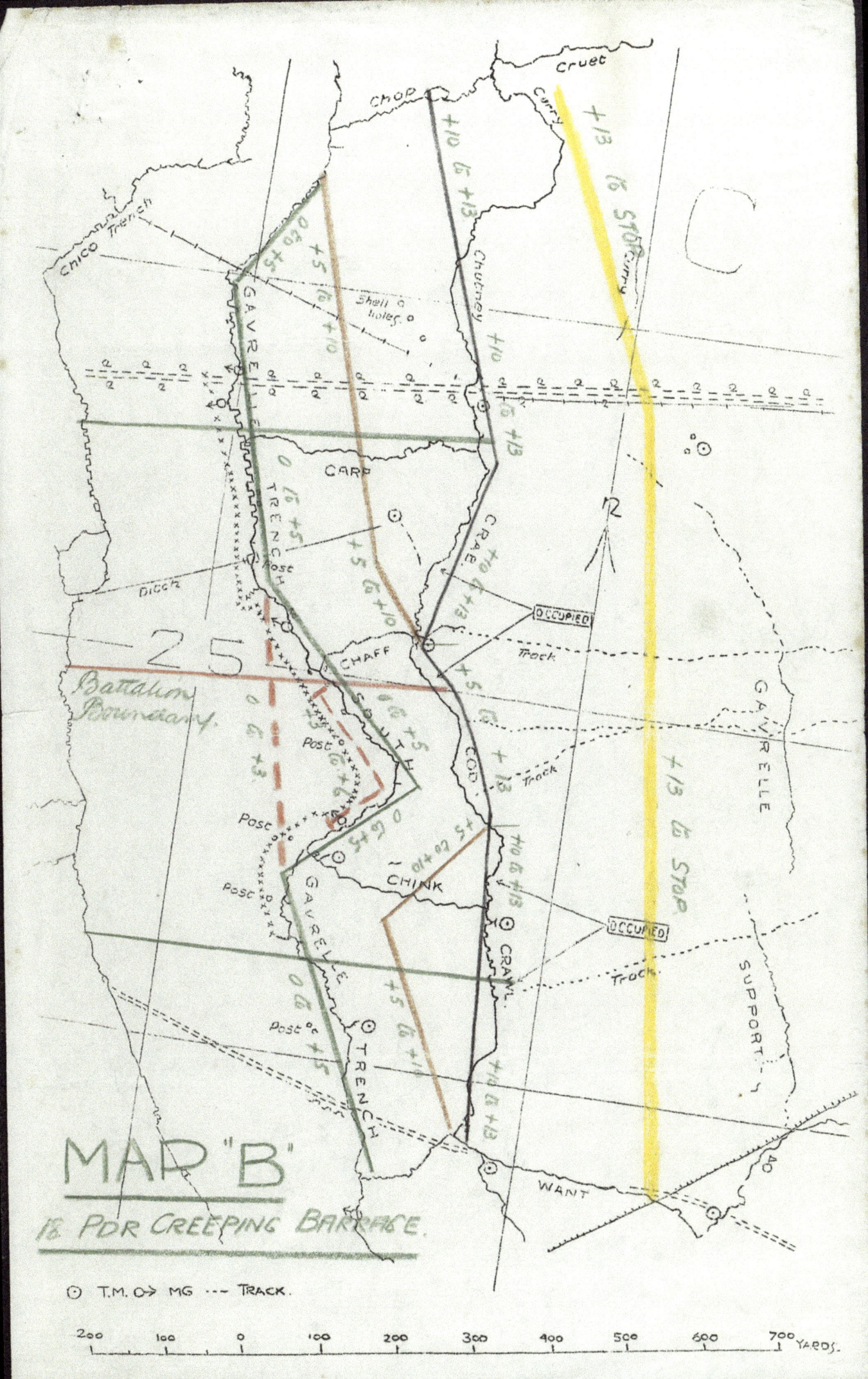

SECRET.   O.O. NO.197.   Copy No.

Refce.O.O. No.196.

1. The following will be conveyed for Raiding Companies and H.Q. by transport to ration dump of RIGHT BN. on the night of November 3/4th, 1917, and will be disposed conveniently for issue on the following morning, under arrangements to be made by O.C. RIGHT BN:-

   (1) LEWIS GUNS and Magazines. (These are to be loaded on limbers by 11 a.m. November 3rd., and report to Armourer Sgt. at Depot by 12 noon for overhaul - Officers' Mess Gear for the line can be carried on these limbers).

   (2) Greatcoats – (to be loaded at 11 a.m. November 3rd.)

   (3) RATIONS. – for following HOT MEALS:-

   DINNERS   —   12 noon.
   TEAS   —   2.45 p.m.
   SUPPERS   —   6.30 p.m. (approx)

   All these meals will be taken in NAVAL TRENCH.
   O.C. RIGHT BN., in conjunction with Q.M. will make necessary arrangements. Sufficient cooks and dixies must accompany.

   (4) RUM – for issue in Front Line before and after operations.
   O.C. RIGHT BN. will provide carrying parties for above.

2. TIME TABLE

   November 4th.

   9 a.m.   (approx) Raiding Companies entrain at ST.AUBIN.
   10 a.m.   Detrain at GUN JUNCTION.
             Move up via TOWY ALLEY, in rear of 23rd.Bn. - "A" Company leading.
             "A" Company moves into NAVAL TRENCH, South of TOWY ALLEY, in place of RESERVE COMPANY of RIGHT BN.
             O.C. RIGHT BN. will move his RESERVE Company, by 10.30 a.m. into area recently occupied by working party.
             "B" Company moves into NAVAL TRENCH, North of TOWY ALLEY, in place of RIGHT Coy. of SUPPORT BN.
             Bn.H.Q. moves to RIGHT Bn.H.Q.

   11 a.m.   Lt.H.S.MITCHELL reports to RIGHT Bde.H.Q., H.1.D.2.5. to synchronise watches.

   2.15 p.m. SUPPORT Company (RIGHT Bn.) starts moving from WILLIE SUPPORT to that part of TOWY ALLEY, West of NAVAL TRENCH – rear of this Company to be clear of junction of TOWY ALLEY and NAVAL TRENCH by 3.10 p.m.

             (Note – When both Raiding Companies are clear of NAVAL TRENCH, this Coy. will move into area vacated by 'A' Company.)

   2.45 p.m. RIGHT FRONT Coy. (RIGHT BN.) will start moving via TOWY ALLEY to WILLIE SUPPORT.

   3.15 p.m. "B" Company starts moving from NAVAL TRENCH into assembly position. - "A" Company follows:
             Both Companies will use TOWY ALLEY ONLY and no other Communication Trench.
             Raiding Companies of 23rd.Lon.Regt., move in via BELVOIR ALLEY.

TIME TABLE. (Continued).

3.30 p.m.   LEFT FRONT Coy. (RIGHT BN.) starts moving via
            COLOUR TRENCH to WATER POST.

            NOTE.   Above times are to be strictly observed
            so that raiding Companies moving into assembly
            positions are not delayed by outgoing Companies.

p.m. ZERO.

            On completion of operations, Raiding Companies
            will return to their previous positions in
            NAVAL TRENCH.
            Front Line and Support Companies, RIGHT BN. will
            then resume their normal positions.

NOVEMBER 5th.

10 a.m.   24th.Bn. will be relieved and proceed to billets
           in MAROEUIL.

3.   DRUMS & BAND. will accompany "A" and "B" Companies respectively
                   as far as NAVAL TRENCH, as carriers.

                        Issued at
                        8.25 p.m. 2.11.17.
     DISTRIBUTION.

     Copy No.1.   File.
            2.   "A" Coy.
            3.   "B" Coy.
            4.   H.Q.Coy.   Captain and Adjutant.
            5.   T.O. & Q.M.
            6.   O.C. RIGHT BN.
            7.   142nd.Inf.Bde. (for personal information of
                                 Brigadier General).
            8.   23rd.Lon.Regt. (for information).

CONFIDENTIAL.

Headquarters,
    142nd. Inf. Bde.

    Herewith War Diary for
December 1917, please.

            [signature]

            Capt. & Adjutant,
    for O.C. 1/24th.Battalion London Regt.,
            "THE QUEENS".

3.1.18.

Army Form C. 2118.

WAR DIARY
or
INTELLIGENCE SUMMARY

(Erase heading not required.)

Instructions regarding War Diaries and Intelligence Summaries are contained in F.S. Regs., Part II. and the Staff Manual respectively. Title Pages will be prepared in manuscript.

Place	Date	Hour	Summary of Events and Information	Remarks and references to Appendices
December 1917.				
	Saturday 1st.		Relieved 17th, 18th and 20th. Battalions in N.E. face of BOURLON WOOD. Relief delayed 2 hours owing to faulty arrangements with regard to guides. Considerable hostile harrassing fire during night. Casualties 4 O.R. wounded.	
	Sunday 2nd.		Brig. Genl. Bailey calls. Considerable artillery activity during afternoon in connection with operation on left of our front. At 4 p.m. under cover of enemy barrage, Cpl. GARRARD and 5 O.R. captured by enemy raiding party. We killed Offizier Stellvertreter of 60th. R.I.R. Line held by "D" Company on left, "B" Company Centre and "C" Company on right with 1 platoon of "A" Company in support of "D" and 1 platoon "B" Company in support of Centre. 2 platoons "A" Company in Battalion Reserve. Casualties 3 O.R. wounded.	
	Monday 3rd.		Lt. Col. GREENWOOD called. Moderately quiet day. Took over command of 1 Coy. 22nd. Bn. on our left thereby increasing front without thinning line. Intense artillery activity throughout afternoon and during night with large proportion of gas. S.O.S. sent up by O.C. "D" Coy. but not responded to by our artillery. 2 enemy shot in No-man's land.	
	Tuesday 4th.		Very quiet day and night. O.C. called to Bde. H.Q. and receives instruction regarding evacuation of BOURLON WOOD and withdrawal to HINDENBURG SUPPORT line S.W. of GRAINCOURT. Battalion less "A" Company (which relieved "B", "C" and "D" Coys. in outpost line about 9 p.m.) withdraws at 11 p.m. "A" Company withdraws at 4 a.m. 5th inst. and occupy previous position.	
	Wednesday 5th.		Lt. Col. Millner having sprained his ankle returns to Transport Lines and Major Bury takes over command. At 9 p.m. Battalion side-steps and relieves 8th. London Regt. in HINDENBURG SUPPORT line with right flank 1400 yds. N.E. of HAVRINCOURT on earth track leading from HAVRINCOURT to GRAINCOURT.	
	Thursday 6th.		Intermittent shell fire on our trenches. Front line held as a line of posts, main line of resistance being old German front line of support system. Dispositions:- Right front line "A" Company. Left front line "B" Company. "C" and "D" Coys in support. Battalion stands to in afternoon on hostile attack near FLESQUIERES. Battalion H.Q. moves to dugout in trench 800 yds. in rear of support trench with advanced H.Q. in main line. Trenches shelled during night.	
	Friday 7th.		Capt. Coleman, R.A.M.C. relieves Capt. Robinson as R.M.O. Fairly quiet day. On orders of Brigade Battalion H.Q. moves again to dugout 500 yds. N. of present H.Q. 40 reinforcements report from Depot. Capt. SAVILL to hospital sick.	
	Saturday 8th.		Brigade Commander and Staff Captain call. Fairly quiet day but intermittent hostile shell fire continued on our trenches.	
	Sunday 9th.		Congratulatory messages from G.H.Q. and Army Commander with reference to the stand made by the 47th., 2nd., and 56th Divs. in BOURLON WOOD and in connection with the withdrawal.	

2449 Wt. W14957/M90 750,000 1/16 J.B.C. & A. Forms/C.2118/12.

Army Form C. 2118.

WAR DIARY
or
INTELLIGENCE SUMMARY

(Erase heading not required.)

Instructions regarding War Diaries and Intelligence Summaries are contained in F. S. Regs., Part II. and the Staff Manual respectively. Title Pages will be prepared in manuscript.

Place	Date	Hour	Summary of Events and Information	Remarks and references to Appendices
	Monday 10th.		G.S.O.3. and Brigade Commander call. At 9.30.a.m. 9 hostile aeroplanes fly over Brigaded Transport lines and drop bombs causing casualties in other units. One dropped in our Camp but did no damage. Move Camp. Major Nadaud and Lieuts Matthews and Burroughs rejoin from reinforcement camp.	
	Tuesday 11th.		Battalion relieved by Composite Battalion of 17th.,18th., and 19th.Battalions under Lt.Col. Hughes,and move into Support trenches N.W. of HAVRINCOURT. H.Q. near Copse 700 yds.N.W. of village. Capt. Williams,M.O. to hospital sick.	
	Wednesday 12th. Thursday 13th.		Under orders of 141st Inf.Bde from 12 noon. Resting and cleaning. Divnl.Commander and Brig.Genl.Erskine Commdg.141st Inf.Bde. call. During day men employed marking out tracks to front line and improving trenches and salvage. Lt.Grose to hospital with gas boils.	
	Friday 14th.		Quiet day.	
	Saturday 15th.		Relieved by 6th.Battalion and move to RUYALCOURT. Relief complete 8 p.m. Very Cold.	
	Sunday 16th.		At 7.30 a.m. Battalion moves by march route to VELU entraining there for AVELUY near ALBERT afterwards marching to billets at BRESLE. Billets of all ranks extremely bad.	
	Monday 17th.		Battalion resting. Heavy snow storm.	
	Tuesday 18th.		Battalion resting. Lt. Turner rejoins from 1st.Army School.	
	Wednesday 19th.		Battalion moves to SENLIS. Billets quite good. Difficulty in moving transport owing to frozen roads. Col.Galbraith calls.	
	Thursday 20th.		Weather still bad. Baths at SENLIS and Company route marches. Brigade Commander and Staff Captain call.	
	Friday 21st.		Weather continues bad. Training confined to route marches. Performance by Divnl."Follies" troop at SENLIS Theatre.	
	Saturday 22nd.		Divnl.and Brigade Commanders inspect billets. Billetting areas altered to allow of 4th.P.W.F. and 520th.Coy.R.E. being accommodated.	
	Sunday 23rd.		C. of E. service at Theatre. Capt.Kilbride, R.A.M.C. reports for duty on being posted as M.O. The following appear in Corps Routine Orders as having been awarded Military Medal in connection with recent operations:- 720143 Pte.C.E.Cole - 721099 Pte.C.R.Weir - 720537 Pte.C.J.Lait. - 720922 L/Sgt.W.J.Neale - 720486 Sgt.G.L.Welch - 722974 L/Cpl.A.Suttle - 720114 Q.Q.M.S.J.Hale. - 720653 Sgt.W.H.Appleton. - 720392 L/Cpl.J.W.Garnham.	
	Monday 24th.		Lt.Col.Thunder calls. C.O. reads Brigade Commander's Christmas message. No.722919 Pte.Taylor. Route marches and Battalion parade. Promulgation of F.G.C.M. on No.722919 Pte.Taylor. C.O. reads Brigade Commander's Christmas message.	
	Tuesday 25th.		No parades. Special Xmas Dinner for N.C.Os and men at R.E. workshop. Half Battalion dining at a time. Brigade Commander calls.	

Army Form C. 2118.

WAR DIARY
or
INTELLIGENCE SUMMARY

(Erase heading not required.)

Place	Date	Hour	Summary of Events and Information	Remarks and references to Appendices
	Wednesday 26th.		Company training. Battalion parade at which Brig.Genl.Bailey presents ribbons of recently awarded Military Medals.	
	Thursday 27th.		C.O. 2nd. i/c, Adjutant, Signalling Officer with Bn.H.Q. Signallers and Runners attend tactical exercise under Divisional Commander in neighbourhood of HENENCOURT. Company training carried out.	
	Friday 28th.		Company and Specialist Training. Company Commanders' Conference. The following names appear in the list of those mentioned by the Commander in Chief for gallant and distinguished service:- Lt.Col.G.E.Milner,M.C. - 2/Lt.P.R.W.Perry - 720750 Sgt.A.J.Beardshaw. - 720234 Cpl.W.H.LeGrove (killed) - 720661 C.S.M.G.W.West.	
	Saturday 29th. Sunday 30th.		Company and Specialist training. Capt.Gill and Lt.Heathcote to England on leave. At 4 p.m. warning order received to move by train from ALBERT. Battalion moves off at 7 p.m. and marches to ALBERT, entraining thence to ETRICOURT. Arrive ETRICOURT at 4 a.m. and move to tents. Conditions extremely uncomfortable owing to hard frost and snow.	
	Monday 31st.		At ETRICOURT. Weather still very cold.	

M. Milner
Lieut.Col.C/g.,
1/24th.Battalion London Regiment,
"THE QUEENS".

Army Form C. 2118.

WAR DIARY
or
INTELLIGENCE SUMMARY.
(Erase heading not required.)

Instructions regarding War Diaries and Intelligence Summaries are contained in F. S. Regs., Part II. and the Staff Manual respectively. Title pages will be prepared in manuscript.

1/24 "A" Loner Ref J.D. 34

Place	Date	Hour	Summary of Events and Information	Remarks and references to Appendices
JANUARY 1918				
Tuesday	1st		C.O. attends conference at Brigade H.Q. and then to METZ and 190th Brigade H.Q. at BEAUCAMP. Ascertain dispositions in case the Battalion should be required to move up. Battalion moves to huts near VALLULARM WOOD (near LECHELLE)	
Wednesday	2nd		C.O. attends conference at Brigade H.Q. to report on previous day's reconnaissance. Warning order received to be prepared to move to-morrow to rejoin the remainder of the Division now in rest in BOUZINCOURT Area. Order received to provide working party to-morrow to bury cable in HAVRINCOURT WOOD for 19th Division - order then cancelled. Lieut F. Goosey reports for duty as a re-inforcement.	
Thursday	3rd		Warning order received to move forward to-night to relieve the left Brigade 19th Division, time to be notified later. At 3 p.m. move to HAVRINCOURT WOOD where tea is issued, then on to HINDENBURG LINE S.W. of RIBECOURT and relieve the 7th Loyal North Lancs (Col Stuart D.S.O.)	
Friday	4th		Major T.O. Bury and Company reconnoitring officers go to 58th Brigade H.Q. and thence to the line. Battalion moves at dusk to relieve the 9th Welch Regt (Major Harrall D.S.O., M.C.) in front line S.W. of MARCOING. B.D.C & A Coys in front line and A Coy 21st London Regt (Capt West) in reserve in old HINDENBURG SUPPORT LINE. Each front line Company with 2 platoons in the line and one in support, except B who have all in front line. C.O. receives D.S.O. in New Years Honours.	
Saturday	5th		C.O. and 2nd in Command reconnoitre the line and meet Brig.Genl Glasgow commanding Brigade. Mention made to G.O.C. that dispositions are not considered satisfactory and he advises seeing own Brigade as soon as [illegible] they take over command. Matter mentioned to Capt. Peel, B.M. Brigadier called. Company Commanders Conference during the afternoon. That night a patrol found by B Company encounters enemy party near DAGO HOUSE.	

Army Form C. 2118.

WAR DIARY
or
INTELLIGENCE SUMMARY.
(*Erase heading not required.*)

Instructions regarding War Diaries and Intelligence Summaries are contained in F. S. Regs., Part II. and the Staff Manual respectively. Title pages will be prepared in manuscript.

Place	Date	Hour	Summary of Events and Information	Remarks and references to Appendices
Sunday	6th		Expected visits from Brigade and Divisional Commanders, but they did not come. C.O. called on Battalion on our right (9th Welch) to establish liaison and discuss patrols. Brigade Major calls. Discussed with him reorganisation of method of holding the line. Submit scheme to Brigade in writing. Lieut H.Gover returns from leave. Major T.C.Burry proceeds on leave. Enemy raid a "C" Company front line post and capture Private Osborne. Working parties from 21st and 22nd London Regt. come to work in our lines. Very wet. Lieut. P.T.Matthews receives M.C. in New Years Honours.	Very wet.
Monday	7th		Brigadier calls during afternoon to make further enquiries about last night's raid. Ordered to assume dispositions submitted yesterday. Working parties from 21st and 22nd London Regt. come to work in our lines. Major H.L.F.B.Nadand comes to Bn.H.Q. to act as 2nd in Command.	
Tuesday	8th		While C.O. and Adjutant are going round the line Divisional and Brigade Commanders call at Bn.H.Q. Lieut May, 7th London Regt. (attached) sniped while examining wire in front line in a blizzard.	
Wednesday	9th		Brigadier goes round line with C.O. C.O. attends conference at Bde.H.Q. 2.30.p.m. to discuss new defence scheme, etc., after which C.O. is informed by G.O.C.Brigade orders are on the way from Division relieving him of the command. Move to reserve at RIBECOURT. Relieved by 22nd London Regt. C.O. hands over command to Major.H.L.F.B.Nadand on receipt of written orders, pending Major T.C.Burry's return from leave. Similarly Lieut Turner hands over command of "C" Company to Lieut B.H.Strachan.	
Thursday	10th		Lt.Col.G.E.Wiltner,D.S.O.,M.C. and Lieut R.V.Turner go to Depot. Lieut S.H.Walker returns from leave. Lieut G.A.Coombe.M.C. returns from leave. Brigadier calls at Bn.H.Q.; subsequently Major H.L.F.B.Nadand visits Bde.H.Q. 150 men working for front line Battalions.	

Army Form C. 2118.

WAR DIARY
or
INTELLIGENCE SUMMARY.
(Erase heading not required.)

Instructions regarding War Diaries and Intelligence Summaries are contained in F.S. Regs., Part II. and the Staff Manual respectively. Title pages will be prepared in manuscript.

Place	Date	Hour	Summary of Events and Information	Remarks and references to Appendices
Friday	11th		Lt.Col.G.E.Milner D.S.O., M.O. reports at Rear Divisional H.Q. at ETRICOURT. The following officer re-inforcements arrive:- 2/Lieut G.R.Ellis posted to "A" Company (Military McCallist) 2/Lieut F.C.B.Holt posted to "A" Company; 2/Lieut E.Whitehead posted to "D" Company The following officer re-inforcement 2/Lieut B.King is notified as having been admitted to hospital. 5 Officers 150 o.rs working by night from 5.p.m. – 11.p.m. : 40 o.r by day.	
Saturday	12th		Day working parties provided for 33rd and R.E's. Working parties provided as usual at night. Battalion relieve by 15th Battalion returned by train to BERTINCOURT.	
Sunday	13th		Resting at BERTINCOURT. Major H.L.F.B.Nadaud inspected horse lines and billets.	
Monday 14th			Major H.L.F.B. Nadaud visited "B" Company at TRESCAULT. Capt.Gamage M.O. inspected billets.	
Tuesday	15th		Lt.Col.G.E.Milner D.S.O., M.C. called to Divisional H.Q. to be seen by Divisional Commander and is reinstated in command of the Battalion. Lieut G.O.Heathcote returns from leave. Capt.F.G.Gill returns from leave. Brigadier inspected horse lines.	
Wednesday	16th		Lt.Col.G.E.Milner D.S.O., M.O. rejoins Battalion. "B" Company rejoin Battalion at BERTINCOURT.	
Thursday	17th		Divisional Commander presents medal ribbons to :- L/Cpl Porter.E.A. M.M. O.S.M. Proud.F. D.C.M. Cpl Neal W.R. M.M. Cpl Theis.O. D.C.M. and certain o.rs of the M.G. Company in a nissen hut where representatives of the Battalion are paraded.	
Friday	18th		Brigade Commander inspects harness. Relieve 19th London Regt in reserve trenches by "A" & "C" Coys S.W. of FLESQUIERES, "D" Coy remaining at TRESCAULT, cable burying, and "B" Coy resting at BERTINCOURT.	

Army Form C. 2118.

WAR DIARY
or
INTELLIGENCE SUMMARY.
(Erase heading not required.)

Instructions regarding War Diaries and Intelligence Summaries are contained in F.S. Regs., Part II. and the Staff Manual respectively. Title pages will be prepared in manuscript.

Place	Date	Hour	Summary of Events and Information	Remarks and references to Appendices
	Saturday 19th		O.O. visited "A" & "O" Coys and also called on 22nd Battalion. Shelling behind Batt. H.Q.	
	Sunday 20th		O.O. and Major Madaud visited "A" & "O" Coys and also the 21st & 22nd Bns. Brigade Major called in afternoon. Desultory shelling all day.	
	Monday 21st		Brigade Commander and Staff Captain call. Inter relief od "B" & "D" Coys.	
	Tuesday 22nd		Heavy enemy shelling throughout the day in Bn.H.Q. area. Major Madaud goes on leave. Capt. Gall assumes duties of 2nd in Command.	
	Wednesday 23rd		Quiet day. Brigade Major calls. Lt. Matthews and reconnoitring party arrange relief of 23rd London Regt.	
	Thursday 24th.		Quiet day. C.O. and 2nd in Command visit all Companies. Major Bury returns from leave and stops at Depot. Relieve 23rd Battalion London Regt. in front line N.E. of FLESQUIERES: "A" & "O" in front line and "D" & "B" Companies in support.	
	Friday 25th.		Capt. & Adjt.L.O.Carage H.Q. to Brigade as Staff Learner. Lieut P.T.Matthews M.C. takes over his duties. Staff Captain and Brigade Intelligence officer call. Major Bray R.E. calls. Lt.Col.Dawes 21st Lon.Regt. calls. Usual patrols and working parties. Conference of Company Commanders at Bn. H.Q. Quiet day and night.	
	Saturday 26th.		C.O. attends Brigadiers Conference at 22nd H.Q. regarding a proposed raid on enemy gunpits. Usual patrols and working parties. Quiet day and night. Bde Major calls. Major Bruce - R.E.Signals calls. Major Duncan R.F.A. calls.	
	Sunday 27th.		Group Commander (Lt.Col.Allen) and Adjt call. G.S.O.1 calls and discusses proposed raid &c., Later informed by Brigade that raid would not be carried out. Lt.Cols.Greenwood (22nd) & Dawes (21st) call. Major Bury goes to 21st London Regt in Command while O.O. goes on leave. Lieut H.S.Mitchell to hospital. Inter relief by front and support Companies. Usual patrols and working parties.	

Army Form C. 2118.

WAR DIARY
or
INTELLIGENCE SUMMARY.
(Erase heading not required.)

Instructions regarding War Diaries and Intelligence Summaries are contained in F. S. Regs., Part II. and the Staff Manual respectively. Title pages will be prepared in manuscript.

Place	Date	Hour	Summary of Events and Information	Remarks and references to Appendices
	Monday 28th		C.Os. of 21st and 22nd call. Patrol encounter during the evening. Lieut Coombe goes to Divisional Wing, Corps Reinforcement Camp as Instructor. Lieut Cadman goes on leave. Lieut E. Gover assumes command of "B" Company. Informed of new organisation by which the following Officers :- Lieut. A.S. Causton, 2/Lieut. (A/Capt) A.C. Alexander M.C., 2/Lieut D. O'Kell, 2/Lieut E.C. Meredith, 2/Lieut E. Day and 350 o.rs of the 8th London Regt. (Post Office Rifles) are coming as a reinforcement on the disbandment of the 1/5th 1/7th and 1/8th Lon.Regts. on reduction of Brigades to 3 Battalions. Usual patrols and working parties. Quiet day and night. Lieut P.W. Burroughs takes over duties of Works Officer.	
	Tuesday 29th		Brigade Commander and Major Duncan R.F.A call. Considerable 6" Newton Mortars activity during the afternoon followed by retaliatory artillery fire. Usual patrols and working parties. Major M.Finney, Major Bray R.E. calls. Capt Wiggles, Corps Intelligence Officer calls.	
	Wednesday 30th		C.Os. calls on 22nd Lon.Regt. C.O. discussed disposal of reinforcement with B.M. Considerable enemy shelling during the afternoon. M.O. to hospital with scabies. No relief available. Usual patrols and working parties.	
	Thursday 31st.		Brigade and Divisional Commanders call. Discuss work, patrols and defensive arrangements. Artillery Group Commander calls. Usual patrols and working parties. Quiet day and night. Capt.C.R.C.Shield.M.C. returns from leave - Capt.G.N.C.Dalziel goes on leave. Staff Captain calls.	

Lieut.Col. cdg.,
1/24th Bn.Lon.Regt.,
"The Queens".

Army Form C. 2118.

1/24 London
1st 35

WAR DIARY
or
INTELLIGENCE SUMMARY.
(Erase heading not required.)

Instructions regarding War Diaries and Intelligence Summaries are contained in F. S. Regs., Part II. and the Staff Manual respectively. Title pages will be prepared in manuscript.

Place	Date	Hour	Summary of Events and Information	Remarks and references to Appendices
February 1918				
Friday	1st.		Quiet day. Reconnoitring party of 15th Lon.Regt. call. C.O. takes Major Woolley round the line.	
Saturday	2nd		Quiet day. Relieved by 15th Lon.Regt. and move from TRESCAULT to BERTINCOURT by rail.	
Sunday	3rd.		Receive a reinforcement of 6 Officers and 243 o.rs from 8th London Regt. which has been broken up on reorganisation of Division and Brigades. Hold conference of Company Commanders on Battalion reorganisation consequent on increase in strength and increase number of Platoons from 3 to 4. 8th London Officers are posted as follows :- Capt. A.C.Alexander M.C. "C" Coy (to command), 2/Lieut E.Day "B" Coy. 2/Lieut C.Witham "B" Coy. 2/Lieut D.O'Neil "D" Coy. 2/Lieut E.G.Meredith "C" Coy. 2/Lieut A.J.L.Causton Signal Officer.	
Monday	4th.		Battalion bathing and refitting. 2/Lieut F.Morgan goes on leave to England. Called on for working party of 30 o.rs. 28 o.rs sent for attachment to Australian Tunnelling Company at RIBECOURT. Col.Thunder D.S.O. A.A.& Q.M.G. calls reference billeting. See Brigade Commander reference difficulty of training and reorganising in view of the large numbers of men required for fatigues and working parties.	
Tuesday	5th.		Reinforcement of 20 o.rs arrives. Working party of 450 o.rs sent to TRESCAULT by light railway to work on reserve trenches and wire. Lieut D.H.Boll reports back from Third Army School.	
Wednesday	6th.		Find working parties of 11 O.Rs. Lieut Sanderson, P.T.A and Intelligence reports for 1 month's line experience. Brigade Commander inspects Transport and Q.M.Stores. M.O. returns to duty from Hospital. A.D.M.S calls. 720224 Sgt Shadgett G.A. awarded Belgian Croix de Guerre. 720367 Sgt Thomas C.B. awarded M.M. 721727 L/Cpl Brennan F. awarded M.M.	
Thursday	7th.		Reconnoitre FLESQUIERES Right Sector at present held by 18th Lon.Regt and arrange details of next relief.	

Army Form C. 2118.

WAR DIARY
or
INTELLIGENCE SUMMARY.
(Erase heading not required.)

Instructions regarding War Diaries and Intelligence Summaries are contained in F. S. Regs., Part II. and the Staff Manual respectively. Title pages will be prepared in manuscript.

Place	Date	Hour	Summary of Events and Information	Remarks and references to Appendices
Friday	8th.		Move into the line. A & C Coys in Front line. D Coy in support in HINDENBURG LINE and B Coy in reserve at RIBECOURT. Major H.O.Kistler 355th U.S.A. Infantry reports for attachment for instruction. Lieut P.W.Burroughs proceeds to 17th Corps Infantry School.	
Saturday	9th.		Brigade Commander calls. Quiet day. G.S.O.1 calls. Conduct Major Kistler round the line.	
Sunday	10th.		Visit front held by 23rd Lon.Regt. on our left with Major Kistler. Quiet day. Daylight patrol by 2/Lieut C.Witham and e.o.rs. Major H.L.F.B.Maland returns from leave. 2/Lieut C.Witham and Lieut D.E.Poll proceed on leave.	
Monday	11th.		C.R.E and Major Laird R.E. call. See M.G.O. regarding their positions. Major Kistler returns to Division. Quiet day with occasional shelling. O.C. 22nd Lon.Regt. calls and arranges details of next relief.	
Tuesday	12th.		Daylight patrol of 2/Lieut. H.C.E.Miller and 8.o.rs - kill 3 of the enemy. B.M. calls. Relieved by 22nd Lon.Regt. and move to RIBECOURT with A Company less 1 Platoon at MOLE TRENCH. Place 1 Company at tactical disposal of 22nd Lon.Regt.	
Wednesday	13th.		Investigated gas casualties to 22nd and 24th men in neighbourhood of MOLE TRENCH with M.O. and Corps Gas Adviser. Report to Brigade Commander. 2/Lieut D.O'Kell reports from leave.	
Thursday	14th.		See Brigade Commander reference proposed daylight raid. O.C. attends demonstration by Third Army Tank Bn. at BRAY SUR SOMME.	
Friday	15th.		O.C. calls on 22nd Lon.Regt. reference proposed raid on enemy post on their front and on 23rd Lon.Regt. to arrange details of next relief. Discuss with Brigade Commander programme of work to be carried out during next tour in the line and details of raid.	
Saturday	16th.		Heavy bombardment of RIBECOURT throughout the day. 2/Lieut. G.R.Ellis, L/Cpls Gard, March and 6.o.rs attack enemy post; no identification obtained owing to enemy having put out new wire since previous reconnaissance but a number of casualties were inflicted. L/Cpl Gard behaved very gallantly during the operation. Relieved 23rd Lon.Regt. in left subsection FLESQUIERES SECTOR. B & D Coys in Front line, A Coy in support and C Coy in reserve.	

Army Form C. 2118.

WAR DIARY
or
INTELLIGENCE SUMMARY.
(Erase heading not required.)

Instructions regarding War Diaries and Intelligence Summaries are contained in F. S. Regs., Part II. and the Staff Manual respectively. Title pages will be prepared in manuscript.

Place	Date	Hour	Summary of Events and Information	Remarks and references to Appendices
Sunday	17th.		O.O. called to Brigade to discuss a proposed raid without artillery preparation. Group Commander called. Lieut. J.P.Cadman and 2/Lieut. E.G.Meredith report back from leave and the former assumes Command of B Company. The following Officer reinforcements report for duty with the Battalion :- 2/Lieut P.G.Hollister. posted to "A" Coy. 2/Lieut W.A.G.Morgan posted to "A" Coy. 2/Lieut A.J.Taylor posted to "B" Coy. 2/Lieut J.E.Collins posted to "B" Coy. 2/Lieut J.N.Summers posted to "C" Coy. 2/Lieut G.B.Poland posted to "D" Coy.	
Monday	18th		Daylight patrol fails to find signs of the enemy. O.O. sees Brigade Commander reference work in the line. Patrol during the night encounters a party of the enemy and drives them in. Lieut E.Gover proceeds to England for 6 months. Quiet day.	
Tuesday	19th		O.O. sees Major Laird R.E. reference tonight's work. Company Commanders Conference at Bn.H.Q. Quiet day.	
Wednesday	20th		Commander Ellis O.C. Hawke Bn. R.N.D calls regarding forthcoming relief. O.O. takes him round the Battalion Sector and the front of the 22nd Bn.Lon.Regt. on our right. Intercompany relief - A & C relieving D & B respectively. B moves into support and A into reserve. Owing to wet weather the trenches fall in badly in many places. Quiet day.	
Thursday	21st.		General Lawrie, G.O.O. R.N.D calls at Bn. H.Q. with Col.Turner,G.S.O.1 and Col.Davis the new G.S.O.1. Patrol of 8 encounters about 30 enemy and drives them in with casualties. 2 of our men wounded. Advance party of Hawke Bn. arrives. Quiet day.	
Friday	22nd.		Major General goes round from line. Relieved by Hawke Bn and move to BERTINCOURT. Quiet day.	
Saturday	23rd.		Move to Rocquigny, marching past the Brigade Commander. 2/Lieut F.Morgan to course at 17th Corps School.	
Sunday	24th.		Church parade. Conference of Company Commanders. Conference of O.Cs at Brigade H.Q. reference training during period in Corps Reserve.	

Army Form C. 2118.

WAR DIARY
or
INTELLIGENCE SUMMARY.
(Erase heading not required.)

Instructions regarding War Diaries and Intelligence Summaries are contained in F. S. Regs., Part II. and the Staff Manual respectively. Title pages will be prepared in manuscript.

Place	Date	Hour	Summary of Events and Information	Remarks and references to Appendices
Monday	25th.		Battalion refitting. Wet day. C.O. attends conference at Division on lessons to be learnt from recent operations, scheme of training while out of the line and the present rôle of the Division.	
Tuesday	26th.		Battalion parade and platoon training. Capt.F.G.Gill on leave to BORDEAUX. 2/Lieut A.C.S Bean to Reinforced Third Army Musketry School. Hon.Lieut.& Q.M.A.J.Beer on leave to England. Corps Commander (Genl.Fanshawe) visits camp while the Battalion is out.	
Wednesday	27th		Battalion parade. Platoon training and Musketry. B.G.C and G.C.O inspects billets during the afternoon. 2/Lieut.A.J.Taylor goes to Divl.Wing, Corps Reinforcement Camp to relieve Lieut.G.A. Coode.M.O. who is to act as Battalion Musketry Officer during training period. 2/Lieut G.R.Ellis to Sniping and Observation Course. 2/Lieut E.Day returns from leave.	
Friday	28th.		350 men inoculated. Bn.H.Q. Officers attend Brigade Instructional Tour in vicinity of Le MESNIL.	

Lieut.Col. Cdg.
1/24th Bn.London Regiment.
"The Queens".

47th Division.

142nd Infantry Brigade.

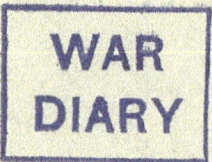

1/24th BATTALION

LONDON REGIMENT

MARCH 1918

Army Form C. 2118.

WAR DIARY
or
INTELLIGENCE SUMMARY.
(Erase heading not required.)

Instructions regarding War Diaries and Intelligence Summaries are contained in F. S. Regs., Part II. and the Staff Manual respectively. Title pages will be prepared in manuscript.

Place	Date	Hour	Summary of Events and Information	Remarks and references to Appendices
MARCH. 1918.				
Friday	1st.		Battalion parade. Lecture by C.O. Riding Instruction for Officers.	
Saturday	2nd.		Battalion parade. Companies train on the assault course. Musketry and Platoon drill. Tactical Scheme for O.C. and 2nd i/c Companies.	
Sunday	3rd.		Church parade in Cinema Hut. Officers reconnoitre Assembly Position behind GOUZEAUCOURT. Entraining point reconnoitred. Guard mounting competition won by "B" Company.	
Monday	4th.		Battalion drill. Band and Drums on range for L.G.A.A. instruction. Coy Reserve L.Gs. on ranges. Battalion in Attack.	
Tuesday	5th.		The C.O. inspects the Battalion on Training Ground. Battalion Training.	
Wednesday	6th.		Physical Training and Bayonet Fighting. Company Training. L.G. Competition won by "C" Coy, second prize "B" Coy. Cooker Competition won by "D" Coy. Captain E.G. Gill returns from BORDEAUX leave.	
Thursday	7th.		Battalion training under Company arrangements. Aeroplane demonstration. Lieut P.T.Matthews goes on leave.	
Friday	8th.		Brigade Tactical Exercise. Guard Mounting Competition won by "D" Coy. Military Medal awarded to the following:- 720584 L/Cpl E.Gard and 720300 L/Cpl V.March.	
Saturday	9th.		Battalion and Company Training. Battalion Concert. Divisional Gymkhana held on RACE COURSE on BUS - BERTHMCOURT ROAD. Band gave a performance.	
Sunday	10th.		Church Parade.	
Monday	11th.		Battalion in Attack. Company Drill. Brigade Boxing Competition - Welter weight, competition won by Pte Brooks - Featherweight won by Pte Ashford.	

Army Form C. 2118.

WAR DIARY
or
INTELLIGENCE SUMMARY.
(Erase heading not required.)

Instructions regarding War Diaries and Intelligence Summaries are contained in F.S. Regs., Part II. and the Staff Manual respectively. Title pages will be prepared in manuscript.

Place	Date	Hour	Summary of Events and Information	Remarks and references to Appendices
Tuesday	12th.		Brigadier inspects Battalion Transport. Demonstration in use of German Light Machine Gun.	
Wednesday	13th.		Battalion provide working party of 300 o.rs to work under R.Es in forward area at TRESCAULT. The following Officers were reposted as follows :- 2/Lieut E.C.Meredith to "A" Coy - 2/Lieut E.Day to "A" Coy. 2/Lieut F.G.B.Holt to "B" Coy - 2/Lieut P.G.Hollister to "C" Coy - 2/Lieut E.Day to "A" Coy.	
Thursday	14th.		The whole Battalion on working party in forward area at TRESCAULT. M.O. goes on leave.	
Friday	15th.		The whole Battalion on working party in forward area at TRESCAULT.	
Saturday	16th.		Battalion and Company training. Divisional Gymkhana held on BUS- BERTINCOURT RACE COURSE.	
Sunday	17th.		Church Parade. Battalion supplies 100 men for working party in forward area. Guard Mounting Competition won by "A" Coy. Brigade Football Competition won by Battalion	
Monday	18th.		Battalion and Company Training.	
Tuesday	19th.		47th Division relieving 2nd Division. Company Officers reconnoitre METZ and WINCHESTER VALLEY. Company Training.	
Wednesday	20th		142 Brigade moves into forward area as Support Brigade. Leave ROCQUIGNY 2.p.m. In position 5.p.m. H.Q. "B" and "D" in village of METZ, "A" and "C" at WINCHESTER VALLEY.— Reconnaissance (Q.21.c.) Lieut H.S.Mitchell and 2/Lieut A.J.Taylor rejoin Battalion. Capt.T.G.Gill leaves for L.G.Course.	
Thursday	21st.		Heavy enemy bombardment and many gas shells - opens about 3.a.m. 6.a.m. Battalion "Standing to". 7.a.m. move up through barrage to 2nd Defence System (about Q.17.a and c.) "A" and "B" front line - "C" and "D" support. In position about noon. Casualties in METZ and moving up :- Lt.Col.G.E.Milner.D.S.O.,M.O.; Wounded - Major H.L.F.B. Madams, Killed - Lieut H.S.Mitchell, Killed. - 2/Lieut G.B.Poland. Killed. - R.S.M., H.W.Norris.D.C.M., Killed. Major.T.O.Bury assumes command Remainder of day we work on trenches. Raids reported on our Divisional Front but actual attacks on flanks to north and south.	

Army Form C. 2118.

WAR DIARY
or
INTELLIGENCE SUMMARY.
(Erase heading not required.)

Place	Date	Hour	Summary of Events and Information	Remarks and references to Appendices
Friday	22nd.		Fairly quiet day. Consolidating our positions. 2/Lieut H.Whitehead to Depot for Course. 2/Lieut D.O'Kell to Depot as T.O. 2/Lieut A.C.Bean from Depot reports for duty. Transport at EQUANCOURT. Bodies of Major H.L.F.B.Nada and 2/Lieut G.B.Poland buried there in civilian cemetery.	
		Midnight.	Front lines retire through us.	
Saturday	23rd.	3.a.m.	Withdraw to positions in METZ SWITCH (Q 14.d and 21 a.) Platoons from "A" and "B" cover same. In position 5.a.m.	
		Morning.	Enemy on our front in HAVRINCOURT WOOD.	
		1.30.p.m.	Withdraw. Our rearguard being in close touch with the enemy.	
		4.p.m.	In position about P.33.b and d. Front lines withdraw through us followed by enemy.	
		6.p.m.	Withdraw to positions N.W. of VALLULART WOOD – enemy being round our right flank – P.26.d. and 32 a.b. "D" Coy and Coy of 23rd Lon.Regt covering right flank of Brigade.	
		9.p.m.	Enemy reported to occupy ETRICOURT, BUS, LECHELLE and VELU.	
		10.p.m.	Withdraw. Fired on from BUS.	
		Midnight.	Whole Battalion with units of other Battalions named East of Railway Embankment at YTRES (P19.b.) Major T.O.Bury holds conference with Company Commanders and Senior Officer Lt.Col.Green.D.S.O.,M.C., 23rd Lon.Regt decides to fight our way out. Dumps at YTRES being exploded. Battalion arrives and takes command. Distance marched this day approx: 7½ miles.	
Sunday	24th.	1.a.m.	Force of approx. 1500 leaves YTRES in column of route. Guides Major BOOSEY, 23rd. London Regiment and Lt. GOOSEY, 24th. London Regiment – marching by Stars and compass. Our C Coy. provides Advance and Flank Guards. Route:– BERTINCOURT – BARASTRE – ROCQUIGNY.	
		7.a.m.	In new positions about U.1.b. and d.	
		2.p.m.	Enemy reported at LES BOEUFS. Withdrawal in North Westerly direction – being fired on from village – to positions EAST of NEW GUEUDECOURT (N.21.a and 27.b.) In position about 3.30.p.m.	
		4.30.p.m.	Ordered to withdraw to COURCELETTE – MARTINPUICH LINE. After moving off destination given as HIGH WOOD – two Companies do not receive this order and Battalion becomes divided as follows:– Northern Half :– D & A Coys. under Capt.O.F.C.SHIELD,M.C. Southern Half:– H.Q., (Major T.O.BURY), C & B Coys. under Capt.A.C.ALEXANDER,M.C.	

Army Form C. 2118.

WAR DIARY
or
INTELLIGENCE SUMMARY.
(Erase heading not required.)

Place	Date	Hour	Summary of Events and Information	Remarks and references to Appendices
Sunday	24th (Cont'd)	6.30.p.m.	South half in position in HIGH WOOD where enemy presses them closely. A/Adjt.Capt G.M.C.Dalziel missing from this point, also Brigade Staff (including Brig.Genl. Bailey and Capt.L.O.Garnage,M.C.)	
		8.30.p.m.	Half Battalion (North) in position N.W. of MARTINPUICH (M.26.b and d.) having marched via EAUCOURT L'ABBAYE passing memorial to men of 47th Division. Oct 1916. Distance covered this day 14½ miles approx. 2/Lieut Witham wounded to-day.	
Monday	25th.	2.30.a.m.	Half Battalion (South) at BAZENTIN – LE – PETIT (S 8 central) having withdrawn from HIGH WOOD.	
		3.30.a.m.	Half Battalion (North) left MARTINPUICH to get in touch with rest of Battalion.	
		6.a.m.	North half Battalion resting at POZIERES.	
		9.a.m.	South half Battalion in CONTALMAISON. Major T.O.Burry evacuated sick. South half Battalion under Capt.A.C.Alexander,M.C. in front line position at X 11 d (CONTALMAISON) – Brig.Genl.Kennedy commanding the line. North half Battalion reports to G.O.C.Division, draws rations, and takes up reserve position (Left half of Divisional Front) at X 9 d and 15 b under Brig.Genl.Mildren.	
		Afternoon & evening	South half Battalion holding up enemy attacks	
		Evening.	North half Battalion extends to left, forming flank to meet enemy who is advancing north of POZIERES – dumps here are exploding.	
			Distance covered this day 3¼ miles approx.	
Tuesday	26th.	2.30.am.	Each half Battalion is ordered to withdraw through LA BOISELLE – AVELUY to BOUZINCOURT.	
		6.a.m.	North half Battalion takes up position and commences digging in on high ground west of AVELUY (W.15 d and 10 a.) Shortly after they are informed that 12th Division are taking over line and proceed by orders of G.O.C. Division towards SENLIS	
		Noon.	Whole Battalion again together at 11 d east of SENLIS. Major A.T.Fearon,M.C., assumes command. Lieut P.T.Matthews,M.C., 2/Lieut G.R.Ellis and Lieut B.H. Strachan rejoin Battalion. Transport joins us here.	
		4.30.p.m.	Leave SENLIS with 142 Brigade. Route:- HEDAUVILLE – FORCEVILLE – ACHEUX – LOUVENCOURT.	

WAR DIARY
or
INTELLIGENCE SUMMARY.

(Erase heading not required.)

Army Form C. 2118.

Place	Date	Hour	Summary of Events and Information	Remarks and references to Appendices
Tuesday	26th (Contd)	10.p.m.	Battalion goes into huts at VAUCHELLES - LES - AUTHIE. Distance covered this day 15 miles approx.	
Wednesday.	27th	9.a.m.	Leave VAUCHELLE route :- RAINEVAL - TOUTENCOURT.	
		1.p.m.	Transport at TOUTENCOURT. Battalion in Brigade Support position West of HARPONVILLE (U.4.c and U.9.d.)	
			Afternoon and evening Battalion resting. Company Commanders reconnoitring this new position. Distance covered this day approx 7 miles. 2/Lieut F.G.B.Holt returns from course.	
Thursday	28th	Midnight	- leave for WARLOY - "D" Coy acting as advance guard to Brigade with "C" Coy in support.	
		2.a.m.	"C" and "D" in position picquetting roads on eastern and southern edges of WARLOY. Remainder of Battalion goes into billets in WARLOY. Rest and re-organise. Distance approx 3 miles.	
Friday X	29th	Night 28/29.	"C" Coy picquets roads with "D" Coy in support.	
		Day	- Rest and reorganise. C.O. reconnoitres front line area.	
		6.45.p.m.	Leave WARLOY. Route :- SENLIS - BOUZINCOURT - MARTINSART.	
		Midnight	- Relief complete of 7th Royal Sussex (12th Div). Battalion now occupies front line positions in AVELUY WOOD (W.4.a and b, and Q.34.d.) Front line "A" and "B". Support "C" and "D".)	
		(Memo)	Distance covered this day approx 6 miles. Distance marched from midnight Mar 22/23 to midnight Mar 29/30 approx 60 miles.	
Saturday.	30th.	Morning	- heavy firing south of ALBERT. Our front fairly quiet. Heavy shelling of village of MARTINSART in our rear at intervals during the day. Rain at intervals and men wet.	
		Evening.	17th Fusiliers on our left relieved by Composite Battn of 2nd Division.	
Sunday	31st.	Night 30/31.	Quiet. Morning :- G.O.C.Div. called at Bn.H.Q. Day:- MARTINSART heavily shelled at intervals. 9.p.m. "D" and "C" relieve "B" and "A" in front right and left respectively latter Companies going in Support.	

Major, Odg.,
1/24th Bn.London Regt.

142nd Brigade.
47th Division.

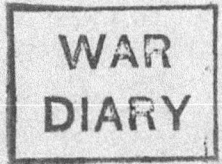

1/24th BATTALION

THE LONDON REGIMENT.

APRIL 1 9 1 8

Report on Operations at AVELUY WOOD

WAR DIARY or INTELLIGENCE SUMMARY.

Army Form C. 2118.

(Erase heading not required.)

Vol 37

Place	Date	Hour	Summary of Events and Information	Remarks and references to Appendices
APRIL 1918.				
MONDAY.	1		3.a.m. – 3.30.a.m. Heavy hostile shelling. Message received that Reserve Division will stand to and enemy attack is expected in morning. 5.15.a.m. – 5.45.a.m. Our artillery put down heavy barrage. 7.a.m. MARTINSART shelled but remainder of day quiet. Morning. G.O.C. Division goes round our line. 7.p.m. MARTINSART shelled and tower of church knocked down. Remainder of the night quiet.	
TUESDAY.	2		Day quiet. D Coy. claims 2 hits on enemy party. Capt. F.G.Gill and Capt.J.L.Kilbride (Medical Officer) report at Depot. 38th. Divisional Officers reconnoitre – Two stay with us. O.C. 4th. Fusiliers. (2nd. Division) now on our left, calls this evening. Night. 2/3rd. Normal. Intermittent shelling. 2/Lieut. G.R. Ellis with party carry out good PATROL to BLACKHORSE BRIDGE, across RIVER ANCRE. No enemy encountered.	
WEDNESDAY.	3		Day quiet. 38th. Divisional Officers leave this morning. Capt. Gill and J.L.KILBRIDE rejoin Battalion this afternoon. Capt. DIXON (acting Medical Officer) returns to Field Ambulance. A Coy. relieves C Coy. and B Coy. relieves D Coy. Capt.F.G.GILL assumes Second in Command.	
THURSDAY.	4		A Patrol of 1 N.C.O. and 7 men of A Coy. under 2/Lt.G.R.ELLIS formed a covering party for R.E's who successfully blow up BLACK HORSE BRIDGE (W.5.b.9.1.) C Coy. supplied a carrying party of 1 N.C.O. and 9 men. Col. CAREY, C.R.E. called – Major WALKER, 7th. Royal Fusiliers called – O. C. 63rd. M.G.Coy. called.	
FRIDAY.	5		Enemy bombardment opened at 6.30.a.m. and continued all day. Enemy attacked at 8.a.m. – put up S.O.S. – D Coy. reinforced B Coy. – two platoons C Coy. reinforced A Coy. – 23rd. Battalion commenced to withdraw – B & D Coys. conformed – A Coy. held – Lieuts. CADMAN and STRACHAN called at Bn. H.Q. and were ordered to regain their original front line – this was not possible and eventually a line was held at about 45 degrees from the old one. Capt. F.G.GILL attended conference at 23rd. Bn. H.Q. with reference to a counter-attack to be made by two Companies of that Battalion to regain original line on right – Counter-Attack was made at 4.30.p.m. but failed – 23rd. Battalion	

WAR DIARY or INTELLIGENCE SUMMARY.

Army Form C. 2118.

(Erase heading not required.)

Place	Date	Hour	Summary of Events and Information	Remarks and references to Appendices
APRIL 1918. FRIDAY	5 Contd.		reinforced us with two platoons at 7.p.m. – these were held in Close Support. At 7.30.p.m. Capt.F.G.GILL called at Brigade H.Q. to explain exact situation and received instructions for the Battalion to hold on at all costs. At 7.30.p.m. A Coy. reported that Battalion on left had fallen back – a defensive flank was formed with one platoon of C Coy. and 1 platoon 22nd. Battalion until touch was regained. At 11.p.m. O.C. 2nd. Battn. Royal Marines called and stated his Battalion had arrived to reinforce 7th. Royal Fusiliers on our left. He, with Capt.F.G.GILL, took one Company to A Coy. where he continued their line on left but on account of enemy fire was forced back behind original line – At midnight Battalion was reinforced by two more platoons 22nd. Battalion – these were held in close support. Casualties:– 2/Lt.F.G.B.HOLT – Killed Lieut.B.M.Streachan – Wounded. Capt.A.C.ALEXANDER,M.C. – N.Y.D.N. 2/Lt.E.DAY – N.Y.D.N. C.S.M.BAXTER – Killed.	
SATURDAY	6		At 6.a.m. two Companies Royal Welsh Fusiliers made a counter-attack with a view to restoring our line on the right, but it failed – 1 platoon A Coy. in conjunction with 2nd. Battn.Royal Marines made counter-attack on left and regained whole of the line capturing at the same time many prisoners. A Coy. secured twenty one prisoners and two machine guns – 2 Platoons of 22nd. Battalion withdrawn and put in close Support. At 7.p.m. enemy attacked from the South – S.O.S. sent up – Front line reinforced on right by two platoons of C Coy. and on left by attached Coy. 22nd. Battalion – Enemy repulsed with heavy losses. O.C. 12th. Bn. Highland Light Infantry, 35th. Division called to arrange relief the same night – Relief complete at 3.35.a.m. on night of 6/7th.	
SUNDAY	7		Battalion arrived in Billets at WARLOY, last Company reaching there at 8.a.m. Battalion rested during rest of the day – C.O. called on Brigade.	
MONDAY	8		Battalion marched from WARLOY to RAINCHEVAL and billeted there.	
TUESDAY	9		C.O. inspects new draft of 90 O.Rs. Divisional Commander and Brigadier called – Companies re-organising and refitting.	

Army Form C. 2118.

WAR DIARY
or
INTELLIGENCE SUMMARY.
(Erase heading not required.)

2⁴ᵗʰ Devon Regt

Instructions regarding War Diaries and Intelligence Summaries are contained in F.S. Regs., Part II. and the Staff Manual respectively. Title pages will be prepared in manuscript.

Hour, Date, Place	Summary of Events and Information	Remarks and references to Appendices
APRIL 1918.		
WEDNESDAY 10th.	Battalion re-organising and refitting. C.O. and Capt. SHIELDS, M.C. reconnoitre BAIZIEUX - FORCEVILLE LINE. 2/Lt.R.G.FURSMAN, 3rd. Corps Cyclist Battalion reports for duty and is posted to B Coy.	
THURSDAY 11th.	Battalion marched from RAINNEVAL to BONNEVILLE - 10 miles.	
FRIDAY 12th.	Battalion marched from BONNEVILLE to VVRENCH - 16 miles.	
SATURDAY 13th.	C.O. inspects Battalion by Platoons - 2/Lt.D.O.Kell transferred from D Coy. to B Coy.	
SUNDAY 14th.	Brigadier and Brigade Major called - Church Parade - draft of 12 arrive.	
MONDAY 15th.	Brigadier and Brigade Major called - Company training - firing on Range - C.O. inspects Battalion Transport - Tactical exercise for Officers and Platoon Sergeants under Brigadier - 2/Lt.C.C.STANESBY and Lt.R.J. PRANKERD report for duty and are posted to A & D Coys. respectively. Lt.Col.R.S.I.FRIEND, D.S.O. arrives and assumes command of the Battn.	
TUESDAY 16th.	C.O. attends Conference at Divisional H.Q. - Coy. training and Musketry - Lt.A.J.L.CAUSTON reports back from Brigade and assumes duties of Signalling Officer - 2/Lt.G.R.ELLIS reports to Brigade for duty. A Coy. win Final in Battalion Football Competition.	
WEDNESDAY 17th.	Company training - Musketry.	
THURSDAY 18th.	Brigadier and Brigade Major call - Lt.W.B.HALL reports for duty and is posted to D Coy. - Company training and Musketry.	

Army Form C. 2118.

WAR DIARY
or
INTELLIGENCE SUMMARY.
(Erase heading not required.)

Summary (4) of Events and Information

Hour, Date, Place	Summary of Events and Information	Remarks and references to Appendices
APRIL 1918		
FRIDAY 19th.	Companies training in the attack - Brigadier and Brigade Major called Capt.C.R.G.SHIELDS, M.C. goes to hospital - Lt.W.B.HALL takes over command of D Coy. - 2/Lt.H.WHITEHEAD leaves for L.G.Course.	
SATURDAY 20th.	Divisional Commander and Brigadier visited the Battalion while training in the attack.	
SUNDAY 21st.	Church Parade - Divisional Sports. The undermentioned Officers reported for duty and are posted as follows:- 2/Lt.F.H.Pledger — posted to A Coy. 2/Lt.H.J.Grose — posted to A Coy. 2/Lt.W.J.N.Moare — posted to B Coy. 2/Lt.L.W.Brown — posted to C Coy. 2/Lt.H.Kelly — posted to D Coy. 2/Lt.H.E.Johnson — posted to D Coy. 2/Lt.A.H.Pyle — posted to D Coy.	
MONDAY 22nd.	Battalion training in the attack. Divisional Commander addressed the Battn. - Brigadier called - Lt.H.J.SANDERS,M.C. arrives and takes over command of C Coy. Lt.A.C.CAMMELL. arrives and takes over command of B Coy. Lt.R.F.STEVERS,M.C. arrives and is posted to B Coy. - Draft 12 arrive.	
TUESDAY 23rd.	C.O. member of Court of Enquiry on claim for damages at WARLOY - MAJOR A.M.FEARON,M.C. President of F.G.C.M. - Battn. training in Advance Guard and Attack. Brigadier visited the Battn. while training - Draft of 12 arrive.	
WEDNESDAY 24th.	Companies training in the attack and Counter-Attack - Brigade Staff Ride. 720735 Pte.C.JACKSON,M.M. awarded Bar to M.M. 720244 Pte.E.HYATT,M.M. awarded Bar to M.M.	

WAR DIARY
or
INTELLIGENCE SUMMARY.
(Erase heading not required.)

Army Form C. 2118.

24th Lon. Regt

Hour, Date, Place	Summary of Events and Information	Remarks and references to Appendices
APRIL 1918. WEDNESDAY 24th. Contd.	724437 Cpl. H.USHERWOOD awarded M.M. 725066 Pte. S.A.BALLS awarded M.M.	
THURSDAY 25th.	Capt.L.BASEDEN,M.O. reports for duty and takes over command of D Coy. Draft of 100 O.Rs. arrive from 19th. Battn.London Regiment - Draft of 35 O.Rs. arrive and are posted to Companies - Brigadier called - Corps Commander called.	
FRIDAY 26th.	Divisional Commander called - Company training & Musketry on Range. 2/Lt.A.J.Taylor reported sick and sent to 6th.London Field Ambulance.	
SATURDAY 27th.	Battalion training = in Advance and Rearguards - Battalion moves to FROMELLES - FONTAIN-SUR-MAVE. Brigadier called - Lt.GOSBY returned from Course - Warning order received to take over sector of Line West of ALBERT - Draft of 9 arrives. The following awarded MILITARY MEDAL:- 720605 Pte.L.W. SCOTT BLOXAM 721043 L/Sergt.E.F.SCOTT 722078 Pte.H.MERLIN 721807 Cpl.H.WOODS 720514 Cpl.J.STANTON 720212 L/Cpl.W.J.HAYMES 725510 Pte.H.W.BARKER 722594 Pte.C.J.V.LANE 720409 Pte.J.BIRD 721849 Pte.J.T.LITTLE	
SUNDAY 28th.	Brigade Church Parade - Sermon preached by the Bishop of KHARTOON - Presentation of ribbons by Divisional Commander - March past. the Divisional Commander - Major A.T.FEARON leaves the Battalion to report to 17th. Battn. London Regiment - Transport leaves for SURCAMPS - 11 miles.	

Army Form C. 2118.

WAR DIARY
or
INTELLIGENCE SUMMARY.
(Erase heading not required.)

24th Lon Rgt

Hour, Date, Place	Summary of Events and Information	Remarks and references to Appendices
APRIL 1918.	(6).	
MONDAY 29th.	Battalion embusses for CONTAY and marches from there to WARLOY - 12 Officers and 121 O.Rs. remain at FROYELLES to report to Divisional Wing - Transport leaves SURCAMPS for WARLOY - 24 miles. Capt. P.W.BURROUGHS Lt. G.C.HEATHCOTE Awarded the MILITARY CROSS. Lt. F.GOOSEN Lt. H.JOHNSON 2/Lt. J.E.COLLINS The following awarded the D.C.M. 720300 L/Cpl. V.MARCH,M.M.	
SUNDAY 30th.	C.O., Signalling Officer and Company Commanders reconnoitred the line to be taken over from 17th.Bn.A.I.F. - Rifle and Kit inspections. Total casualties from March 21st to April 30th. inclusive:- KILLED 34 MISSING 15 WOUNDED 123 WOUNDED(GAS) 20 WOUNDED at DUTKIA 8 N. Y. D. N. 8	
2nd. May 1918.	R.M.Reid Lieut.Col., Cdg., 1/24th.Battn.London Regiment, 'The Queens'.	

H.Q.
142 Inf. Bde.

HEADQUARTERS GENERAL STAFF No. G90/7/49 Date 17.4.18 47th (LONDON) DIVISION

The narrative of Operations at Aveluy Wood from March 29 to April 4th 1918 is enclosed please.

S. Mathew

April 16. 1918.
CAPTAIN & ADJUTANT,
2/4 (COUNTY OF LONDON) BN.
THE LONDON REGIMENT.
"THE QUEEN'S"

47 Div.
Forwarded for information please.

S. Graham Capt.
Brigade
(for) B.G.C.

HEADQUARTERS 142ND INFANTRY BRIGADE.
No. ....
Date 17/4/18

1/24th. BATTALION LONDON REGIMENT.

"THE QUEENS".

N A R R A T I V E

OF

OPERATIONS at AVELUY WOOD

MARCH 29th 1918 to APRIL 7th 1918.

―――――――――oooooooooo―――――――――

On the night March 29th/30th the 1/24th Battalion LONDON REGIMENT relieved the 7th ROYAL SUSSEX (12th Division) in positions at AVELUY WOOD (W4 a and B and Q 34 d). "A" and "B" Companies were in front line and "C" and "D" in Support. Relief complete 3.30 a.m. During 30th and 31st March our front was comparatively quiet except for the heavy shelling of MARTINSART at intervals. On night of 31st March /1st April "C" and "D" Companies relieved "A" and "B" Companies in the front line. At 3.30 a.m. on the 1st April message received that an attack was expected on V Corps front. Our own artillery put down a heavy barrage at 5.15 - 6 a.m. On night 2nd/3rd April a fighting patrol under 2/Lt ELLIS patrolled our Battalion front to Blackhorse Bridge across River Ancre but no enemy was encountered. On night 3rd/4th April "A" and "B" Companies relieved "C" and "D" Companies in front line. The same fighting patrol as previous night formed a covering party for R.E's who successfully blew up Blackhorse Bridge.

At midnight 4th/5th April the disposition of the Battalion was as follows:-
"A" Company   Left Front   "B" Company   Right Front
"C" Company   Left Support   "D" Company   Right Support
At 6.30 a.m. 5th April an exceedingly heavy hostile bombardment was opened on our front line and Back areas; this continued without ceasing until 8 a.m. when the bombardment ceased on the front line and the enemy attacked on the whole front in mass formation offering exceedingly good targets.

The S.O.S. was fired from "A" and "B" Companies and repeated at B.H.Q. Our Artillery which had been heavy all the time increased in volume. The attack was met with successful results with Lewis Gun and Rifle fire but about 8.30 a.m. it was noticed that the right Battalion were being forced back necessitating our right Company (B) to form a defensive flank at about 45 degrees from original line to cover the gap thus occasioned. In the meanwhile a platoon of "C" Company moved forward to reinforce "A" Company and two platoons of "D" Company to reinforce the right flank of "B". The line was therefore at 9 a.m. on 5th held as follows:- "A" Company and one platoon of "C" in its original line and "B" company and two platoons of "D" in a line forming the defensive flank. It was then found that the position of the extreme right was very grave and the remaining two platoons of "D" were brought forward to continue the defensive flank until in touch with the right Battalion.

This position was held during repeated attacks throughout the whole day with the exception that the left platoon of the centre company (B) was forced to evacuate its position owing to heavy rifle bombing about 9.30 a.m. This made a gap of about 50 yards between "A's" right and "B's" left; this was successfully rectified by advancing one platoon of "C" Company which occupied the gap thus once more creating a continuous line. The line was at 11 a.m. as follows:- "A" Company, One platoon "C" Company, "B" Company, "D" Company.

At the opening of the original attack a forward L.G. post of "A" Company had been withdrawn to a position to command a drive through the wood. At 11.30 a.m. during a lull a fighting patrol left the front line in order to go forward in order to ascertain the whereabouts of the enemy; this patrol encountered the enemy in occupation of the forward L.G. post. It proceeded to attack and drove the enemy back to their own lines killing 3 of them.

At 4 p.m. the Support Battalion moved forward in S formation to counter attack on the right flank. This was done under covering fire on the right of "D" Company. This counter attack was launched at 4.30 p.m. but was unsuccessful in retaking the lost ground. It was noticed that directly the enemy got into our line it became almost impossible to shift him. At 6 p.m. it was observed that the right Battalion of the Division on our left were withdrawing; this left our flank unprotected, so the platoon of "C" Company which had been sent up to reinforce "A" Company was moved to the left flank to form a defensive flank. This was found to be insufficient to link up with the other Division. Two platoons of the Support Battalion came up to reinforce the Battalion. One of these was used to continue the defensive flank on the left. It was still found that the left flank was yet unprotected. On this information being sent back to B.H.Q. from the left Company, they got into communication with the Battalion on our left who at 11p.m. sent up two Companies of the R.M.L.I. who occupied a line 300 yards behind their original position thus getting into touch once more with our left Company, enabling the platoon of the Support Battalion and the platoon of "C" Company to take up their original positions.

At midnight April 5th/6th the situation became quiet and remained so until 5.55 a.m. 6th April when two Companies of the 4th R.W.F counter attacked on the front of the right Battalion, and our centre Company (B) and right Company (D) were ordered to conform with their movement thus endeavouring to regain original line. This counter attack proved a failure owing to the fact that the enemy had brought up numerous M.Gs. and had them established in good positions. The line therefore remained as heretofore. At 10 a.m. the enemy attacked the left of the left Company (A) and the Division on the left. This attack was sucessfully repulsed M.G. and Rifle fire causing a very large number of casualties to the enemy, who shewed signs of disorganisation. Therefore the left Company (A) in conjunction with the Division on the left made a counter attack, keeping in touch with the centre Company (B) throughout the whole operation, and captured two M.Gs. and 21 prisoners. The forward position was found to be unsuitable owing to the difficulty of keeping touch on the flanks so the left Company (A) withdrew to its original line. In conjunction with the counter attack of the left Company the centre Company sent out a patrol and got into close touch with the enemy. This patrol is outstanding owing to the fact that one of its number (L/c March) went forward and personally entered into an engagement with a hostile patrol, the officer of which he shot and brought back his papers and maps containing information of great importance. The situation regained tranquility until 6 p.m. when the enemy again attempted to attack in force. This attack was met at once by our Artillery and Stokes mortars together with M.G. and Rifle fire and repelled causing great casualties to the enemy. At 8 p.m. the situation again became normal and remained so until the Battalion was relieved by the 12th H.L.I. at 3 a.m. on the morning of the 7th April.

Army Form C. 2118.

WAR DIARY
or
INTELLIGENCE SUMMARY.
(Erase heading not required.)

2nd R. Fus. Regt.

Vol 38

Instructions regarding War Diaries and Intelligence Summaries are contained in F. S. Regs., Part II. and the Staff Manual respectively. Title pages will be prepared in manuscript.

Place	Date	Hour	Summary of Events and Information	Remarks and references to Appendices
1918. MAY.				
Wednesday	1st		Relief complete at 10.45 p.m. of 17th Batt'n A. I. F. Quiet night except for our artillery.	
Thursday	2nd		C.O. went round line with I.O. Brigade Major called 6.30 a.m. Brigadier General called 8 p.m. and commanding officers round line with him. Brigadier General slept at Battalion Headquarters. Quiet night except for our own Artillery. MILLMOUNT, SELLIS and BOUZINCOURT shelled at intervals. Warning of attack by enemy in near future. 2nd Lieutenants Johnson and Brown posted to 22nd Battalion The London Regiment.	
Friday	3rd		Divisional Commander called at 7 a.m. 2nd Lieut. Collins proceeds on leave from Divisional Wing. Four Tanks reported just S of ALBERT. ALBERT shelled by number of squadrons from 6 to 7 o'clock p.m. ALBERT invisible on account of smoke and dust. Brigadier General slept at Battalion Headquarters. Lieut. Coombe M.O. reports from Divisional Wing.	
Saturday	4th			
Sunday	5th		G.S.O.1 called. BOUZINCOURT shelled. Lieut. Coombe M.O. reports to Bde as galloper to Brigadier.	
Monday	6th		O.C. 18th Batt'n London Regiment called in reference to accommodation for two Companies. SELLIS MILL and BOUZINCOURT shelled at intervals. Very wet night - working parties cancelled by Brigade.	
Tuesday	7th		Excavations for new Battalion and Brigade Headquarters commenced by 253rd Tunnelling Company. We find 9 men for them. 2nd Lieut V.L. Gale accidentally wounded. Brigade Major called. Very misty all day until 5 p.m. O.C. A.C.1.O. commence to lift Batt'n Sector of Brigade Front prior to relief of 23rd Batt'n on night of 8/9th Inst. 2nd Lieut F. Morgan reports from Divisional Wing and is detached to act as liaison officer between our Batt'n and Division on our Left.	
Wednesday	8th		Quiet day until 11.30 p.m. when enemy opened a heavy bombardment until 11.50 p.m.	
Thursday	9th		S.O.S. sent up by Left Coy of Brigade Front at 3.30 a.m. Their left post was raided and captured. Batt'n stood to at 3.30 a.m., the Divisional General and Brigadier called 4.45 a.m. "A" Coy.pn was placed at disposal of 23rd Batt'n. At mid-day they were ordered 10 a.m. pm to position close to left Batt'n Headquarters. Also reported this complete at 3.45 p.m.	

(A704) Wt. W2771/M2937 750,000 5/17 Sch.52 Forms/C2118/14
D. D. & L. London, E.C.

Army Form C. 2118.

WAR DIARY
or
INTELLIGENCE SUMMARY.
(Erase heading not required.)

Instructions regarding War Diaries and Intelligence Summaries are contained in F. S. Regs., Part II. and the Staff Manual respectively. Title pages will be prepared in manuscript.

Place	Date	Hour	Summary of Events and Information	Remarks and references to Appendices
	10th Friday		Orders received for relief of Bat'n less "A" Company by 1/20th Bat'n London Regiment at 6 p.m.; these orders were cancelled at 7 p.m. Our "A" Company moved up to Reserve positions of the Left Bat'n and our "B" Company moved up to the area vacated by them, the area reported to be in position at 11.30 p.m. The 3rd Bat'n counter attacked the position lost about 11p. regaining all that was lost dead – capturing 1 Officer, 10 R. and two Machine Guns.	
	11th Saturday	9 a.m.	Quiet morning and heavy mist. Brigade on our left attacked in AVELUY WOOD 9 a.m. Orders received for relief by 1/20th Bat'n London Regiment 4.30 p.m. During the day the C.O. and I.O. visited the whole area occupied by the Bat'n.	
	12th Sunday	1.30 a.m.	Relief complete 1.30 a.m. Bat'n moved to billets in WARLOY. Day occupied in inspections, kit, etc. and cleaning up. Capt. Baseden M.C. detailed as Member F.G.C.M. "A" Company loss one platoon rejoins the Bat'n.	
	13th Monday	9.30 a.m.	"B" and "C" Companies ordered up to Reserve positions in MURRAY TRENCH and THE MAZE. Major Gill and the S.C. proceeded with them and formed advanced Bat'n Headquarters. "A" and "D" Companies sent up to reserve positions on working party at 9 a.m. They returned to billets at 8.30 a.m. 2nd Lieut Whitehead M.M. reports from Divisional Wing.	
	14th Tuesday		Working parties at night. "B" Company remain in line, "A" Company returning to WARLOY. Quiet day, very wet.	
	15th Wednesday	11.15 p.m.	Major Green and reconnoitring party of 22nd Bat'n London Regiment call at Bat'n Headquarters in reference to relief on night of 14/15th. Relief complete at 11.15 p.m.	
	16th Thursday		C.C., 2nd I/C, and Company Commanders reconnoitre Corps Line prior to relief of 12th London Regiment on evening of 16th. Brigadier called.	
	17th Friday		Battalion relieves 12th Bat'n London Regiment in CORPS LINE in WARLOY - BAIZIEUX Sector. Brigadier called. One O.R. wounded.	
			Brigadier goes round line with C.O. Cable buried in HENENCOURT. "A" and "B" Companies by day and "C" and "D" by night. Weather very hot.	

Army Form C. 2118.

WAR DIARY
or
INTELLIGENCE SUMMARY.
(Erase heading not required.)

Instructions regarding War Diaries and Intelligence Summaries are contained in F.S. Regs., Part II. and the Staff Manual respectively. Title pages will be prepared in manuscript.

Place	Date	Hour	Summary of Events and Information	Remarks and references to Appendices
Saturday	18th		O.O. and 2nd I/O attend Divisional Commanders conference. Ground round LAVIEVILLE SPUR reconnoitred. Battalion working on WARLOY. - BAIZIEUX sector of Corps line. Very hot.	
Sunday 19th	19th		Musketry training. Brigadier called. 2nd Lieut Summers proceeds to BOUCHON to attend Trench Mortar Course. Very hot.	
Monday	20th		Capt. Sanders M.O., Capt. Burroughs M.O., Lieuts Cadman and Hall, 2nd Lieuts Meredith, Morgan and Collins M.C. report for duty from Divisional Wing. 2nd Lieut Briggs reports for duty and is posted to "A" Company. Divisional Commander visits Corps line at WARLOY. Brigadier called. Large working parties under R.E. supervision. Training in counter attack by "A" and "B" Companies, Company drill and Musketry.	
Tuesday	21st		Large working parties under R.E's. Musketry on range, Company drill and training in counter attack by "C" and "D" Companies. Baths.	
Wednesday	22nd		Musketry on range. All Companies under R.E's. Baths.	
Thursday	23rd		O.O., 2nd I/O and Company Commanders reconnoitre right sector of Corps Front prior to relief of 6th Northampton Regiment on night of 24/25th. All Companies working on Corps Line under R.E's. Baths!	
Friday	24th		Major Burt reports for duty and assumed 2nd I/O. Battn relieves 6th Northampton Regiment in Right Sector of Corps Front. Relief complete 1.40 a.m. Two casualties. Disposition "C" and "B" Companies in Front Line, "D" Company in Support and "A" Company is Reserve.	
Saturday	25th		Divisional Commander and Brigadier go round line. Intermittent hostile shelling in Battn Area. Lieut. Turner reports for duty and is posted to "C" Company.	
Sunday	26th		Severe bombardment from 3 a.m. to 3.45 a.m. Brigadier called. C.S.O. 1 called. "A" Company moves into NEW TRENCH. Casualties 1 killed, 5 wounded.	
Monday	27th		Brigadier called. Lt. Col. Payne, Heavy Artillery called. Lt. Col. Marshall, Royal Welsh Fusiliers called. Front and Support line heavily shelled between 11 and 12 midday.	

Army Form C. 2118.

WAR DIARY
or
INTELLIGENCE SUMMARY.
(Erase heading not required.)

Instructions regarding War Diaries and Intelligence Summaries are contained in F. S. Regs., Part II. and the Staff Manual respectively. Title pages will be prepared in manuscript.

Place	Date	Hour	Summary of Events and Information	Remarks and references to Appendices
Tuesday	28th		O.C. 5 4th Army called. "D" Company relieves "C" Company. "A" Company relieves "B" Company. "A" Company patrol of 9 O.R's under 2nd Lieut. Grose was fired on. Casualties- 2nd Lieut. Grose and 4 O.R's wounded, 3 missing. Lt. Col. Marshall M.G. called.	
Wednesday	29th		Brigadier called and goes round line with O.C. O.C. 47th Batt'n M. G. C. calls. O.R.E. calls. "D" and "A" Coy send out patrols. Quiet day.	
Thursday	30th		O.C. 23th Batt'n Australian Infantry calls. Lt. Col. Payne, Heavy Artillery calls. Brigade Major 140th Brigade calls. Major Daly D.S.O.; G.S.O.2, 23rd Corps calls. Divisional Commander goes round line with Brigadier and O.C. Casualties two wounded. Quiet day.	
Friday	31st		Battalion Headquarters shelled during morning also Front Line. O.C. 47th Batt'n M.G.C. calls. 2 Lewis Gun Sections of 23rd Batt'n sent up to occupy positions in WELCH TRENCH. Lt. Col. Priend D.S.O. goes on leave. Major Bury assumes command.	

T. Ormeerong
Major, Cdg.,
1/24th. Batt'n.London Regiment,
The Queens

Army Form C. 2118.

WAR DIARY
or
INTELLIGENCE SUMMARY.
(Erase heading not required.)

Vol 3 2nd R. Ln Regt

Place	Date	Hour	Summary of Events and Information	Remarks and references to Appendices
June.1918.				
	Saturday 1st.		Officers of 15th Bn.London Regt., reconnoitre sector prior to relief on night of 1/2nd. Relief complete 1.30.a.m.	
	Sunday 2nd.		Battalion occupies LA HOUSSAYE System behind FRANVILLERS. Cleaning up. Baths.	
	Monday 3rd.		Lewis Gun Training. Interior economy. Baths.	
	Tuesday 4th.		Major Alexander D.A.A and Q.M.G called. Lewis Gun Training. Musketry. Interior economy.	
	Wednesday 5th.		Brigadier General inspects the Battalion by Companies. Lewis Gun Training. Gas Drill. Baths.	
	Thursday 6th.		Battalion moves to trenches in BAIZIEUX System. Bn.H.Q. in BAIZIEUX.	
	Friday 7th.		Battalion "stood to" at 3.a.m. but anticipated attack did not take place. Range practice. Tunnelling parties.	
	Saturday 8th.		C.O. and Company Commanders reconnoitre front line on left of Divisional Sector.	
	Sunday 9th.		Battalion relieves 18th Bn.Lon.Regt in Left Sector of Divisional Front. Relief complete 3.30.a.m. Dispositions :- "C" Coy Right Front : "B" Coy Left Front: "D" Coy Support : "A" Coy Counter Attacking Company.	
	Monday 10th.		Brig.Genl., visits Battalion Front. G.S.O.2 and G.S.O.3 Fourth Army called. Quiet day.	
	Tuesday 11th.		Divl.Commander and Brig.Genl visit Battalion Front. C.R.E called. Group Commander R.F.A called. Lieut Bradley, 520th Field Coy.R.E. reports for duty as supervisor of work.	
	Wednesday 12th.		G.S.O.1 111rd Corps called. Lt.Col.Bailey, R.F.A. called. Divl.Signalling Officer called. Battalion does musketry training in the line. 2/Lieut.J.N.Summers reports for duty from Divl. Wing.	

Army Form C. 2118.

WAR DIARY
or
INTELLIGENCE SUMMARY.
(Erase heading not required.)

Instructions regarding War Diaries and Intelligence Summaries are contained in F.S. Regs., Part II. and the Staff Manual respectively. Title pages will be prepared in manuscript.

Place	Date	Hour	Summary of Events and Information	Remarks and references to Appendices
	June 1918.			
	Thursday 13th.		G.S.O.3. IIIrd Corps called. C.O.Tunnellers called. O.C.520th Field Coy.R.E.called. "A" Coy. relieves "B". "D" Coy relieves "C". Lieut.A.C.Alexander.M.C. rejoins for duty from Divl.Wing.	
	Friday 14th.		Gas projected by us at 2 a.m. on night of 14/15th. Our artillery shelled heavily all night. Enemy shelling light. O.C.520th Field Coy.R.E. called. Capt P.W.Burroughs M.C. goes to Depot prior to going on leave. Lieut.A.C.Alexander.M.C. assumes command of "A" Coy. Lieut. A.J.L.Causton returns from Transport Course and takes over duties of Transport Officer.	
	Saturday 15th.		Bn.H.Q. shelled - 3 o.r wounded - 1 died of wounds. Lt.Col.Lee, U.S.Army reports to Battalion and stays night. G.S.O.3 called. "A" Coys patrol proceed 1000 yards forward of their Coy front.	
	Sunday 16th.		G.S.O.1 called. Lt.Col.Lee goes round line and leaves for Brigade at 6.30.a.m. Major Tollerton, O.C. 23rd Bn.Lon.Regt called. Quiet day.	
	Monday 17th.		Div. and Brigade Commanders go round line. Bn.H.Q. shelled. 22nd Bn.Lon.Regt., raid enemy line on our right.	
	Tuesday 18th.		Officers of 3rd Lon.Regt. reconnoitre sector prior to relief on night 19/20th. Lt.Col.R.S.I. Friend.D.S.O. returns from leave. 2/Lieut H.J.Grose returns from hospital.	
	Wednesday 19th.		Battalion relieved by 3rd Lon.Regt. Relief complete 1.45.am. Battn.proceeds to BEHENCOURT.	
	Thursday 20th.		Bn. in billets in BEHENCOURT cleaning and resting. Capt.S.H.Walker goes to 142nd Inf.Bde. 2/Lieut C.H.V.Kempton reports for duty and is posted to "C" Coy.	
	Friday 21st.		Battn. embusses for PISSY at 7.p.m. Battn. arrives at PISSY at 11.30.p.m.	
	Saturday 22nd		Brig.Genl. called C.O.attends Conference at Div.H.Q. Company Training.	
	Sunday 23rd.		Church Parade. Company Commanders Conference reference Training Programme.	

Army Form C. 2118.

WAR DIARY
or
INTELLIGENCE SUMMARY.
(Erase heading not required.)

Instructions regarding War Diaries and Intelligence Summaries are contained in F.S. Regs., Part II. and the Staff Manual respectively. Title pages will be prepared in manuscript.

Place	Date	Hour	Summary of Events and Information	Remarks and references to Appendices
	June 1918.			
	Monday 24th.		Three Officers reconnoitre round BOVES. Battn Drill. Coy and Platoon Training. Major.T.O.Bury leaves to assume command of 20th Bn.Lon.Regt. Capt.F.G.Gill assumes Second in Command. No.9 Platoon commanded by Sgt G.A.Copps wins A.P.A Competition in 142nd Inf.Bde.	
	Tuesday 25th.		Battalion Drill. Coy and Platoon Training. "A" Coy on Range. Brig.Genl. and Bde Major called.	
	Wednesday 26th.		Coy and Platoon Training. Baths. "B" and "C" Coys on Range. Div.Commander inspects Battn. while training.	
	Thursday 27th.		Brig.Genl. called. Battalion Drill. Baths. Musketry on Range.	
	Friday 28th.		Brig.Genl. called. Div.A.R.A.Competition - No.9 Platoon 3rd. Battn Drill Musketry on Range. C.O. and Adjutant take part in Bde Tactical Exercise.	
	Saturday 29th.		C.O. and Adjutant take part in Bde Tactical Exercise. Coys practise attack as a drill. Musketry on Range. Capt.F.G.Gill member of a Court. of Enquiry on 5 men of 22nd Lon.Regt. missing since raid on 17th inst.	
	Sunday 30th.		Bn.Church Parade. During month Bn attacked by epedemic of P.U.O - 18 Officers and over 300 O.r suffering from same.	

R.L. Freid
3.7.1918. Lt.Col., Cdr.,
1/24th Bn.London Regiment.
"The Queens".

1/24TH BATTALION,
LONDON REGIMENT,
THE QUEEN'S.

Army Form C. 2118.

Vol 40
142/47
2nd Bn. Lon. Regt.

WAR DIARY
or
INTELLIGENCE SUMMARY.

(Erase heading not required.)

Instructions regarding War Diaries and Intelligence Summaries are contained in F. S. Regs., Part II. and the Staff Manual respectively. Title pages will be prepared in manuscript.

Place	Date	Hour	Summary of Events and Information	Remarks and references to Appendices
July 1917	Monday 1st		Battalion carried out Field Firing Practice on range A by Rere. Report received of portable Frant Forman relieving from Ground.	
	Sunday 2nd		Major General MONTGOMERY, Chief of Staff visited Battalion training in Advance and Rear Guard Tactics over range. Brigadier called.	
	Wednesday 3rd		Battalion Drill. Our Roles Garrison at PROUCQY.	
	Thursday 4th		Field Firing Practice on range. Battalion sports in afternoon.	
	Friday 5th		Brigadier called.	
	Saturday 6th		Battalion Drill — Platoon training. Field Firing Practice on range. Army and Divl Commander inspected route the Battalion will be training.	
	Sunday 7th		Church Parade. Brigade Sports at OISSY. Lt Col FRIEND arrived. Officers Jumping Competition.	
	Monday 8th		Battalion Drill and Company Training. D by Sports.	
	Tuesday 9th		Attack tactics on range — Brigade Transport Competition. Lecture on Reserve Military Division.	
	Wednesday 10th		Second in command took Company Commanders and signalling officers reconnoitre division left sector of Corps Front. 18 Pl by Sports	

D. D. & L., London, E.C.
(A200) Wt.W1771/M2031 750,000 3/17 Sch. 52 Forms/C2118/4

Army Form C. 2118.

WAR DIARY
or
INTELLIGENCE SUMMARY.
(Erase heading not required.)

2nd Bn. Lon. Regt.

Place	Date	Hour	Summary of Events and Information	Remarks and references to Appendices
July 1918	Thursday 11th		Divl. Commander visits the Battalion whilst training – Battalion Drill and Coy training – HQ Coy sports in afternoon.	
	Friday 12th		Battalion inspected by MAJ. ROYAL who relieves 2nd Bn. East Surreys Ribbont with left sector of Corps front. Scheme in company, LIEUT. GOOSEY M.C., 2/LIEUTS F. MORGAN E.G. MEREDITH, R.G. FURSMAN with 127 ORs Spared to training camp at MOLLIENS-AU-BOIS. Relief complete at 11.30 p.m. Brigadier called.	
	Saturday 13th		Quiet day. O.R.E. Allen. Tunnelling parties and usual work on trenches. Brigadier called.	
	Sunday 14th		Quiet day. Tunnelling parties as before.	
	Monday 15th		The Divl. Commander and Brigadier called and visited Battalion Area.	
	Tuesday 16th		The Divl. Commander and Brigadier visited Battalion Area. B. Coy left forward in POSSUM TRENCH and took over position in MURRAY TRENCH from D. Coy. 2/2 Bn. LONDON REGT. Two Garrying Battalion in report.	
	Wednesday 17th		2nd Lieut. C.B. SEGRAVE D.S.O. board 1/5th Bn. LONDON REGT reconnoitred Battalion Area. Usual daily programme carried out.	
	Thursday 18th		Usual daily programme carried out. Reconnoitring parties of 1/5th Bn. LONDON REGT visited Coy areas. Battalion relieved by 1/5th Bn LONDON REGT. Relief complete 12.30 a.m. Battalion took up position HENENCOURT – SENLIS ROAD. "A" Battalion of Reserve Brigade left sector. Move Ambulance 2 a.m.	
	Friday 19th		All Companies tunnelling under R.E. Supervision.	

WAR DIARY or INTELLIGENCE SUMMARY

Army Form C. 2118.

24th Bn. Lon. Regt.

Place	Date	Hour	Summary of Events and Information	Remarks and references to Appendices
July 1918	Saturday 20th		Tunnelling parties continued. Major Burnard 236 Battery called.	
	Sunday 21st		A & B Coys Commanders reconnoitred Signalling Officers reconnoitre Lyle Trench. Left to Bde recon. Advance parties took over from 2/5th London Regt in Shelters in Warloy. Battalion relieved by 2/5th London Regt Relief complete 1.30pm Battalion proceed to Warloy.	
	Monday 22nd		Cleaning up. Interior economy.	
	Tuesday 23rd		Interior economy. Left Battalion Rifle Brigade reconnoitred by Adjutant and O.C. Coy Commanders.	
	Wednesday 24th		Battalion relieved 1/9 London Regt in left of Rifle Brigade Relief Complete 12.20 am. A Coy in front line. B Coy in support. C & D in Reserve. Major Gillen commanding. H. Lewis OC R.S.I. Friend DSO proceeds to Molliens au Bois and commands Bde Training Cadre while Lieut Col R.W. Turner A.G. Alexander MC Von Paulsen Darling Ball & Lieut J.F. Cadman proceed on leave to Paris.	
	Thursday 25th		Brigadier called. Warning Capt A.G. Cattell to regain EU Battery Company Commanders source here by 58th Division. S.W. Albert - Amiens Rd ac to at. Enemy retaliation on outpost. 1 casualties (killed & wounded) Gas attacks by us at 2am	
	Friday 26th		(Quiet day. Battalion relieved by 1 Coy of 106 BN 131 American Regt Relief completed 3am. Battalion relieved 2/8 BN London Regt in support) in night of new Outpost line. Albert - Amiens Road. Relief complete 4.45 am - relay amphalaxia Dispositions: A Coy in Millie Trench, B Coy in Dodo Trench, C Coy in Hill Row, D Coy in Darling Reserve. Casualties - 1 wounded.	

Army Form C. 2118.

WAR DIARY
or
INTELLIGENCE SUMMARY.
(Erase heading not required.)

Instructions regarding War Diaries and Intelligence Summaries are contained in F. S. Regs., Part II. and the Staff Manual respectively. Title pages will be prepared in manuscript.

Place	Date	Hour	Summary of Events and Information	Remarks and references to Appendices
July 1917	Saturday 27th		Brigadier called. Two Australians attached to Battalion Instructors in Patrolling. Quiet day	
	Sunday 28th		S.I.O. called also Brigadier and Bde Major. Lieut Sperry American Army paid friendly visit from direction of M.O.	
	Monday 29th		Brigadier and Staff Capt. called also Major Lowe 520 Field Coy R.E. Have a covering party proceeding to work on emplacement on new trench from MELBOURNE TRENCH to BRISBANE TRENCH. Lieut D.E. Poll and Capt H. Solomon report for duty from Orders	
	Tuesday 30th		Same working parties as for 29th. 6.0. by Commander arranged for arrangements front line trench to relief of 23rd BN LONDON REGT on night of 31 July/1st Aug. Lieut D O'Keefe leave Battalion to join A.V.C. at ABBEVILLE. Congrats. Lieut O'Keefe Casualties wounded	
	Wednesday 31st		Battalion relieved 1/23rd BN LONDON REGT in Right Reserve Right Sub sect. Relief complete 12 midn't W. Dispositions. C Coy Right front. D Coy Left front B Coy Support (Sunken sunken bay) A Coy in Reserve. Lieut FIRSMAN reports for duty from Rest Camp Draft of 95 OR arrived.	

3.8.18

R.O.I. Frink Lieut.Col., Coy,
1/24 BN LONDON REGT
The Queens

142nd Bde.
47th Div.

1/24th BATTALION,

LONDON REGIMENT,

AUGUST 1918.

WAR DIARY or INTELLIGENCE SUMMARY

Army Form C. 2118.

14/47

2nd Bn. Som. L.I.

Place	Date	Hour	Summary of Events and Information	Remarks and references to Appendices
Thursday	Aug 1		Bn HdQrs Coy Commanders and Bn Clerks. Usual working parties. Coy patrol until 1pm to 4 OR of Australians by extr enemy kneed on our front and came in 1.50 × No more enemy found.	
Friday	2		Bn patrol recd Pm totr. Enemy cleared throwing up dumps, dug into S of ALBERT. Enemy of ALBERT CATHEDRAL shelled. Suggest that enemy went dating from to first line system Daylight patrols by the main right (12, LOB) sales enemy found. S of ALBERT - AMIENS road and just to but journey further fought which advanced with Bn on right of our own patrols reached enemy line front. Bn front another went thro' POW cage to NE and there at head working parties in gap leading down Pls. Enemy bombed his own tire will Pr shells. 4.40 Scaltd B M called	
	3		[illegible] that enemy bombarded the front line system. Enemy Daylight patrol consisting of 2 Offrs & 2 OR (APR) and pound an extra uses. AMCRE and found no trace of enemy. Advanced from Postr to occupy enemy front line by our outpost by between gros. Lines E. 2.3 m to E.8.9.10. & Coy attached to that by in forder by 12.30 am Patrol working out to " wire enemy seen on E side Coy centre on Bn by to westward	

Army Form C. 2118.

WAR DIARY
or
INTELLIGENCE SUMMARY.
(Erase heading not required.)

7th Bn. London Regt

Place	Date	Hour	Summary of Events and Information	Remarks and references to Appendices
Saturday	Aug	3	Coml. returned with 2nd in no left in billeting. Inspection of the Lines. A. Coy just B. Coy sent D. Coy for D. Coy sent B. Coy o.c. Coy Lt Roberry R.E. gabion making instruction given to e.s. ANCRE	
Sunday		4	Major CURTIN D.S.O. Battery. Major EDEN Cav Battery called. Officers of the 18th LONDON Regt reconnoitred Line prior to relief on night of 5th/6th. B. Coy relieved C. Coy in old German trenches.	
Monday		5	Brigadier called. Patrols active in front of A.G. system. 2/Lt BEARDSHAW, FOSTER & STANTON patrol went to the Quarry. 2/Lt BEARDSHAW wounded. 2/Lt STANTON missing. 2/Lt PYLE taken out three covering parties one of which Pte HICKS was wounded. Pte EDWARDS was killed. Bn relieved by 18th LONDON REGT. Relief complete 1.10 a.m. H.Q. C & D Coys proceed to billets in WARLOY and Coys to trenches in HENENCOURT system.	
Tuesday		6	Lt Col FRIEND D.S.O. assumes temp command of 140 Bde. Brigadier called. Major GILL assumes command of Bn. Baths reform enemy etc.	
Wednesday		7	WARLOY. Handed training till night, no casualties. Bath. Interior economy	

WAR DIARY or INTELLIGENCE SUMMARY

Army Form C. 2118.

2/4th Lon. Regt.

Place	Date	Hour	Summary of Events and Information	Remarks and references to Appendices
Thursday	Aug 8		C.O. inspected Coys in WARLOY by Platoons. C.O. & 2nd i/c went by Lorry to LIMEUX to see LEWIS GUN system. WARLOY shelled in afternoon & evening.	
Friday	9		H. COOMBE returned from leave. Battalion relieved from MOLLIENS-au-BOIS. Quiet. Bullet ammunition by 1/ Platoon 1 2/3 Bn. LON. REGT. Officers & N.C.O. attend lecture on contact patrols at COYTAS. B & C Coys relieved A & D Coys in LAVIEVILLE 78. 1 Remained to proceed to MOLLIENS-au-BOIS.	
Saturday	10		Battn relieved by S.W.E. SURREYS. Battn Relief complete 3.15 a.m. Battn marched to LA HOUSSOYE. Last Coy arriving there 9 a.m.	
Sunday	11		C.O. proceeded with Brigadier to reconnoitre O.B. System. W.O. MORLANCOURT Sector. Relief of 1st Batt 3rd Bn. London Infantry Batt Lewis LA HOUSSOYE at 6.30 p.m. but owing to complete disorganisation in the take-over relief is not complete till 8 a.m. following morning. Capt Warden the Hendrike, Gray and 100 O.R.s proceed to MOLLIE NS au BOIS as Battn support.	
Monday	12		C.O. reconnoitred Brigade MORLANCOURT sector from trench some right of 10th LONDON REGT on left of letter Batt Lewis O.B. Line at 6.30 p.m. Relief complete 1.10 a.m. Disposition of Coys. B right front C left front D support A Reserve. No casualties although heavy shelling.	

WAR DIARY
or
INTELLIGENCE SUMMARY.
(Erase heading not required.)

Army Form C. 2118.

2nd Bn The Bev Regt

Place	Date	Hour	Summary of Events and Information	Remarks and references to Appendices
Tuesday	Aug	13	Under Bde left attack at 4.45 am reached objective but failed to hold it. Enemy shelling front line system heavily all the morning and throughout and its vicinity during afternoon. Brigade HQ on limber called & 6 O 2 called	
Wednesday		14	Remainder of Brigade had daught. 29 Bn returned to support 8th Can taking up position in our support. Enj sufft at B by rifle & M.G. Right supported A by. Hostile D by enemy shell heavy during aft.	
Thursday		15	Enemy gas alarm came up at 1 a.m. All told. D.O. signal was but on annoyed at 5.30 a.m. Bombarded Major Enr D.O. called Major Gillespie at 5.35 pm to his company of Battle Surplus took body with him to H.G. G.S.O. called and questioned us base.	
Friday		16	Relieved by 31st Bn Royal Nick complete 1.30 a m 21st Pen Leuvre Lin church Bivon up and to & expangents held to dress.	
Saturday		17	Proceeded to O B 2 will HQ in Barn behind	
Sunday		18	Conference at Bde. HQ. CO adj. OC Coys attend	
Monday		19	CO adj OC Coys attend conference at Bde HQ. Tactical General explained Re engaged in table shoving at night	
Tuesday		20	CO held conference to discuss Tactical General carried out in afternoon. Bn proceeded to HEILLY Area and took over from 2/8 Ch London Dist. LONDON took over from us	

WAR DIARY
or
INTELLIGENCE SUMMARY.

(Erase heading not required.)

Army Form C. 2118.

Place	Date	Hour	Summary of Events and Information	Remarks and references to Appendices
Wednesday	Aug 21		Bn still in HQ area 11am Bn preparing to move	
Thursday	22		A.O.E. at HAPPY VALLEY Bn moves forward at 3.30am. Bde HQ at KIODO 6.15am Advance of Bn ready, the bombs established in support 6.12a. 8.10am HQ established L1 a 3 2. Advance HQ established L1 a 3 2. Runner sent forward lying at 10am. B now forming from Coys. by HQ answers A & B in extreme line. 4 & 3 in front line withdrawn Y Bn advancing to internal exploits MG fire and heavy shelling SOS received at 5.30am. C O of 23rd with a steadier return to Bde and at of our artillery there a covering barrage in front of Bn line along the Ridge. Bullecy 14th & Bde on withdrawn at 11.30pm.	
Friday	23	6am	Burying to complete casualties Killed 2 Off Lt Morgan. Died of wounds Lt Yell, wounded Capt Bowden, 2Lt Alexander, Sadiman, 2Lt Tunnman, 2Lt Pledge 4 Off. Prisoner Lt R Stevens	
Saturday	24		Major Gill again Bn Brigadier called Roll meeting	
Sunday	25		Bn resting and refitting	

Army Form C. 2118.

WAR DIARY
or
INTELLIGENCE SUMMARY.
(Erase heading not required.)

Instructions regarding War Diaries and Intelligence Summaries are contained in F. S. Regs., Part II. and the Staff Manual respectively. Title pages will be prepared in manuscript.

2nd Bn Irish Regt

Place	Date	Hour	Summary of Events and Information	Remarks and references to Appendices
	Monday Aug	26	Battn move at 7.30 a.m. to Genl. Cmm. Lg. MESSITZ and billeted. 11/0 Bn. Coy dig trenches in Brigades sub area	
	Tuesday	27	Battn Battn ditto from found for General Brigades out area.	
			2/Lt Y. Greenhalgh from base. Strays 340 Rts arrive. BO attends conference at Bde HQrs. CO goes to Depot and Major Ect assumes command	
	Wednesday	28	Brigade called 2/B.O. 2nd 3rd called by emergency. Warning orders received. Lecture on 29/W.	
	Thursday	29	Battn moves to MURREPAS to take up covering position at LE FOREST for attack on 3rd Army. Activity unjustified arouse casualties on B. Coy. B.O. attends conference at Bde. HQ. Intruders on move for attack	
	Friday	30	B.O. & other Coy commands conference at 16 am and instruction given	
			1.43 Lg Bn attack. Bn objective Hill 150. Zero 6 am. All objectives except E. 5.30 a.m. A. Coy Right front. C. Coy Left front B. Coy Rght. Support D. Coy Reserve. All objectives were gained by 8 am Batt H Q advanced to LE FOREST valley 10 a.m. Casualties killed 2/Lt. Van der Veide. Wounded 9/Lt Ray, 2/Lt Chaves	

Army Form C. 2118.

WAR DIARY
or
INTELLIGENCE SUMMARY.
(Erase heading not required.)

1st Bn The Queens Regt

Place	Date	Hour	Summary of Events and Information	Remarks and references to Appendices
Satisfied	Aug 31		142 Bde was relieved by the 141 Bde. but the returned to previous assembly positions in front of MAUREPAS. A hostile counter attack from FALFEMONT was assembled during the afternoon. C.O. 1/19th Bn sent a verbal message at 5 pm that enemy had taken though actually the attacks were crowded by rifle, M.G. and artillery fire. 2 Platoons of D Coy covered LE FOREST valley during night - got up	

F.G.W.
Major
comdg 1/4th London Regt.
4th Queens.

Army Form C. 2118.

WAR DIARY
or
INTELLIGENCE SUMMARY.
(Erase heading not required.)

Instructions regarding War Diaries and Intelligence Summaries are contained in F.S. Regs. Part II. and the Staff Manual respectively. Title pages will be prepared in manuscript.

Place	Date	Hour	Summary of Events and Information	Remarks and references to Appendices
September 1918	1st		Batln relieved 16 Hill 150 Bn & that are reorganised. Regimental orders to attack St. PIERRE VAAST WOOD next morning. Orders received at 10 p.m. Verbal orders issued to Coy Commanders at 11 p.m. Battn to proceed to assembly positions via Intermediate Assembly pt. between NEEDLE WOOD and St PIERRE VAAST WOOD. Route pole NEEDLE VALLEY and BOUCHAVESNES. Embussed 10/11.30 am. Zero 5.30 am.	1st R.W. Fus. Rgt Vol 42
	2nd		Attack on BORROWITZ, HILT and LINS trenches - front of St. PIERRE VAAST WOOD in conjunction 12th Division. No Wood D Coy Right front. B Coy Left front. C Coy in support. A Coy occupied HILT TRENCH after clearing LONEY CORE. Battn Commander (Lt. Col. of LINS and HILT TRENCHES) at 8 am. B. Coy in pushing forward on our [?] to West of St. PIERRE VAAST WOOD Suffered [?] when right Company met with [?] LtCol B. C. HORN-SMITH the telephone officer was [?] dead. Capt K. GORDON, Lieut G. C. HEATHCOTE, 2nd Lieuts R.A. [?], R. W. F. cleared St. PIERRE VAAST WOOD and finally found ??? with R.W. F. on road near Rettin London near [?] Boundaries. Bn JUPITER TRENCH B Coy attained part HILT TRENCH Ashy E and HILT TRENCH D. C Coy was to aid R. W. F. in BORROWITZ TRENCH. The following messages from Kent Codley Commanding W. Corps "Please convey to 1st Midd. Durk and 1st R.W. Fus and Major F. G. Bill and 2nd LONDON My Hearty congratulations on the brilliant [?] of above [?] which resulted in the capture of Zero prisoners two 5.9 guns and 1 Bty of Mum Guns.	
	3rd		Orders received at 3 to attack position H.B. NODEM MONASTIR TRENCH and away W and of Canal before dusk. C Coy assembled in VAUX WOOD, D Coy in BORROWITZ TRENCH. Values of Borrow[?] in MONASTIR was covered. A Coy to secure crossing was built up on [?] W. bank of Canal. Owing to visibility of D.F. Btn [?] Moment the last Battn and two Coys of R.W. F. relieved by 7th QUEENS Battn returned to JUPITER PREP field companies by 10 am.	

D. D. & L. London, E.C.

Army Form C. 2118.

WAR DIARY
or
INTELLIGENCE SUMMARY.
(Erase heading not required.)

Instructions regarding War Diaries and Intelligence Summaries are contained in F. S. Regs., Part II. and the Staff Manual respectively. Title pages will be prepared in manuscript.

Place	Date	Hour	Summary of Events and Information	Remarks and references to Appendices
September 1918	4th		Batln. rested in JUPITER AREA. Orders received at 8 p.m. to occupy Canal de MOISLAINS and move forward Labr. E. Essex Regt and 1/5 KSLI on MOISLAINS were all night. A Coy occupied the Pill & Ridge and took the private track of army OP S.5. of TREVOR Hill Copse. During the attack answered a mild rifle and M.G fire + patrols to Coy occupied ridge north eastwards MOISLAINS.	
	5th	at 8 a.m.	Batln moved westward to own at 141 Rte attacked PERONNE - CAMBRAI ROAD	
	6th		2/E and 1/5 Rifles attacked LIERAMONT. Batln took up position to defend S.E. end of ERNETTE WOOD in conjunction with 13th LONDON. Lt. R.W. TOWNER having command of "D" Coy. Division in reserve. 2/L Ball relieved by 1/5 LONDON RIFLES. Completed relief at 11.30 a.m. Batln marched to BOUCHAVESNES Between Aug Posts and Pill Box & Batln casualties 2 m.k.a. offrs & others 4 men gun + 4 m. Gns. P.O H.Q. 360 Tournes.	
	7th		Batln marched to CLERY	
	8th		Batln entrained for HERICOURT. Move completed before Batln bivouacs in HERICOURT AREA.	
	9th		Rally for D. Coy entrainment for Linens at 9 p.m. D. Coy acted as battalion guards for M.T of Bde. 3/Lt 2/Lt. FRENO 9/10 Sener Batln arce 6/147 Inf Bde.	

Army Form C. 2118.

WAR DIARY
or
INTELLIGENCE SUMMARY.
(Erase heading not required.)

1/2nd the Lon Regt

Place	Date	Hour	Summary of Events and Information	Remarks and references to Appendices
September 1918	10th		Arrived at LIEVRARD 12 NOON, and marched to BOIS RIEUX in billets by 4 p.m.	
	11th		Interior economy.	
	12th		Battn. moved by march route to ALLOUAGNE. Interior economy.	
	13th		Bde. order for training programme. 1.Hour Battn. Parade and Show Company Training. V.P.O's (Pannero reports to 2/Lt E.C. HERBOTHAM for duty to 142 Inf. Bde. V.P.O (PANNERO reports to 4/LON SIGn L Coy	
	14th		Battn. carries on training	
	15th		Church Parade. Draft of 10 O.R's arrived	
	16th		Battn. carries out training. Bde Commander attended Battn. Parade and inspected morning	
	17th		Battn. carries out training. XIII Corps Commander inspected Battn. at training	
	18th		Battn. moved by march route to HUCLIER at 9am. as entraining point for ITALY. Arrived and billets at 12.30pm.	
	19th		Battn. carries out training. Dump for stable etc at BRIG. Station.	
	20th		Training under Company arrangements including Lewis Gun instruction and Range Practice.	

WAR DIARY or INTELLIGENCE SUMMARY

Army Form C. 2118.

Place	Date	Hour	Summary of Events and Information	Remarks and references to Appendices
September 1918	21st		Bn. carried out training. The following Officers reported for duty: 2/Lt. W.D. Mort, 2/Lt. H.H.A. Nitz, posted to Coy. 2/Lt. D.A. Christmore, 2/Lt. S.F. Brooks posted to B.Coy.	
	22nd		Church Parade.	
	23rd		Coy training carried out on Aerodrome CONTEVILLE, and range practices	
	24th		Coy training. 14's & 1 Bn. Gymkhana on Aerodrome at 2 p.m. Divl. Lottery 6 p.m.	
	25th		Coy training. Draft of 44 ORs arrived.	
	26th		Bn. Tactical exercise for dealing with enemy Machine Gun posts and for forming strong flank. Bde. Commander attended operations. Lieut. P.T. Cruston relieved from leave.	
	27th		Division moved to the P. &. L. AREA. Bn. on leave HUCLIER at 9.30 am fr. MONCHEAUX will a bay at MONT-EN-TERNOIS.	
	28th		Training under bay arrangements in billets. Bde Commander called. Capt. S.H. Watkis returned from leave.	
	29th		Church Parade. Cross country run in afternoon 96 entries. B.Coy. team won.	

Army Form C. 2118.

WAR DIARY
or
INTELLIGENCE SUMMARY.

(Erase heading not required.)

1/24 Bn The Lon R[egt]

Instructions regarding War Diaries and Intelligence Summaries are contained in F. S. Regs., Part II. and the Staff Manual respectively. Title pages will be prepared in manuscript.

Place	Date	Hour	Summary of Events and Information	Remarks and references to Appendices
September 1918	30th		Coy training. Semi final of Battn Football Competition	

N. Bull
Majr. Coy.,
1/24 Bn London Regt
The Queens

WAR DIARY
or
INTELLIGENCE SUMMARY.
(Erase heading not required.)

Army Form C. 2118.

Instructions regarding War Diaries and Intelligence Summaries are contained in F.S. Regs., Part II. and the Staff Manual, respectively. Title pages will be prepared in manuscript.

2nd Bn Lon Regt

Place	Date	Hour	Summary of Events and Information	Remarks and references to Appendices
October 1918	1st		Orders received for Bn. to move by rail to HEDONCHELLE. Transport to leave at 11.30. Marching Order required for Batt. to proceed to entrain. Bn. Comm. addresses Coy. Their very two boys on range.	
	2nd		Batt. leaves MONCHEAUX at 01.00 & marches to St. ROL & entrains at 11.30 for MERVILLE. Railway billeted LYNKEN.	
	3rd		Batt. received orders at 00.75 to move at 06.30 & march to positions at WINDEN. Batt. moves off at 06.45 arriving at new positions at 11.10. Philosophy mess formed in WINDEN (S. ex. as of ORCHARD HOUSE). N.35 & 3 a 2 0 proceed to report Batt. S.H. under command of Batt.	
	4th		Batt. leaves ORCHARD HOUSE area at 06.30 following LONDON R. at LE MENIL SECONDON for attack of Railway Embankment 500' W of ERQUINGHEM at of 50 meeting heavy M.G. fire. B. moves in support at 09.00 B.H.Q. fires likely 975 stiffen hill 4 Bde on left and Lg. London Regt at 11.00. In support & chiefly lights (A Coy) O. son. & own immediate limited A Coy. Immediate support (opp x 17 Wy Chateau at Pl. 1117.6) B. support LE MENIL LINIER LE MENIL ROAD B coy.	
	5th		A Coy. Officer Commander lines. B Coy and supt. Lines a bright 4 lights, bn. lay men to LANDRY BOUTERN, one man killed. Enemy artillery about jumpy and very dazed. Hist off 4/5th 140 Bed. Carried to Bde on left front. B Coy 2nd Bn London Scottish. B Coy ad Bn Lon R 6 a 0 c Rifle ample is 12.00 hours. Moving up in B Lond was incomm. lines and 2 Soch who lacks particulars.	
	6th		Hostile line changed BRUNTEEN. 21.02 BN Bn WAR CHAFER, advanced relay have established at CHANGE OF ZONE at 09.00. A hill has been taken up by enemy use oppositely by Coy. and in reserve of our respective lines. [illegible] gets a fire broadway of Raulin Form.	

Army Form C. 2118.

WAR DIARY
or
INTELLIGENCE SUMMARY.
(Erase heading not required.)

Instructions regarding War Diaries and Intelligence Summaries are contained in F. S. Regs., Part II. and the Staff Manual respectively. Title pages will be prepared in manuscript.

2nd Bn KOSB

Place	Date	Hour	Summary of Events and Information	Remarks and references to Appendices
Beaurepaire	Feb.	8.15	Advance Battn HQ established at Chateau de Flandre. Major 1/6 KOSB now assumes command of Battn. Lieut Colonel F. Stevenson Balfour Comg. Major Grant now Brigadier and 2nd in Comd Battn	
		9.15	Main supply line examined and stretched 22 Grosvenor Bn remained in the trenches. Battn HQ 22 Bn relieved 2.8 Bn and 2 Bn in the line & they completed the night.	
			Battn billeted in Poff Wabaye LE MENSIL as "C" (Reserve) to 1/6 Bde. Brigade HQ HQ two Coys moved to Chocolet H.Q. of Bn & H.Q.	
		10.15	Coys carry out ordinary training & All ranks	
		11.15	Coy party out & show Victoria 6.0 and bombardier commanders free here by 22 Bn. 1 Batt relieved 2 Bn, relief completed by 21.40.	
		12.00	2/10 attack was attempted, but weather became too hazardous, but dropped on account of weather. Enemy actively very little	
		13.15	Lieut Lt. ARCHER O'CO recce comm'd and of Battn Brigaded makes Battn near	
		14.15	06.00 Day quiet ordinary reconnaissance. Orders of relief arrived. Relief Battn General ERQUINGHEN, the relief General begin at 06.15 during Battn general attack from the front, several decided. They were fired on while out of our own wire Pot. 09.30 failed to relieve HC a 9.2 Bn Coy over and HQ by 10.00. Later 15' Monday 11 Monday 15' Tuesday 11 moves arr. 15'. Coys relieve in Company by 22 Bn. Evening Bn relieved by 2/8 Bn and relieved by 7/Bn Battn & Br. Billy Bn filled by 21.30	

Army Form C. 2118.

WAR DIARY
or
INTELLIGENCE SUMMARY.
(Erase heading not required.)

24th Bn. Lon. Regt.

Instructions regarding War Diaries and Intelligence Summaries are contained in F. S. Regs., Part II. and the Staff Manual respectively. Title pages will be prepared in manuscript.

Place	Date	Hour	Summary of Events and Information	Remarks and references to Appendices
October 1918	15th		Enemy on our left Batln Bombarded by our C. Coy. supposed to be relieved, repelled by 25th Bn. at 07.30. Later our Bn. was relieved when it started to strike. Evening 15th Supply train was to entrain one provision. Not related till Relief at 05.30 next morning however present by B Coy when entrainment finished.	
	16th		Relieve Holding line Name S. of Fm de Maisdeanne. 00.30 Advance of Bn. Recommenced. By 02.30 OUTPT Line 05.30 2nd Bn. Kepe and 28th Bn. 25th Bn. to our Right limit B Coy. then A Coy support a Coy in Reserve. 06.30 Commanding established to Artill Bn. HQ. 10.00 No Reserves. HQ in front. Summary of Reports received by 10.30. Rolls. D and B by 16.0 Per Arm. support advanced though advanced. b Coy may not though advance B Coy Nothing on supporting on 'A' supporting on D supporting on B. Orde Dahlius this flank under 12.30 Artillery engaged on later attack. Roll was Bn. supported by 25th Bn. commence the attack. The line from N. of ENGLOS and ERQUINN 15.00 25th Bn. unable to advance E of FORT D'ENGLOS. Disposition of Batln. B Coy. Vert BERLOT-HASBUG on FORD. D Coy. N.E. of HALLENNE. A Coy supporting B not in need D Coy 300 Yd W. of HALLENNE. 2/Lieut K. W. HUTCHINS and M.H. 39th left at 07.30 of commence Right 16/4 M. Ball relieved by the Huntington Regt. Batln. marched to FROMELLES, and left by Light Railway at 11.00 for Feres arrived at 18.00 Coys. Billetes arranging for leave	
	17th		Batln. moved to MANQUEVILLE arriving at 16.30 #E.E. HEREDITH H.C. reports from 14th Bde.	
	18th			
	19th		Which Enemy Brigades relief and unpredictable.	

WAR DIARY or INTELLIGENCE SUMMARY

Army Form C. 2118.

24th Bn London Regt

Place	Date	Hour	Summary of Events and Information	Remarks and references to Appendices
October 1917	20th		Work hindered owing to weather	
	21st		Coys carried out training in billets owing to weather	
	22nd		Bath parade. Bde Divisional Baths	
	23rd		Bulls parade. Beginning 23rd Bn Coys at Instant Relief on R VENANT training area. Officers on R60 attitude	
	24th		Bulls Coys out Instant relief on R VENANT Training Area	
	25th		49th Bn Cal events medal retn. Europe moved from bivouacs	
	26th		Bath and aircraft attacks at 0905, & later at 2005 to 2100, and reached to 1900 arrived at 1900 in billets	
	27th		Holding parade. Day devoted to cleaning up. Brigadier came to tea	
	28th		Divisional Artillery, R.A., Gen. Birdwood and Major Gen. J.J. is in Grand Place Lille and proceeded billets at HELLEMER	
	29th		Coys at disposal of OC Coys. 92nd. A.R. Ellis claims for horses	
	30th		Brigade inspection Brigade	
	31st		Coys at disposal of OC Coys	

Major

Lieut Col & by
1/24 Bn London Regt
The Queens

Army Form C. 2118.

WAR DIARY
or
INTELLIGENCE SUMMARY.
(Erase heading not required.)

Instructions regarding War Diaries and Intelligence Summaries are contained in F. S. Regs., Part II. and the Staff Manual respectively. Title pages will be prepared in manuscript.

1/24 London R.

Place	Date	Hour	Summary of Events and Information	Remarks and references to Appendices
1918 NOVEMBER.				
	Friday 1st	—	Bn marched to LE BREUKE, arriving at 13.00 hrs. Carried out exercises on the way. Brig Genl called in afternoon. 2/Lt H.J.GROSE.M.C left for leave.	
	Saturday 2nd	—	Companies carried out tactical training. Major K.R.O'BRIEN.M.C left for leave	
	Sunday 3rd	—	Church Parade at 11.30 hrs. Capt A.E.COTTRELL.M.C left for leave.	
	Monday 4th	—	Companies carried out tactical training. Brig Genl visited Battn area	
	Tuesday 5th	—	Companies carried out tactical training. 2 Portuguese Padres arrived. I attached to D Coy, 1 to C Coy. Coy HQ to C Coy.	
	Wednesday 6th	—	Companies cleaned up billets and moved to TEMPLEUVE in afternoon to relieve 1/19th Bn in reserve. On arrival relief was cancelled	
	Thursday 7th	—	Bn moved to TEMPLEUVE arriving at 15.30 hours to relieve 1/19th Bn in reserve.	
	Friday 8th	—	Companies at disposal of Coy Commanders. Capt P.T.MATTHEWS.M.C returned from leave after course	

WAR DIARY
or
INTELLIGENCE SUMMARY.
(Erase heading not required.)

Army Form C. 2118.

Place	Date	Hour	Summary of Events and Information	Remarks and references to Appendices
1918. NOVEMBER. SATURDAY	9th		Information received at 06.30 that the enemy had withdrawn. At 10.30 hrs orders were received to move forward to FOURCROIX, where dinners were eaten. At 14.30 hrs. orders were received to proceed to PARADIS ORMONT area for the night. Bn arrived at 16.30 hrs, crossing canal by buckboard bridge at PONT-A-CHIN. 2/LIEUT. F.A. BRIGGS, M.C. left for leave.	
SUNDAY	10th		Bn moved forward at 09.00 hrs. See KAIN - BIZENCOURT - MELLES to QUARTIES where dinner was had. 22 & 23 Bns went in front - 24 Bn in Reserve. After dinner Bn proceeded to FRASNES, arriving in billets at 16.30 hours.	
MONDAY	11th		Bn marched to PARADIS - HAYRON area arriving at 16.30 hrs in billets. 3 Coy were left at REBUT to fill in craters. ARMISTICE DECLARED.	
TUESDAY	12th		Conferences at disposal of O.C. Coys. 2/LT. C.H.V. KEMPTON left for leave. B. Coy moved to NOURCOURT.	
WEDNESDAY	13th		Bn moved to LA TOMBE area, arriving in billets at 18.00 hrs. B. Coy joined Bn.	
THURSDAY	14th		Bn billets cleaned out and mess rooms prepared. Portuguese Platoons left Bn. Captain H.J. SANDERS, D.S.O., M.C. left for leave.	

WAR DIARY or INTELLIGENCE SUMMARY

Army Form C. 2118.

Place	Date	Hour	Summary of Events and Information	Remarks and references to Appendices
1918. NOVEMBER				
	FRIDAY 15th		Bn moved to CYSOING, arriving in billets at 15.30 hrs.	
	SATURDAY 16th		Companies at disposal of Coy Commanders for kits cleaning etc. Brig. Gen. inspected billets.	
	SUNDAY 17th		Church Parade in CINEMA HALL at 11.00 hrs.	
	MONDAY 18th	—	Bn Parade 10.00 hrs. Bn Commander visited area. Following Officers reported in duty from ENGLAND:- LIEUT. B.G. BUSBY - 2/Lt. W.A.G. MORGAN - 2/Lt. A.H. PYKE - 2/Lt. F.W. HILTON - 2/Lt. C.H. STUBBINGS - 2/Lt. A. LINDSALL - STEWARD. Football - Officers v Sgts - Result 3-1.	
	TUESDAY 19th		Bn Parade 10.00 hrs. Bn Cross Country run and 1st round of inter-platoon football competition. Brig. Gen. visited Bn area whilst Bn training. 2/Lieut M.T. ROSE. M.C. reported back from leave.	
	WEDNESDAY 20th		Bn's at CYSOING. Final of Inter-Coy matches A Coy v Transport. Result 3-1. Officers played 22 - Bn Officers. Result 2. Bn won 1-0. Capt J.K. KILBRIDE, R.A.M.C. proceeded on leave.	
	THURSDAY 21st		Bn Training 09.30 hrs. 2/Lt. T.R.S. ROSS awarded M.C. Capt. R.N. TURNER. M.C. proceeded on leave. Capt. A.G. CATTELL. M.C. reports from leave. Lt. C.Y. KEEBLE. M.C. reports for duty from ENGLAND.	

Army Form C. 2118.

WAR DIARY
or
INTELLIGENCE SUMMARY.
(Erase heading not required.)

Instructions regarding War Diaries and Intelligence Summaries are contained in F.S. Regs., Part II. and the Staff Manual respectively. Title pages will be prepared in manuscript.

Place	Date	Hour	Summary of Events and Information	Remarks and references to Appendices
1918. NOVEMBER.				
	FRIDAY 22	—	Cols. F. GOOSEY. M.C. and Lt. A.J.L. CAUSTON proceed on PARIS leave. Bn. parade 10.00 hrs. – leaves non Classes. Lieuts H. GODFREY – F/Sgt TODD and W.J.H. DUNN reported for duty from ENGLAND.	
	SATURDAY 23	—	Bn parade 11.00 hrs. C.O. presented Major DEPOT and Lt. R. ROSS with M.C. ribbon. Coys at disposal of OC Coys. 09.30 – 10.45 hrs. Bn team won Bde cross country race and also 2nd place. Lt. H. NITZ proceeded on smoking course. Band concert 18.00 hrs.	
	SUNDAY 24	—	Church parade 10.15 hrs. Bde Transport Competition 10.15 and 15.15 hrs. C.O. and Adjt attended Bench Church – Special Peace service. Billeting parties left for HARBOURDIN.	
	MONDAY 25	—	Bn left CYSOING at 09.30 hrs. – arrived HARBOURDIN 15.00 hrs. Distance marched 11½ miles.	
	TUESDAY 26	—	Bn left HARBOURDIN at 09.30 hrs. – arrived FOUQUEREUIL at 16.00 hrs. Distance travelled 21 miles.	
	WEDNESDAY 27	—	Bn left FOUQUEREUIL at 10.35 hrs arrived ALLOUAGNE 13.00 hrs. Distance marched 5½ miles.	

WAR DIARY
or
INTELLIGENCE SUMMARY.

(Erase heading not required.)

Army Form C. 2118.

Place	Date	Hour	Summary of Events and Information	Remarks and references to Appendices
1918 NOVEMBER				
	THURSDAY 28		Day devoted to cleaning-up and arranging billets. No.7oMg Sgt NEW awarded M.M. Cpl ACCATTELL awarded M.C. Capt. R.C. HEATHCOTE awarded bar to M.C.	
	FRIDAY 29		Alphabet Parade 11.00 hrs. Coys at disposal of O.C. Coys 09.00 - 11.00 hrs. L.G. - N.C.O.s - and Education classes. C.O. attends conference at Bde H.Qrs. 685147 Pte O'HEARN - 770800 Pte A. ROBINSON 770549 Sgt. C.H. RAYCE awarded M.M.	
	SATURDAY 30		R.S.M.s parade 10.30 hrs. L.G. - N.C.O.s and Education Classes. Coy Imprest accounts closed and new Imprest Account opened. 2/LT C.H.V. KENPTON returned from Leave.	

R.Gordin Major
for Lieut. Col. Cmdg.
1/24 Bn. London Regt. "The Queens"

H. 12. 9. 18

1/24th BATTALION
LONDON REGIMENT.
No. S 385
Date 4/12/18

Army Form C. 2118.

1/24 London Regt
Vol 45

WAR DIARY
or
INTELLIGENCE SUMMARY.
(Erase heading not required.)

Instructions regarding War Diaries and Intelligence Summaries are contained in F. S. Regs., Part II. and the Staff Manual respectively. Title pages will be prepared in manuscript.

Place	Date 1918	Hour	Summary of Events and Information	Remarks and references to Appendices
Sunday	Dec. 1st		Church Parade 09:00 hrs. Lecture by Sir Francis Younghusband attended by Officers in Theatre ALLOUAGNE.	
Monday	2nd		Coys at disposal of O.C. Coys 09:00 to 10:30 hrs. Physical Drill, L.G, NCOs and Education Classes. Adjutants parade 11:00 hrs. Capt. H.J. SANDERS. D.S.O. M.C. reported back from leave.	
Tuesday	3rd		Coys at disposal of O.C. Coys 08:00 - 10:00 hrs. On Range 10:00 - 13:00 Physical Drill, L.G, NCOs and Education Classes. Capt. F. GOOSEY MC and Lt. A.J. CAUSTON reported back from PARIS leave.	
Wednesday	4th		NCOs, L.G, Physical Drill, and Education Classes. 1st day of BDE Rifle Meeting. Div: Maj: General presented V.C. ribbon to Pte HARVEY, of 22nd LONDON REGT. One Platoon of each Coy attended.	
Thursday	5th		Holiday. Eleven platoons entered for "DAILY TELEGRAPH" competition at Rifle Meeting. 4th M.G. HOLLINGTON reported for duty.	
Friday	6th		Coys at disposal of O.C. Coys. 09:00 - 12:00 hrs. Baths for whole Bn.	
Saturday	7th		Coys at disposal of O.C. Coys 09:00 - 12:00 hrs. Football - Officers v Sergts. Result 2-3	

Army Form C. 2118.

WAR DIARY
or
INTELLIGENCE SUMMARY.
(*Erase heading not required.*)

Instructions regarding War Diaries and Intelligence Summaries are contained in F. S. Regs. Part II. and the Staff Manual respectively. Title pages will be prepared in manuscript.

Place 1918	Date Dec.	Hour	Summary of Events and Information	Remarks and references to Appendices
Sunday	8th		C of E. Parade 11.30 hrs.	
Monday	9th		Coys at disposal of O.C. Coys. 08:00 – 12:00 hrs. i.e. NCOs Education and Physical Drill Classes.	
Tuesday	10th		Coys at disposal of O.C. Coys. 08:00 – 12:00 hrs. i.e. Physical Drill and Education Classes.	
Wednesday	11th		Coys at disposal of O.C. Coys. 09:00 – 12:00 hrs. Physical Drill and Education Classes. 2/Lt MIRAILLE. R.P. returns from PARIS PLAGE.	
Thursday	12th		Coys at disposal of O.C. Coys. 09:00 – 12:00 hrs. Usual Classes. Lt Col. PARGITER. D.S.O. proceeds on PARIS leave.	
Friday	13th		Coys at disposal of O.C. Coys. 09:00 – 12:00 hrs. Usual Classes.	
Saturday	14th		Baths and interior economy.	
Sunday	15th		Church Parade 09.30 hrs. Football 23rd v 24th Result 23rd – 3 24th – 1	
Monday	16		"A" Coy on Range, Coys at disposal of O.C. Coys Usual Classes. 1st performance of Battn Concert Party 16:- RED SPADES. 2/Lt. E.C. MEREDITH, M.C. J.N. SUMMERS. G.R. ELLIS report from PARIS leave.	

E.C. MEREDITH, M.C.

Army Form C. 2118.

WAR DIARY
or
INTELLIGENCE SUMMARY.
(Erase heading not required.)

Place	Date	Hour	Summary of Events and Information	Remarks and references to Appendices
1918	Dec.			
	Tuesday 17th		"B" Coy on Range. Coys at disposal of Coy Coys. 09:00-12:00 hrs. Usual Classes	
	Wednesday 18th		Battn Parade. 08:00-10:30 hrs. Coys under Coy Commanders. 10:30 - 12:30. Usual Classes.	
	Thursday 19th		Brigadier inspects Battn on Auchel Aerodrome at 10:00 hrs. 2/Lt Ellis. G.B. to hospital	
	Friday 20th		"C" Coy on Range. Coys under Coy Comdrs. 09:00-12:00 hrs. Usual Classes. Lt W.F. Wettone reports from England for duty.	
	Saturday 21st		"D" Coy on Range. Coys at disposal of Coy Coys. 09:00-12:00. Usual Classes. Lt. Col. Pargiter. DSO. returns from Paris Leave.	
	Sunday 22nd		C of E. Parade. 11:00 hrs.	
	Monday 23rd		Baths and clean change for whole Battn. Bde Transport Competition. Capt. J.L. Kilbride returns from leave	
	Tuesday 24th		Result of Platoon rifle competition. 1st. /C Allen 2nd /C 3 Plln. Coys preparing for Xmas dinner. Major S.C. Marriott takes over command of Battn. Lt. Col. Pargiter, DSO proceeds to 1st Battn Middlesex Regt.	

Army Form C. 2118.

WAR DIARY
or
INTELLIGENCE SUMMARY.
(Erase heading not required.)

Place 1918	Date DEC.	Hour	Summary of Events and Information	Remarks and references to Appendices
Tuesday	24th (contd)		Lt. G.A. COOMBE. M.C. proceeds on leave. 2/Lt. F.W. HILTON to PARIS PLAGE.	
Wednesday	25th		C of E Parade 1100 hrs. Extra pork, nuts, fruit and beer bought for Xmas dinners from Canteen profit.	
Thursday	26th		Physical Drill and cleaning up. Rifles 09.30 - 10.00 hrs. Capt. KILBRIDE. R.A.M.C. leaves for England, 2/Lt. A.H. PYLE to 1st Army School (BOULOGNE)	
Friday	27th		Wet all day training cancelled.	
Saturday	28th		Coys under Coy Comdrs, 08.00 -12.00. Usual Education Classes. Lt. B.G. BUSBY. (proceeds to Musketry Course - MATRINGHAM)	
Sunday	29th		Parade C of E. 11.00 hrs, HQ. move into new Batt Officers Mess	
Monday	30th		Coys under Coy Comdrs. 09.00 - 12.00 hrs. 2/Lt W.J. WEST proceeds to PARIS PLAGE. Combined band - concert with 6 L.F.A.	
Tuesday	31st		Coys at disposal of Coy Comdrs. 09.00 - 12.00 hrs. Usual Classes.	

Blackley (?) Lt/Major
for Major
Cmdg. 1/24 Bn LONDON REGT
The Queens.

Army Form C. 2118.

WAR DIARY
or
INTELLIGENCE SUMMARY.
(Erase heading not required.)

Instructions regarding War Diaries and Intelligence Summaries are contained in F. S. Regs., Part II. and the Staff Manual respectively. Title pages will be prepared in manuscript.

Place	Date	Hour	Summary of Events and Information	Remarks and references to Appendices
January 1919.				
Wednesday	1st		Coys at disposal of Coy Commanders 09.00 to 12.30 hrs for Coy training. Education Classes	
Thursday	2nd		Baths and Interior Economy.	
Friday	3rd		Coys at disposal of Coy Commanders 09.00 to 12.00 hrs for Coy training. Education Classes.	
Saturday	4th		Coys at disposal of Coy Commanders 09.00 to 12.30 hrs for Coy training. Education Classes. 2/Lieut. R.P. MURRALLE to ENGLAND for leave.	
Sunday	5th		Church Parade 11.00 hrs. 2/Lt. H.A. HARRISON to ENGLAND for leave.	
Monday	6th		Coys at disposal of Coy Commanders 09.00 to 12.00 hrs for Coy training. Education Classes. 2/Lt. R.S. ROSS M.C. returned from leave in ENGLAND. 2/Lt. E.W. HILTON returned from leave in PARIS. PLAGE. 2/Lt. R.I. AGATE to ENGLAND for leave. Blankets disinfected	
Tuesday	7th		Coys at disposal of Coy Commanders 09.00 to 12.30 hrs for Coy training. Education Classes. C.O. inspects "B" Coy. C.O. attends conference at Bde. Hqrs. at 16.00 hrs. Blankets disinfected	
Wednesday	8th		Coys at disposal of Coy Commanders for Coy training. Education Classes. C.O. inspects "C" Coy. Batln. Boxing Tournament in Recreation Room. Major K.B. O'Brien M.C. leaves for S.O.S. Course at ALDERSHOT.	
Thursday	9th		Baths and Interior Economy. "Red Shades" at Theatre 18.00 hrs.	
Friday	10th		Coys at disposal of Coy Commanders 09.00 hrs to 12.30 hrs for Coy training	

Army Form C. 2118.

WAR DIARY
or
INTELLIGENCE SUMMARY.
(Erase heading not required.)

Instructions regarding War Diaries and Intelligence Summaries are contained in F. S. Regs., Part II. and the Staff Manual respectively. Title pages will be prepared in manuscript.

Place	Date	Hour	Summary of Events and Information	Remarks and references to Appendices
January 1919				
Friday (contd)	10th		Education Classes. C.O. inspects "D" Coy. Lt. V.G. KELLY reports for duty from ENGLAND.	
Saturday	11th		2/Lt. W.J. WEST returns from PARIS-PLAGE, Bde. Boxing Contest.	
Sunday	12th		Battn Parade and Route march 09.15 to 12.30 hrs.	
Monday	13th		C of E Parade 09.30 hrs. Lt. L.G.D. COOMBE. M.C. returns from leave.	
			Battn Parade 09.15 to 10.30 hrs, Education Classes. Coys at disposal of Coy. Comdrs.	
Tuesday	14th		10.30 to 12.30 hrs. 2/Lt. H. WHITEHEAD to leave and duty. 2/Lt. D.D. CHESHIRE to PARIS PLAGE	
			Coys at disposal of Coy Commanders 09.00 to 12.30 hrs Education Classes. "D" Coy	
			on Range. 2/Lt. G.R. ELLIS to leave and duty.	
Wednesday	15th		Bde. Route March 09.00 to 12.30 hrs.	
Thursday	16th		Baths and Interior Economy. 2/Lt. F.C. MEREDITH. M.C. returns from XI Corps Hqrs.	
Friday	17th		Coys at Disposal of Coy. Commanders 09.00 to 12.30 hrs. Capt. F. GOOSEY. M.C. to ENGLAND for leave.	
Saturday	18th		Battn Parade 09.15 to 10.30 hrs. Education Classes. Coys under Coy Commanders	
			10.30 to 12.30 hrs. 2/Lt. H.M.B. NIXX and 2/Lt. S.F. BROOKER to leave and duty.	
Sunday	19th		C of E Parade 10.30 hrs.	
Monday	20th		Battn Parade 09.15 to 10.30 hrs. Coys at disposal of Coy Commanders. 10.30	
			to 12.30 hrs, Education Classes. 2/Lt. W.J. WEST to leave and duty.	

Army Form C. 2118.

WAR DIARY
or
INTELLIGENCE SUMMARY.
(Erase heading not required.)

Place	Date	Hour	Summary of Events and Information	Remarks and references to Appendices
January 1919.				
Tuesday	21st		Coys at disposal of Coy Commanders 09:00 to 12:30 hrs. Education Classes. Lt. H.W. Allison. M.C. takes over "B" Coy. Lt. B.G. Busby takes over transport. Capt. D.E. Poad. M.C., Lt. A.L.L. Colston, 2/Lt. J.N. Summers, to leave and duty.	
Wednesday	22nd		Capt. A.G. Gates. demobilized. Coys at disposal of Coy Commanders 09:30 to 12:30 hrs. Education Classes. 2/Lt. E.C. Meredith M.C. to leave and duty.	
Thursday	23rd		Baths and Interior Economy.	
Friday	24th		Coys at disposal of Coy Commanders 09:30 - 12:30 hrs. Education Classes. 2/Lt. W.A.G. Morgan to leave and duty.	
Saturday	25th		"2" officers and "50" O.Rs to guard at La Pierrette. Coys at disposal of Coy Commanders, 09:00 to 12:30 hrs. Education Classes. Lt. J.E. Collins. M.C. returns from leave. 2/Lt. E.W. Hinton, Lt. H.F. Nettone, 2/Lt. L.A. Steward, 2/Lt. C.H. Stubbings, to leave and duty.	
Sunday	26th		C of E parade 10:30 hrs. Capt. R.W. Turner. M.C. and F&C.M. Lt. V.G.F. Kelly to leave and duty. C. Adjt. visited guard at La Pierrette.	
Monday	27th		Batn on Fatigue parties. Education Classes. Lt. H.W. Allison, M.C. and 2/Lt. W. Hossington. to leave and duty.	

Army Form C. 2118.

WAR DIARY
or
INTELLIGENCE SUMMARY.
(Erase heading not required.)

Place	Date	Hour	Summary of Events and Information	Remarks and references to Appendices
January 1919				
Tuesday	28th		Battn on Fatigue parties, Education Classes.	
Wednesday	29th		Battn on Fatigue parties, Education Classes. Adjt and 2nd i/c visit guard at LA PIERRETTE. Corker sent to guard. F.G.C.M. promulgated.	
Thursday	30th		Baths and Interior Economy.	
Friday	31st		Coys at disposal of Coy Commanders 09.00 to 12.30 hrs Education Classes.	

Cummings
Lt Col.
Comdg 1/24 LONDON REGT

Army Form C. 2118.

WAR DIARY
or
INTELLIGENCE SUMMARY.
(Erase heading not required.)

Instructions regarding War Diaries and Intelligence Summaries are contained in F. S. Regs., Part II. and the Staff Manual respectively. Title pages will be prepared in manuscript.

Place	Date	Hour	Summary of Events and Information	Remarks and references to Appendices
1919 FEBRUARY				
SATURDAY	1ST		Battn on fatigues. Guard of 50 ORS return from LA PIERRETTE 2/LT H. GODFREY to leave and duty	
			2/LT A.H. PYLE returns from course.	
SUNDAY	2ND		Church of England parade 11:30 hours.	
MONDAY	3RD		Battn on fatigues	
TUESDAY	4TH		Battn on fatigues	
WEDNESDAY	5TH		C and D companies to LA PIERRETTE guard.	
THURSDAY	6TH		Baths. 2/LT A.H. PYLE to leave and duty	
FRIDAY	7TH		B. COY 2/LT R.S. ROSS. to LA PIERRETTE guard 2/LT F.S.G. JUDD to leave and duty	
SATURDAY	8TH		LT C.V. KEEBLE. MC. to leave and duty	
SUNDAY	9TH		2/LT C.H.V. KEMPTON to leave and duty. Capt F. GOOSEY. MC and 2/LT H.M.A. NITZ return from leave and duty. C of E parade 10.30 hours.	
MONDAY	10TH		2nd in command visited LA PIERRETTE guard.	
TUESDAY	11TH		Cmdg Officer visited LA PIERRETTE guard CAPT. D.F. POLL. MC from leave and duty	
WEDNESDAY	12TH		2/LT J.N. SUMNERS from leave and duty	
THURSDAY	13TH		Baths cancelled.	

Army Form C. 2118.

WAR DIARY
or
INTELLIGENCE SUMMARY.
(Erase heading not required.)

Place	Date	Hour	Summary of Events and Information	Remarks and references to Appendices
1919 FEBRUARY				
FRIDAY	14TH		Officer in charge of LA PIERRETTE guard relieved. Guard at LILLERS found daily from today	
			LT. E.C. MEREDITH. M.C. from leave and duty	
SATURDAY	15TH		24 ORS on coal fatigue at BRUAY. 2/LT H.WHITEHEAD returned from leave and duty	
SUNDAY	16TH		C of E parade at 10.30 hours	
MONDAY	17TH		Orders received to move to FLORINGHEM on 19TH CAPT. DE. POLE. M.C. reconnoitred	
TUESDAY	18TH		Fatigues	
WEDNESDAY	19TH		Move to FLORINGHEM complete at 16.30 hours. 2/LT F.W.HILTON from leave and duty. MAJOR H.J.SANDERS.D.S.O.	
			M.C. and 2/LT H.M.A.NITZ to demobilization	
THURSDAY	20TH		Day spent in rearranging camp. 2/LT J.N.SUMMERS to demobilization. CAPT. H.W. ALLISON. M.C. and 2/LT V.G.F. KELLY	
			from leave and duty	
FRIDAY	21ST		Comdg Officer attends Brigade conference	
SATURDAY	22nd		2/LT W. HOLLINGTON and LT. H.F. NETTONE from leave	
SUNDAY	23rd		C of E parade 10.00 hours. 1 Officer 3 NCOs and 24 men to guard at LA PIERRETTE guard.	
MONDAY	24TH		CAPT. R.W. TURNER. M.C. visits guard. Guard mounted at FLORINGHEM aerodrome. 2/LT. M. GODFREY from leave	
TUESDAY	25TH		LA PIERRETTE guard relieved	

Army Form C. 2118.

WAR DIARY
or
INTELLIGENCE SUMMARY.
(Erase heading not required.)

Place	Date	Hour	Summary of Events and Information	Remarks and references to Appendices
FEBRUARY 1919				
	WEDNESDAY 26TH		Fatigues	
	THURSDAY 27TH		Baths. 2/LT. W. HOLLINGTON to demobilization. 2/LT. A.H. PYLE from leave and duty.	
	FRIDAY 28TH		Baths 2/LT. L. LINDSELL-STEWART from leave. Summer time commences at 2300 hours.	

[signature]

3.3.19.

1/24th (COUNTY OF LONDON) Bn.
THE LONDON REGIMENT.
THE "QUEENS."

Army Form C. 2118.

WAR DIARY
or
INTELLIGENCE SUMMARY.
(Erase heading not required.)

Instructions regarding War Diaries and Intelligence Summaries are contained in F. S. Regs., Part II. and the Staff Manual respectively. Title pages will be prepared in manuscript.

Place	Date	Hour	Summary of Events and Information	Remarks and references to Appendices
MARCH 1919				
SATURDAY	1st		2/Lt F.S.G. JUDD and CAPT C.V. KEEBLE MC from leave.	
SUNDAY	2nd		4470 francs allotted from divnl canteen funds. LT J.F. COLLINS MC and 2/LT. STUBBINGS to 235 Brigade, R.F.A.	
MONDAY	3rd		All available men on fatigues.	
TUESDAY	4th		LT A.J.K. CRUSTON to Boulogne on leave. Visit to forward areas, Vimy, Lens, and Douai	
WEDNESDAY	5th		2/LT S.F. BROOKER and 2/LT C.H.V. KEMPTON from leave	
THURSDAY	6th		All available men on fatigues	
FRIDAY	7th		——— do ———	
SATURDAY	8th		LT A.J.K. CRUSTON returns from leave	
SUNDAY	9th		1494 francs allotted to battalion from divnl funds	
MONDAY	10th		Baths at RAIMBERT. Brigadier inspected Battn Transport Park.	
TUESDAY	11th		Band and Drum instruments despatched to depot via Cox + Co.	
WEDNESDAY	12th		All available men on fatigues	
THURSDAY	13th		All available men on fatigues	

Army Form C. 2118.

WAR DIARY
or
INTELLIGENCE SUMMARY.
(Erase heading not required.)

Instructions regarding War Diaries and Intelligence Summaries are contained in F. S. Regs., Part II. and the Staff Manual respectively. Title pages will be prepared in manuscript.

Place	Date	Hour	Summary of Events and Information	Remarks and references to Appendices
MARCH 1919				
	FRIDAY 14TH		Draft of A.O.14 personnel to 1ST BN. MIDDLESEX with LT. J.E. COLLINS. MC. LT. E.C. MEREDITH. MC. 2/LT. R.S. ROSS. MC. 2/LT. S.F. BROOKER. 2/LT. STUBBINGS. 2/LT. G.R. ELLIS.	
	SATURDAY 15TH		10 Officers and 10 ors attend lecture by CAPT. COLYAR at PERNES. CAPT. ALLISON. MC. demobilized.	
	SUNDAY 16TH		Church parade at PERNES and FERFAY. Trip to forward area LA BASSEE.	
	MONDAY 17TH		Warning order for entraining received	
	TUESDAY 18TH		2/LT. A.H. PYLE for demobilization	
	WEDNESDAY 19TH		Removal of transport park to PERNES. STATION	
	THURSDAY 20TH		Removal of transport park to PERNES STATION	
	FRIDAY 21ST		Removal of transport park to PERNES STATION	
	SATURDAY 22nd		Removal of transport park to PERNES STATION	
	SUNDAY 23rd		Removal of transport park to PERNES STATION	
	MONDAY 24TH		Removal of transport park to PERNES STATION	
	TUESDAY 25TH		CAPT. G.A. COOMBE. MC. to demobilization	
	WEDNESDAY 26TH		CAPT. R.W. TURNER. MC to demobilization	
	THURSDAY 27TH		C.O. attends farewell dinner to MAJOR-GENERAL GORRINGE at DIVNL. HDQRS.	

Army Form C. 2118.

WAR DIARY
or
INTELLIGENCE SUMMARY.
(Erase heading not required.)

Instructions regarding War Diaries and Intelligence Summaries are contained in F. S. Regs., Part II. and the Staff Manual respectively. Title pages will be prepared in manuscript.

Place	Date	Hour	Summary of Events and Information	Remarks and references to Appendices
1919	MARCH			
	FRIDAY 28TH		Major-General's inspection at 1215 hours	
	SATURDAY 29TH		All available men on fatigues	
	SUNDAY 30TH		All available men on fatigues	
	MONDAY 31ST		CAPT. F. GOOSEY M.C. CAPT. C.V. KEEBLE M.C. 2/LT. L. LINDSELL-STEWART. 2/LT. O.H.V. KEMPTON. 2/LT. E.W. HILTON to demobilization	

1/24TH BATTALION
LONDON REGT.
No. 6705
Date 1st April 19

[signature]
Comdg 1/24 London Regt.

2/K 2/m. Reg.

Army Form C. 2118.

ML 49

WAR DIARY
or
INTELLIGENCE SUMMARY.
(Erase heading not required.)

Instructions regarding War Diaries and Intelligence Summaries are contained in F. S. Regs., Part II. and the Staff Manual respectively. Title pages will be prepared in manuscript.

Place	Date	Hour	Summary of Events and Information	Remarks and references to Appendices
APRIL 1919				
	TUESDAY 1ST		All available men on fatigue	
	WEDNESDAY 2nd		Baths at RAIMBERT	
	THURSDAY 3RD		2/Col. S.C. MARRIOT to ENGLAND for leave. CAPT. P.T. MATTHEWS, M.C. takes over command. All available men on fatigues	
	FRIDAY 4TH		All available men on fatigues	
	SATURDAY 5TH		All available men on fatigues. Officers of 142nd Bde Cadre Group play 47th divn officers - result draw 1-1	
	SUNDAY 6TH		Voluntary Services	
	MONDAY 7TH		All available men on fatigues	
	TUESDAY 8TH		Baths at RAIMBERT	
	WEDNESDAY 9TH		All available men on fatigues. Officers of 142nd Bde Cadre Group play 47th divn officers - result 3-1 (142nd GROUP won)	
	THURSDAY 10TH		All available men on fatigue. 2/4 Battn play 73rd French infantry Bn. result 3-0. 2/4 Battn won	
	FRIDAY 11TH		All available men on fatigues. LT. A.J. BEER to ENGLAND for leave	
	SATURDAY 12TH		All available men on fatigues	

Army Form C. 2118.

WAR DIARY
or
INTELLIGENCE SUMMARY.
(Erase heading not required.)

Instructions regarding War Diaries and Intelligence Summaries are contained in F. S. Regs., Part II. and the Staff Manual respectively. Title pages will be prepared in manuscript.

Place	Date	Hour	Summary of Events and Information	Remarks and references to Appendices
APRIL 1919				
	SUNDAY 13TH		Voluntary Services	
	MONDAY 14TH		CAPT. D.E. POLL. MC. LT. H.F. HETTONE. 2/LT H. WHITEHEAD MM. 2/LT F.S.G. JUDD 2/LT W.A.G. MORGAN to demobilization. Draft of ORs to HAVRE transferred to 13TH MIDDLESEX 2/LT W.J. WEST conducting officer.	
	TUESDAY 15TH		All available men on fatigues	
	WEDNESDAY 16TH		Cadres of BDE HQRS 22ND and 23RD Battns move to FLORINGHEM CAMP	
	THURSDAY 17TH		LT. A.J. BEER and LT-COL. S.C. MARRIOTT return from leave. LT-COL. S.C. MARRIOT resumes command of Battn.	
	FRIDAY 18TH		Voluntary Services	
	SATURDAY 19TH		Baths at PERNES	
	SUNDAY 20TH		All men on fatigues	
	MONDAY 21ST		All men on fatigues	
	TUESDAY 22ND		All men on fatigues	
	WEDNESDAY 23RD		All men on fatigues	
	THURSDAY 24TH		All men on fatigues	
	FRIDAY 25TH		All men on fatigues 2/LT W.J. WEST returns from conducting duty	
	SATURDAY 26TH		All men on fatigues	

Army Form C. 2118.

WAR DIARY
or
INTELLIGENCE SUMMARY.
(Erase heading not required.)

Instructions regarding War Diaries and Intelligence Summaries are contained in F. S. Regs., Part II. and the Staff Manual respectively. Title pages will be prepared in manuscript.

Place	Date	Hour	Summary of Events and Information	Remarks and references to Appendices
1919 APRIL				
SUNDAY	27TH		Voluntary Services	
MONDAY	28TH		Baths at PERNES. Cadres of 1st Bn. Hyss and 22nd and 23rd Battns to HAVRE	
TUESDAY	29TH		Battn transport moved from wagon park to PERNES station. 3 Companies of R.E's move to FLORINGHEM Camp. LT. V.G.F. KELLY to 1st ARMY HQRS. as education officer. 2/LT. W.J. WEST to XI Corps Cyclists as a Cadre Officer	
WEDNESDAY	30TH		All men on fatigues	

30.4.19. [signature] Lieut Col.
Cdg. 1/24th (COUNTY OF LONDON) Bn.
THE LONDON REGIMENT,
THE "QUEENS."

Army Form C. 2118.

WAR DIARY
or
INTELLIGENCE SUMMARY.
(Erase heading not required.)

1/24 Croydon Bn.

Instructions regarding War Diaries and Intelligence Summaries are contained in F. S. Regs. Part II. and the Staff Manual respectively. Title pages will be prepared in manuscript.

Place	Date	Hour	Summary of Events and Information	Remarks and references to Appendices
1919 May				
	1st		All available men on fatigues.	
"	2nd		Loading schedules at FERNES STN.	
"	3rd		Entrained at 19.45 hrs. for HAVRE.	
"	4th		Arrived at HAVRE 13.30 hrs. Arrived at HARFLEUR CAMP 17.30 hrs.	
"	5th		Delousing and baths.	
"	6th		Awaiting orders for embarkation	
"	7th	"		
"	8th	"		
"	9th	"	Loading party report at docks at 09.00 hrs. Cadre embarked at 16.15 hrs. Arrived at SOUTHAMPTON 1.30 hrs. 10.5.19.	

Lieut Col.
A/g 1/24 Bn London Regt
The Queens.